Paddling Northern California

FALCONGUIDES ®

GUILFORD, CONNECTICUT
HELENA, MONTANA
AN IMPRINT OF THE GLOBE PEQUOT PRESS

To buy books in quantity for corporate use
or incentives, call **(800) 962–0973**
or e-mail **premiums@GlobePequot.com.**

FALCONGUIDES®

Cover photo © Larry Prosser
All interior photographs by Charlie Pike

Text design by Amy Bransfield/Bransfield Design

Library of Congress Cataloging-in-Publication Data
Pike, Charles W.
    Paddling northern California / by Charlie Pike.
        p. c.m.
    Includes bibliographical references.
    ISBN 978-1–56044–968–3
        1. Canoes and canoeing—California—Guidebooks. 2. California—Guidebooks.
    I. Title.
GV776.C2 P55 2001
797.1'22'0974—dc21   00–049029

♻ Printed on recycled paper.
Manufactured in the United States of America
First Edition/Fourth Printing

CONTENTS

Map Legend vi

Northern California Map vii

Acknowledgments viii

Introduction 1

    Lay of the Land 1

    How to Use This Guide 3

    Planning Your Trip 9

    Safety on the Water and Paddling Etiquette 10

    Minimum Impact Camping 11

    Wild and Scenic Rivers Protection 12

    Marine Mammal Protection Act 13

The Paddling

    1. Monterey Bay—Cannery Row 15

    2. Elkhorn Slough 18

    3. Chesbro Reservoir 22

    4. Lexington Reservoir 24

    5. Lake Del Valle 26

    6. Lafayette Reservoir 28

    7. Berkeley Aquatic Park 30

    8. East San Francisco Bay—Emeryville to Berkeley 32

    9. San Leandro Bay 34

  10. San Francisco Bay—Angel Island 36

  11. China Camp Shoreline 39

  12. Drakes Estero 43

  13. Tomales Bay 48

  14. Estero Americano 52

15. Lake Sonoma 55

16. Navarro River 58

17. Navarro River Estuary 62

18. Albion River 64

19. Big River 67

20. Mendocino Coast 70

21. South Fork Eel River—Leggett to Redway 76

22. South Fork Eel River—Sylvandale to Weott 83

23. Eel River 87

24. Trinity River—Lewiston to Junction City 89

25. Trinity River—Junction City to Cedar Flat 96

26. Trinity River—Hawkins Bar to Willow Creek 101

27. Sacramento River—Redding to Balls Ferry 105

28. Sacramento River—Balls Ferry to Red Bluff 109

29. Sacramento River—Red Bluff to Woodson Bridge 114

30. Sacramento River—Woodson Bridge to Colusa 118

31. Feather River—Oroville to Wildlife Refuge 124

32. Yuba River 129

33. Cache Creek—North Fork to Bear Creek 134

34. Cache Creek—Rumsey Canyon 138

35. Cache Creek—Capay Valley 142

36. Folsom Lake—North Fork Arm 144

37. Lake Natoma 148

38. American River Parkway 152

39. Cosumnes River Preserve 159

40. Mokelumne River—Electra Run 165

41. Mokelumne River below Camanche 167

42. Stanislaus River—Knights Ferry to McHenry Recreation Area 170

43. Tuolumne River—La Grange to Roberts Ferry 176

44. Tuolumne River—Roberts Ferry to Fox Grove Park 180

45. Ahjumawi Lava Springs State Park 183

46. Eagle Lake 185

47. Juniper Lake 189

48. Round Valley Reservoir 192

49. Mountain Meadow Reservoir 194

50. Antelope Lake 196

51. Middle Fork Feather River—Sloat to Nelson Point 198

52. Little Grass Valley Reservoir 201

53. Bear River—Colfax to Dog Bar 204

54. Lake Spaulding 207

55. Lake Valley Reservoir 210

56. Sugar Pine Reservoir 212

57. North Fork American River—Colfax to Lake Clementine 214

58. Lake Clementine 219

59. French Meadows Reservoir 221

60. Middle Fork American River—Greenwood Bridge to Mammoth Bar 223

61. South Fork American River—Chili Bar to Folsom Lake 226

62. Truckee River—Tahoe City to River Ranch 231

63. Truckee River—River Ranch to Floriston 235

64. Lake Tahoe near Emerald Bay 241

65. East Fork Carson River 246

Appendix A: Flows, Tides, Waves and Storms 251

Appendix B: For More Information 254

Appendix C: Further Reading 269

Appendix D: California Paddling Organizations 270

Index 273

About the Author 280

Map Legend

Interstate Highway	(00)
U.S. Highway	(00)
State or County Road	(00) (000)
Forest Road	120
Interstate Highway	===⟹
Paved Road	⟹
Gravel/Unimproved Road	⟹
Featured Route	〜〜〜
Other Waterways	〜〜〜
State Boundary	▬▬ ▬ ▬
Access Site/ Put-in or Take-out	◄ Access here
Dam	▬
Diversion Dam	〜
Lake, River/Creek, Rapids/Waterfall	〜〜
Tributary	〜〜
Bridge	
Parking Area	Ⓟ
Marsh or Wetland	〜
Peak	Mount Moran

Mileage Marker	*26*
Gate	•—•—•
Ranger Station	♣
City or Town	Craig or Craig
Campground	⛺
Cabin or Building	■
Railroad	┼┼┼┼┼┼┼┼┼
Overlook/Point of Interest	◘
Trail	− − − −
Stream Gauge	⊗
National or State Forest/Park Boundary	
Map Orientation	N ↑
Scale	0 0.5 1 Miles
Map Locator	★

Northern California Map

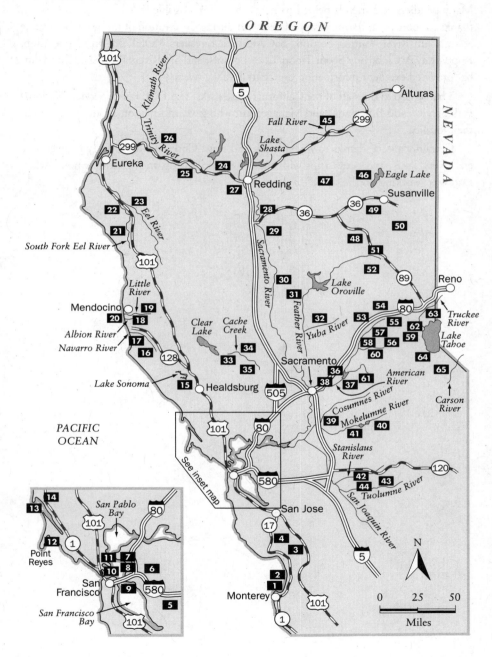

OREGON

NEVADA

101

5

Alturas

Fall River 45 299

Klamath River

Trinity River

26

Lake
Shasta

299

Eureka

25 24

27 Redding

46 Eagle Lake

47

Susanville

23

22

Eel River

28

36 36 49

50

21

29

South Fork Eel River

101

48

51

Little
River

30

Sacramento River

Lake
Oroville

52

89

Reno

Mendocino 19

31

Feather River

Yuba River

54

80

63

Truckee
River

20 18

32

53 55 62

Albion River 17

Clear
Lake

Cache
Creek

57 59

58 56

Lake
Tahoe

Navarro River

16

128

34

60

64

33

35

Sacramento

36

American
River

65

Lake Sonoma 15 Healdsburg

505

38 37 61

Carson
River

PACIFIC
OCEAN

101

80

39 Mokelumne River

Cosumnes River

40

41

Stanislaus
River

580

42 43

120

44

Tuolumne River

San Joaquin River

San Jose

17

4

3

5

2

1

Monterey

101

1

N

0 25 50

Miles

Inset map

14

13

San Pablo
Bay

80

101

12

1

Point
Reyes

11 7

10 8 6

San
Francisco

9

580

5

San Francisco
Bay

101

See inset map

Acknowledgments

Many paddlers and friends helped to make this book possible. I'd like to extend special thanks to some organizations I've paddled with during the creation of this guidebook: The Sierra Club River Touring Section, Bay Area Sea Kayakers, POST, Marin Canoe Club, Koppa Kayak Club, Boy Scout Troop 12 of Loomis, and Six Rivers Paddlers. Chet Dunbar provided excellent information on Central Valley rivers.

Thanks also to the staff of the California State Parks, U.S.D.A. Forest Service, National Park Service, and Bureau of Land Management who gave information about waterways in their locality.

Certainly special thanks to my wife AJ, and sons, Chris and Russ. They enjoyed several rivers, lakes, and ocean trips with me. They also put up with countless hours when Dad was "working on the book!"

Introduction

Lay of the Land

California is a place of diverse climates and landforms. Along the immediate coast, winter weather ranges from mild temperatures with light winds between storms to heavy wind and rain for days at a time. Snow and sub-freezing temperatures are rare. Summer weather is typically cool with foggy mornings and northwesterly winds building in the afternoons. Summer rains are rare. To escape summer fog, go a few miles inland where the sun is often shining. Enjoy summer daytime temperatures in the 80s. In general, spring and autumn weather is best for paddling along the coast.

The rugged Coast Ranges separate the Pacific Ocean from the Central Valley. Formed by the collision of the North American and Pacific plates, the Coast Ranges enfold the San Andreas Fault, which can easily be seen at waterways such as Tomales Bay. Coastal mountains collect heavy winter rainfall that swells the rivers into flood stage. Snow covers the higher areas for most of the winter and spring. Summer weather is comfortable, with warm, sunny days and cool evenings. Summer rain is infrequent, and the flows in most of the undammed rivers quickly dwindle.

Between coastal hills, San Francisco Bay surges with the rhythm of California's rivers and tides. Before Europeans arrived, the 50-mile-long bay mixed river water from the Central Valley with the Pacific Ocean to form one of the nation's most productive estuaries. For the past decade, San Francisco Bay and the tributary Sacramento–San Joaquin Delta have been the focus of massive state and federal efforts to restore endangered species, restore habitats devastated by dams and twentieth-century land use, and protect the ecosystems from invasions of flora and fauna from exotic parts of the world.

San Francisco Bay offers great paddling. Protected from Pacific Ocean swells, the bay has great scenery with hundreds of miles of waterways to enjoy. The nearby reservoirs are great places to learn and practice paddling. The weather is moderate year-round. Summer winds and morning fog blow through the Golden Gate. The same winds that delight sailors and windsurfers will challenge sea kayakers. You must plan for it.

In the delta and nearby portions of the Central Valley, marine winds blowing from the Bay, create cool summer days.

The Central Valley is a flat, alluvial basin more than 400 miles long and about 50 miles wide, bounded by the Coast Range on the west and the Sierra Nevada on the east. Most rivers draining from the Sierra Nevada and Coast Ranges flow onto the Central Valley floor to join with the Sacramento or San Joaquin Rivers. The Sacramento and San Joaquin Rivers meet in the Sacramento–San Joaquin Delta before flowing through a gap in the Coast Range to San Francisco Bay.

Central Valley winter weather is cool and often foggy or rainy. Summer days become hot. Summer temperatures of 90 degrees F are normal, and 100-degree days are frequent. Summer evening temperatures often remain above 80 degrees F near Red Bluff and Redding. Closer to the delta, ocean breezes and marine fog moderate temperatures.

Beautiful Caspar Cove on the Mendocino Coast.

Dams and reservoirs affect flows on most Central Valley rivers. Reservoir releases sustain summer flows. Winter floods may raise Central Valley rivers to unsafe levels for extended periods.

Nearer the California-Oregon border, the rugged Klamath Mountains are the meeting place of the Coastal Range, Cascade Range, and the Sierra Nevada. Mount Shasta and Lassen Peak are the most distinctive Cascade volcanic cones in California. Until the 1980 eruption of Mount St. Helens in Washington, Mount Lassen was the most recently active volcano in the continental United States. The Modoc Plateau in Northeastern California is a broad area of lava flows and small volcanic cones extending into eastern Oregon and Washington. In winter, these northern mountains experience a cold continental climate with ample snow and sub-freezing temperatures. Summer weather moderates with warm days and cool nights.

The Sierra Nevada is a fault block mountain range whose eastern slopes are steep and dry, while deep, river-cut canyons mark the western slopes. Winter snows normally pile 15 to 20 feet deep, making Sierra lakes and rivers inaccessible. Spring snowmelt swells the canyon and foothill rivers with some of the state's best clear cold whitewater. Since Sierra rivers are mostly dam controlled, boatable releases persist through summer and sometimes into autumn.

Sierra summer weather is delightful. Daytime temperatures are often in the 70s, and skies are usually clear except for some late-summer thunderstorms. At the lower-elevation foothills, temperatures climb to 90 degrees F and higher. Most of the rivers flow to the west, and paddlers usually encounter westerly afternoon winds.

As you paddle Northern California rivers, you will visit streams dramatically altered by the California Gold Rush. According to the U.S. Geological Survey, the Gold Rush of 1849 through the 1960s left a legacy of detrimental environmental effects. Miners disturbed at least four billion cubic meters of material in the Sierra Nevada and left mercury still found in some California streams.

Placer mining, which yielded most of the gold in the early years, used large amounts of mercury to aid in separating the gold from other materials. Hydraulic mining directed powerful streams of water from huge nozzles that washed away entire hillsides. Later, giant floating dredges excavated to bedrock wide swaths of streambeds. The dredges dumped mountains of loose rocks, known as dredger tailings, along many miles of rivers. Elsewhere, tunnels diverted stream channels.

How to Use This Guide

This book describes a variety of the state's finest lakes, streams, and coastal waterways for the beginning and intermediate paddler. Included are waterways known for wonderful scenery, good fishing, calm relaxation, historical importance, practice spots close to home, remote overnight trips, whitewater to thrill and test the skill of experienced boaters, and marine wildlife.

Each trip description highlights the waterway attributes needed to select and plan a trip. *Paddling Northern California* divides longer waterways into several trips based on character, access, and difficulty. (For example, I have separated the flatwater from the whitewater sections on some rivers.) Each chapter begins with capsulized bits of information meant to be read "at a glance" to help determine if the entire waterway description is of interest to you. Different headings are included or excluded for different trips, depending on the nature of the paddling (ocean, lake, or river). The information includes:

Character: A short description of the waterway and what makes it worth inclusion in *Paddling Northern California*.

Length: Distance of the route in miles.

Average run time: The time it takes to paddle the route at an average pace. Generally it is based on a paddling speed of 2 to 3 miles per hour plus lunch breaks. Plan to travel more slowly if your group is large or inexperienced, or if there are difficult rapids to scout or portage, adverse tides, or winds.

Size: The length and width of a body of water.

Elevation: The elevation (in feet) of a body of water.

Class: The difficulty level of the water is based on two scales. The International Scale of River Difficulty applies to rivers. The Sea Conditions Rating System (SCRS) applies to marine waters and large lakes. The scales run from Class I to Class VI. Generally rapids get more difficult as flow levels increase. Sea conditions and large lakes grow more difficult with high winds, large surf, and rocky shorelines. Boating along any waterway becomes more hazardous in cold water. Calm waterways with little difficulty are referred to as "flatwater."

International Scale of River Difficulty

Updated in 1998 by the American Whitewater Affiliation. Reprinted with permission.

Class I: Easy. Fast-moving water with riffles and small waves. Few obstructions, all obvious and easily missed with little training. Risk to swimmers is slight; self-rescue is easy.

Class II: Novice. Straightforward rapids with wide, clear channels that are evident without scouting. Occasional maneuvering may be required, but rocks and medium-sized waves are easily missed by trained paddlers. Swimmers are seldom injured and group assistance, while helpful, is seldom needed. Rapids that are at the upper end of this difficulty range are designated "Class II+."

Class III: Intermediate. Rapids with moderate, irregular waves which may be difficult to avoid and which can swamp an open canoe. Complex maneuvers in fast current and good boat control in tight passages or around ledges are often required; large waves or strainers may be present but are easily avoided. Strong eddies and powerful current effects can be found, particularly on large-volume rivers. Scouting is advisable for inexperienced parties. Injuries while swimming are rare; self-rescue is usually easy but group assistance may be required to avoid long swims. Rapids that are at the lower or upper end of this difficulty range are designated "Class III-" or "Class III+" respectively.

Class IV: Advanced. Intense, powerful but predictable rapids requiring precise boat handling in turbulent water. Depending on the character of the river, it may feature large, unavoidable waves and holes or constricted passages demanding fast maneuvers under pressure. A fast, reliable eddy turn may be needed to initiate maneuvers, scout rapids, or rest. Rapids may require "must" moves above dangerous hazards. Scouting may be necessary the first time down. Risk of injury to swimmers is moderate to high, and water conditions may make self-rescue difficult. Group assistance for rescue is often essential but requires practiced skills. A strong Eskimo roll is highly recommended. Rapids that are at the lower or upper end of this difficulty range are designated "Class IV-" or "Class IV+" respectively.

Author's note: Only three runs described in this guide have this level of difficulty.

Class V: Expert. Extremely long, obstructed, or very violent rapids that expose a paddler to added risk. Drops may contain large, unavoidable waves and holes or steep, congested chutes with complex, demanding routes. Rapids may continue for long distances between pools, demanding a high level of fitness. What eddies exist may be small, turbulent, or difficult to reach. At the high end of the scale, several of these factors may be combined. Scouting is recommended but may be difficult. Swims are dangerous, and rescue is often difficult even for experts. A very reliable Eskimo roll, proper equipment, extensive experience, and practiced rescue skills are essential. Because of the large range of difficulty that exists beyond Class IV, Class V is an open-ended, multiple-level scale designated by Class 5.0, 5.1, 5.2, etc. Each of these levels is an order of magnitude more difficult than the last. Example: Increasing difficulty from Class 5.0 to Class 5.1 is a similar order of magnitude as increasing from Class IV to Class 5.0.

Author's note: No streams of this difficulty are included in this guide.

Class VI: Extreme and Exploratory. These runs have almost never been attempted and often exemplify the extremes of difficulty, unpredictability, and danger. The consequences of errors are very severe and rescue may be impossible. For teams of experts only, at favorable water levels, after close personal inspection and taking all precautions. After a Class VI rapids has been run many times, its rating may be changed to an appropriate Class 5.x rating.

Author's note: No streams of this difficulty are included in this guide.

Conceptually similar to the American Whitewater Affiliation's International Scale of River Difficulty, the **Sea Conditions Rating System (SCRS)** was developed by Eric Soares and Michael Powers of the Tsunami Rangers to gauge the hazards of coastal paddling. This guidebook uses SCRS to indicate the "Class" of coastal waterways and large lakes. Originally published in *Extreme Sea Kayaking*, by Eric Soares and Michael Powers, Ragged Mountain Press, 1999. Reprinted with permission.

Factor	Computation Method	Maximum Points	Score
1-Water Temperature	1 point for each degree below 72°F	40	____
2-Wind Speed	1 point per mph of wind speed	50+	____
3-Wave Height	2 points per vertical wave foot	40+	____
4-Swim Distance	1 point per 100 meters	20	____
5-Breaking Waves	30 points if waves are breaking	30	____
6-Rock Garden	20 points if rocks are present	20	____
7-Sea Cave	20 points if entering sea caves	20	____
8-Night	20 points if it is night	20	____
9-Fog	Up to 20 points if fog is dense	20	____
10-Miscellaneous	10 points or more for other danger	10+	____

TOTAL POINTS = ____

Divide total points by 20 to obtain CLASS LEVEL = ____

Scoring Directions:

Assess the conditions using instruments or conservative estimates, and rate each of the ten factors. Add up the scores and divide the sum by 20.

Score	Class	Skill Level
Up to 1.9	Class I	Easy to moderate difficulty, danger, and skills required.
2.0 to 2.9	Class II	Intermediate difficulty, danger, and skills required.

Score	Class	Skill Level
3.0 to 3.9	Class III	Advanced difficulty, danger, and skills required (e.g. a reliable roll and self-rescues a must).
4.0 to 4.9	Class IV	Extreme conditions, advanced techniques required, loss of life possible in a mishap.
5.0 to 5.9	Class V	Very extreme, life-threatening conditions suitable only for a team of experts.
6.0+	Class VI	Nearly impossible conditions, loss of life probable in a mishap.

The following Beauford Wind Scale is useful to estimate wind speed since it is such an important factor.

Beauford Force #	Wind Speed mph	Wind Term	Sea Surface Conditions
1	1–3	light air	slightest ripples
2	4–7	light breeze	noticeable ripples
3	8–12	gentle breeze	ripples everywhere with scattered whitecaps
4	13–18	moderate breeze	numerous whitecaps, hinders paddling progress
5	19–24	fresh breeze	many whitecaps, some spray, for skilled kayakers only
6	25–31	strong breeze	small craft advisories, whitecaps everywhere, more spray
7	32–38	moderate gale	white foam from breaking waves begins to be blown in streaks

Skill level: Related directly to the American Whitewater Affiliation and SCRS scales of paddling difficulty, the skill levels are based largely on difficulty and perceived hazard. Add an extra level of difficulty if the waterway is remote or the weather and water temperature is extremely cold. The different levels of paddling skill are an approximation, based on the following parameters:

Beginner: Knows the basic strokes and can handle craft competently in smooth water. Knows how to bring a boat to shore safely in fast current, can negotiate sharp turns in fast current, can avoid strainers and other obstacles, and understands the difficulties of the stream to be floated. A beginner is not a person who is picking up a paddle for the first time. Those folks should get some practice on a lake or with an experienced paddler before taking their first trip. Streams with many obstacles or streams used for teaching whitewater skills are noted "beginners with whitewater experience."

Intermediate: Knows basic strokes and uses them effectively. Can read water well, can negotiate fairly difficult rapids with confidence, and knows how to safely catch an eddy. Won't panic and knows what to do in the event of an upset. Can come to shore quickly to inspect dangerous spots and knows when to portage. The tandem paddler knows how to coordinate strokes between bow and stern and can paddle at either end.

Expert: Has mastered all strokes and uses them instinctively. Confident of own ability even in very difficult situations. Skillful in heavy water or complex rapids. Knows when a rapid is not runable and has a deep respect for all safety precautions.

Marine weather: Radio channels or telephone numbers for marine weather advisories specific to that location. Offshore buoy locations report sea swell and wave conditions. Fog, wind, building ocean swells, and high surf can dramatically alter the safety of your trip. Check the weather that day before you set out.

Optimal flow: Included in trip descriptions with the name of the stream gauge stations. Appendix A provides Internet and telephone sources for these stream gauge readings and flow forecasts. Optimal flows are omitted where they are not relevant. "Optimal flow" is an inexact term. At the very least, optimal flow indicates a level with enough water to float over most obstructions. Anglers may prefer lower flows, when fish are concentrated in pools. On the other hand, exuberant whitewater paddlers may seek higher water levels, when rapids are turbulent and more difficult. Generally speaking, the range provided in this book is low for commercial-style rafts, which require more water than canoes, kayaks, or inflatable kayaks. The upper limit indicated in these descriptions is the level at which most paddlers consider the river higher than ordinary and requires higher skills than suggested here. Be advised that all rivers are hazardous during high spring runoff and flood stages.

Water source: Indicates if the streamflow results only from rain runoff, snowmelt, or is controlled by reservoirs.

Tide differences: Tides dramatically influence waterways closely connected to the ocean. "Tide differences" tell the length of time that high or low tides occur before (-) or after (+) that tide at a place referenced by published tide tables. This book usually refers to those published for the Golden Gate Bridge. For California, high and low tides alternate on cycles that last a little more than 6 hours. The times for high and low tides change every day. Just as important, the height of the tide changes. When extreme high tides (flood tides) and extreme low tides (minus tides) follow each other, strong currents are induced in estuaries and channels. Plan your trip to go upstream with an incoming tide and return with an outgoing tide, so you will add to the enjoyment of the experience and will also avoid getting stuck on mudflats. Make wide channel crossings at slack tide (get "current table") so you don't get swept away. Obtain tide tables for the current year. Daily tide tables are readily available from many sport fishing shops, marine boating suppliers, and on the Internet (see Appendix A).

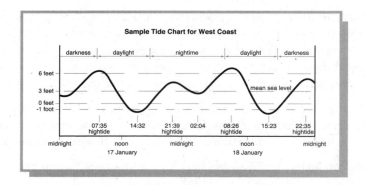

Average gradient: The steepness of the streambed calculated as vertical feet per mile.

Best season: Time of year when favorable conditions exist to make the trip. On some streams, rainfall or snowmelt dictates favorable conditions. On other waterways, wind, temperature, or fog may be a greater influence.

Craft: Type of watercraft most frequently used or encountered on this waterway.

Hazards: Any risks that require your attention. You can pay attention before you paddle through the hazardous waters or pay later when you need emergency rescue and/or medical care.

Maps: A list of detailed maps that will help you navigate your way to and along a waterway. Maps illustrated in this book are designed for trip planning to give you a general idea of the water route. **They are not meant to be navigational aids.** They show only a few of the rapids or navigational hazards.

Access: Provides directions for legal approaches to waterways. Some are improved with launch ramps, paved parking, and rest rooms. Others are informal sites with roadside parking and stream banks suitable only for hand-carried craft. Most require fees for use.

Shuttle: Tells the **one-way** driving distance and driving time to travel from the put-in to the take-out. For river trips, the most common way to regroup your vehicles and boat at the end of the trip is to "run a shuttle." That is: put a vehicle at the take-out, then return to the put-in with your gear. Alternative shuttle methods are bicycling, jogging, hiring a commercial shuttle driver, catching a ride with a commercial outfitter shuttle, or using a bus service available for paddlers on some rivers. Remember the vehicle keys!

For more information: Gives the names of organizations or agencies that can provide more specific information and may be able to answer questions. For specific addresses, phone numbers, and websites, this section will refer you to Appendix B in the back of the book.

Planning Your Trip

The most detailed maps available are topographic quadrangles published by the U.S. Geological Survey and sold at many land survey and outdoor supply houses. Check the Internet at ask.usgs.gov/maps.html or telephone the Earth Science Information Center (ESIC) at 1–888–ASK–USGS (1–888–275–8747). These maps show land contours, roads, and water courses and are especially useful in previewing remote waterways. The downside is that many maps are 25 years old and do not show current roads, bridges, and urban developments. Electronic versions are available via the Internet and CD-ROM from several vendors, such as Maptech (www.maptech.com) and R.E.I. (www.rei.com).

Before you leave on your trip, get up-to-date weather and water level information. Ocean conditions change dramatically when the winds increase. Some streams are runable only under certain circumstances. Regularly updated river level readings are provided by the California Department of Water Resources (cdec.water.ca.gov/river/rivcond.html) and the U.S. Geologic Survey (waterdate.usgs.gov/ca/nwis/rt). Appendix A lists marine buoys, marine weather sites, stream gauges, and websites pertinent to this book.

Hydrographs

A picture of a stream's average annual ups and downs as measured in cubic feet per second (cfs) are included with trip descriptions where appropriate. Most of this information comes from the U.S.G.S. and DWR websites. Hydrographs show the size of a river (the greater the flow, the larger the stream) and the times water flows are usually greatest and least. When

Good planning can make your trip a little easier. These smart paddlers brought a cart to transport their boats.

you are on the DWR or U.S.G.S. websites, use the station provided in the "Optimal flow" heading to quickly find the present flow for a particular site.

Outfitters conduct guided tours and rent paddling equipment that will enable you to travel along rivers or lakes at almost any level of comfort. To learn about outfitters near the river you are running, call the land management agency listed in the "For more information" section of the trip description, or see Appendix B.

Safety on the Water and Paddling Etiquette

In California, county sheriffs coordinate search and rescue with appropriate land management agencies. If you need help, call 911 and ask for search and rescue. Before the trip tell someone where you are going, when you expect to return, and where to call if you do not.

The American Whitewater Affiliation updated its paddling safety code, which includes the following:

- Be a competent swimmer with the ability to handle yourself underwater.
- Wear a snugly fitting vest-type life preserver.
- Wear a solid, correctly fitted helmet when upsets are likely.
- Do not boat out of control. Be able to stop or reach the shore before reaching danger.

- Whitewater rivers contain many hazards: high water, cold, strainers, broaching, dams, weirs, ledges, reversals, holes, and hydraulics. These hazards may change.

- Boating alone is discouraged. The recommended minimum party is three people or two craft.

- Have a frank knowledge of your boating ability, and don't attempt rivers or rapids that lie beyond that ability. When in doubt, stop and scout. If you are still in doubt? Portage.

- Be practiced in self-rescue.

- Be trained in rescue skills, CPR, and first aid. Carry a first aid kit. Know how to avoid poison oak and rattlesnakes. Be prepared to deal with these hazards.

- Carry equipment needed for unexpected emergencies, including good footwear for walking out. Approach remote rivers through isolated wilderness with caution, since aid is difficult or impossible to obtain in case of an accident.

- Be prepared for extremes in weather. Know about the dangers of hypothermia and how to deal with it. When air and water temperature add up to 120 degrees or less, hypothermia is a high risk. Wear wetsuits (drysuits) for protection from cold water and cold weather.

- Know early signs and symptoms of heat exhaustion and dehydration in hot weather. Remember that certain medications can complicate these types of environmental injuries.

- Allow the craft ahead of you to pass through the rapid before you enter it. This will avoid a double disaster if the leading boat blocks the channel.

Minimum Impact Camping (Adapted from the California Department of Boating and Waterways)

Bring your own drinking water or be ready to filter and treat the water you find. As in most of the world, pathogens now infect California's surface waters.

Summer camping in California is very popular and you need reservations for developed campgrounds. For most state parks contact ReserveAmerica. For Forest Service campgrounds contact the National Recreation Reservation Service. For the Internet addresses and telephone numbers, see Appendix B. Some locations (like Point Reyes) have specific procedures with contact information described in the trip description.

Although rivers are public waterways, always respect private property and obey posted *No Trespassing* signs.

Public campgrounds and facilities often have special rules designed to protect the natural resources and the public. Learn about the regulations governing the sites you plan to visit.

Pack out what you pack in, including food items such as fruit peels. Keep trash bags handy in your camp area or watercraft. Pack the bags and all nonburnable materials with you. Carry out all solid human waste. If you are unable to transport human waste, dig a hole at least 6 inches deep and 150 feet above high water mark for this purpose. Put wastewater from cooking in the same hole and cover it.

Select a campsite that will cause a minimum impact to soil and vegetation.

Locate your shelter so that rainwater will drain away naturally, avoiding the need to dig a ditch around your tent or sleeping bag.

Minimize impacts by using a firepan. Carry a grill so no rocks will be blackened for a fire pit. Use dead and down fuel wood for your fire. If cooking with charcoal, take excess charcoal with you when you leave.

Be careful of extreme fire hazards that develop in summer and autumn. Consider the use of a fuel stove.

Use biodegradable soap for your diswashing and bathing needs. Be sure to bathe and wash dishes well away from the waterway.

Wild and Scenic Rivers Protection

In 1969, Congress passed the National Wild and Scenic Rivers Act. The Act declared that certain rivers that possess extraordinary scenic, recreational, fishery, or wildlife values shall be preserved in their free-flowing state, together with their immediate environments, for the benefit and enjoyment of the people.

Waterways selected for the National Wild and Scenic Rivers were designated wild, scenic, or recreational. Different reaches of the same river may have different designations.

"Wild" rivers are those rivers or segments of rivers that are free of impoundments (dams) and generally inaccessible except by trail, with watersheds or shorelines essentially primitive and water unpolluted.

"Scenic" rivers are those rivers or segments of rivers that are free of impoundments, with shorelines or watersheds still largely primitive and shorelines largely undeveloped, but accessible in places by roads.

"Recreational" rivers are those rivers or segments of rivers that are readily accessible by road or railroad, that may have some development along their shorelines, and that may have undergone some impoundment or diversion in the past.

California has created its own Wild and Scenic Rivers system. People who enjoy rivers and would like to continue paddling with future generations should encourage the legislature to add more streams to the protected Wild and Scenic Rivers status. Do it soon. There are already more than 1,300 dams in California. Support your local and statewide conservation groups like Friends of the River to achieve these goals.

A great blue heron looks over the Trinity National Wild and Scenic River.

Marine Mammal Protection Act

Ocean and marine estuaries offer close encounters with marine wildlife. In the past, hunting severely reduced the population of many of these species. To protect the remaining populations and to restore their numbers, Congress enacted the Marine Mammal Protection Act. The Act makes it illegal to kill, hunt, injure, or harass marine mammals. The marine animals protected include dolphins, whales, seals, sea lions, sea otters, polar bears, manatees, dugongs, and walruses. Harassment is defined as human activity having the potential to disturb a marine mammal in the wild by causing disruption of behavioral patterns, including, but not limited to, migration, breathing, nursing, breeding, feeding, or sheltering. Examples of harassment: paddling by a group of sleeping harbor seals a hundred yards away and causing nervous alarm postures such as head lifting or sitting-up, or causing them to panic and flee into the water. Likewise, harassment would include paddling toward the path of a swimming sea otter so that the otter changes course away from you. Continual disruption of the animals may cause them to abandon a previously frequented area.

The Point Reyes National Seashore advises that "Harbor seals are extremely sensitive to human disturbance. Harbor seals and other pinnipeds need to 'haul out' for several hours every day to rest. Give them a berth of at least 300 feet when the seals are on land and 50 feet in the water. Never handle seal pups found anywhere." Some outfitters recommend staying a minimum of 50 feet from sea lions and otters. The National Marine Fisheries Service requires a minimum of 10 yards between whales and boats. On the other hand, if the

Give lots of space to sea lions and other species protected by the Marine Mammals Protection Act.

animal swims up to you, it's not your fault. The Bay Area Sea Kayakers have posted an extensive discussion on the Internet at www.bask.org. The Elkhorn Slough Foundation recommends that people avoid sudden changes in course and speed. Refrain from standing, shouting, or making sudden gestures, such as waving and pointing. Avoid boating too close to shore when approaching a haul-out area.

Monterey Bay—Cannery Row

Character: A beginning kayaker's delight offering seaside views of Cannery Row while paddling among sea otters, seals, whales, and sea lions. Marine Mammal Protection Act applies.

Length: 2 miles each way.

Average run time: 1 to 3 hours.

Class: SCRS I to III.

Skill level: Beginner to intermediate.

Marine weather: Monterey radio or telephone.

Sea conditions and offshore wave heights: NOAA Monterey buoy.

Tide differences from Golden Gate: Monterey Bay: high tides: –1 hour, 8 minutes; low tides: –47 minutes.

Best season: Year-round.

Craft: Sea kayaks.

Hazards: Large powerboats frequent Monterey Harbor. Although the Monterey Peninsula protects this coast from the Pacific swells, the peninsula seaward of Lovers Point and especially beyond Point Pinos is exposed to the full waves, winds, and force of the Pacific Ocean. Since Monterey Bay water seldom warms above 55 degrees F, even summer weather warrants a wetsuit in case of an upset. Strong northerly winds increase the size of the shore break at the put-in/take-out. Thick fog sometimes reduces visibility and makes navigation difficult. Check marine weather forecasts for fog and wind before starting.

Maps: USGS 7.5 Monterey, AAA Monterey.

Overview: As you paddle along the scenic Monterey peninsula, try to envision the coastline as it used to be: first when Sebastián Vizcaíno discovered it in 1602; later as the backwater capital of Alta California (1775 to 1846); and then in Steinbeck's day as a bustling sardine-fishing center. Today, the tourist Mecca of Monterey Bay is the nation's largest marine sanctuary, and the Pacific Grove State Marine Gardens Fish Refuge protects the shoreside waters north of Pacific Grove. Together they provide a protected habitat that is rich in marine life.

Tour the Monterey Bay Aquarium before you paddle the bay. The aquarium's marvelously detailed exhibits will greatly add to your appreciation of the critters that you meet and see on the water.

Today's 2,000-plus California sea otters have all bred from a colony of less than 50 animals that survived near Big Sur. During the 1700s and 1800s, fur traders hunted sea otters for their rich pelts, with as many as one million hairs per square inch.

The paddling: The Municipal Wharf and Monterey Harbor protect this broad section of Monterey State Beach from wave action. The beach also avoids the busy harbor lanes. Added luxuries are the adjacent facilities of Monterey Bay Kayaks.

Monterey Bay—Cannery Row

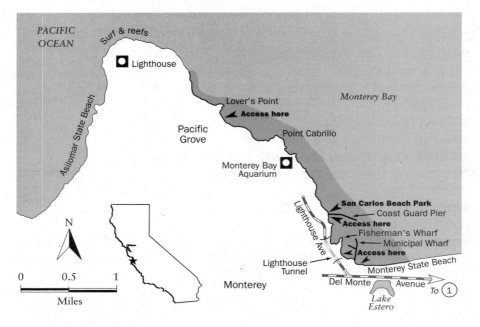

Paddle toward the end of the Municipal Wharf, taking care where commercial fishing boats unload their catch. Large sea lions bark loudly from under this commercial wharf. Some bolder ones may swim close to your boat, then usually dive under it.

Toward the ocean from the Municipal Wharf is the end of the Coast Guard Pier and breakwater. When they are not visiting warmer waters in breeding seasons, hundreds of male California sea lions congregate on the rocks. Sea lions have large front flippers that they use to lift themselves. Stay out of the way of the many large boats using the entrance to the harbor.

Inside the harbor, a concrete sea wall protects the marina. At low tides, the wall offers a display of sea stars, barnacles, and small sponges. On the rocks and kelp beds between Fisherman's Wharf and the Coast Guard Pier, harbor seals and sea otters bask.

Outside the breakwater, head toward the bulky, gray Monterey Bay Aquarium. The route takes you through the kelp beds frequented by sea otters. When not swimming, they look like pairs of brown bumps floating amid the kelp. The otters wrap themselves and their young in kelp to stay stationary and use rocks to break shellfish held on their chest. Remember to keep your distance from sea otters and other marine mammals. (See Introduction regarding Marine Mammal Protection Act.)

Few easy landing sites lie beyond Point Cabrillo except a small surfers' beach next to Lovers Point. Beyond, rocks and reefs line the shore where the surf breaks constantly. Pacific swells crash directly on Asilomar beach.

Even a return to the harbor can be exciting. One time, three gray whales surfaced within 50 yards of us just outside the breakwater. That was a great day!

Access: To get to Monterey Beach State Park adjacent the Municipal Wharf, follow Del Monte Avenue into Monterey. Pass the Sloat Avenue traffic signal. With El Estero Park on the left and the beach on the right, turn into the parking area on the right. The friendly folks at Monterey Bay Kayaks have a place to change, shower, and wash your boat. Otherwise, it is metered parking.

Fisherman's Wharf is at the next stoplight west of Monterey Beach. Look for the parking signs. Turn right toward the parking lot and Municipal Wharf, then left toward the marina. The free boat ramp is beside the harbor master's building. Monterey enforces metered parking 24 hours a day. Beware of motorized and sail craft in the marina.

To get to the Coast Guard Pier Ramp, continue west toward Cannery Row and go through the tunnel. Immediately after the tunnel is the Coast Guard Pier on the right. Adjacent to the jetty is a free boat ramp into the harbor. If you do not like the boat ramp, and if the surf is calm, sandy San Carlos Beach lies just past the jetty. It avoids the harbor traffic and is right next to the kelp beds. Like the other places in Monterey, the city meters parking.

Shuttle: None.

For more information: (See Appendix B for street addresses, Web addresses, and phone numbers.) For rentals and guided tours, telephone Monterey Bay Kayaks or visit the website. For state parks camping reservations, contact ReserveAmerica. To learn other conditions at the Monterey Bay State Seashore, call them or view their website. Contact Monterey Peninsula Visitors and Convention Bureau for accommodations, dining, and activities.

▣ Elkhorn Slough

Character: Paddling calm water in the Elkhorn Slough is an unforgettable experience for viewing marine wildlife. Marine Mammal Protection Act applies.

Length: Up to 5 miles each way.

Average run time: 3 to 7 hours.

Class: Flatwater estuary.

Skill level: Beginner.

Tide differences from Golden Gate: Elkhorn Slough California Highway 1 bridge: high tides: –1 hour, 6 minutes; low tides: –49 minutes. Kirby Park: high tides: –43 minutes; low tides: –39 minutes.

Best season: Year-round. Best bird watching is in the winter.

Craft: Canoes and kayaks.

Hazards: Many fishing and pleasure boats ply Moss Landing Harbor. Strong ebb tides, up to 3 knots, can sweep unwary paddlers into the CA 1 pilings or carry you into the open ocean.

Maps: USGS 7.5 Moss Landing, Prunedale.

Overview: Expect to spend lots of time enjoying the marine and avian wildlife at one of the largest salt marshes between San Francisco and Morro Bay. "Rolling hills with coastal oak and Monterey pine overlook tidal creeks and salt marshes in this outstanding Monterey Bay wetland with more than 250 bird species" (*California Wildlife Viewing Guide* by Falcon Publishing). Six endangered species inhabit the mudflats, marshes, and uplands surrounding the slough.

Moss Landing State Wildlife Area borders 3 miles of the slough along the north and west sides. East of the power generating plant, the National Estuarine Research Reserve manages 1,400 acres on the south and east shores. Elkhorn Slough is one of only two National Estuarine Research Reserves in California. Plan to explore the visitor center at 1700 Elkhorn Road.

Plan your trip to take advantage of the winds and currents. Strong afternoon winds blowing inland from Monterey Bay can make the paddle to Moss Landing difficult. Please help protect all plant and animal life in the slough. East of the railroad tracks, the Elkhorn Slough Reserve and connected waterways are off-limits. Posted areas on the west side are closed to boaters. The Reserve allows no camping or fires. Landing and toilets can only be found at Kirby Park and the Moss Landing put-in. Rubis Creek dock and the nearby outhouses are on private property and were closed effective January 1, 2000. The state permits seasonal waterfowl hunting in the main waterway and Moss Landing Wildlife Area.

Ask the folks at Monterey Bay Kayaks (MBK) to recommend nearby restaurants in Moss Landing. That harbor town sits at the mouth of the slough. A prominent whaling center in the nineteenth and early twentieth centuries, the marinas are home to hundreds of pleasure boats, commercial fishing vessels, and two marine research institutes.

Elkhorn Slough

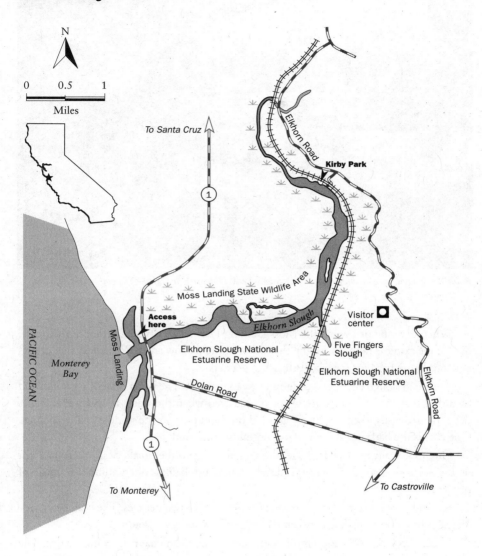

The paddling: Consult your tide tables to plan this trip. The slough's tides can give you a free ride back to your launch site, leave you stranded on a mudflat, or even wash you out to sea. Start at Moss Landing Harbor with an incoming tide. Start at Kirby Park when the tide is high. With favorable wind and tides, you can float the entire distance from Kirby Park to Moss Landing. Otherwise start and end at the same place.

Rubis Creek winds its way through Moss Landing State Wildlife Area at Elkhorn Slough.

When entering or leaving the Moss Landing Harbor, observe the "rules of the road." Stay to the extreme right side of the channel or in the shallow areas. Remember that canoes and kayaks are hard for large boats to see and avoid.

The main slough channel is wide and easy to navigate. The water is usually smooth and so turbid that the bottom is impossible to see even when the water is only a few inches deep. Don't be surprised if you go aground on a mud bar in the middle of the channel. One clue is the harbor seals hauled out on midstream mud bars.

One mile from the CA 1 bridge, the slough bends to the north. Seals often haul out on the north side, so keep 100 yards distant. The south bank is often home to a lineup of pelicans.

Sea otters have returned to the slough during the past two decades. They can be incredibly cute, but do not paddle between the adult otters and their young.

Rubis Creek forms a loop on the north side of the main channel. At higher tides, the tidal creeks offer close-up views of marsh birds, crabs, and other mudbank-dwelling critters. Birds and fish prey upon these invertebrates, so they are an important part of the food web. The many sinuous turns test your maneuvering ability and get more difficult as the tide ebbs. If you get stranded at low water, you may have to wait for the next high tide to get out. The gluey goo under the pickleweed is too soft to support a person, and the salt marsh is sensitive to trampling.

A wide mouth under a shaded oak hillside proclaims the east end of the Rubis Creek loop. Look across the broad expanse of water to the east. You can probably see the visitor center far up the hillside.

Five Fingers Sloughs open to the south. Paddle only as far as the railroad trestle. Returning to the main slough, you can paddle another two miles to Kirby Park. Marshland, with attendant bird life, borders both sides. Near the shallows look for the dorsal fins of smoothhound and leopard sharks or the wingtips of bat rays slicing the water. The two islands splitting the distance are closed to visitors. To the east, farmers have planted strawberries on several hillsides.

Start your return to Moss Landing by early afternoon. Especially in summer, the northwest winds build into a stiff headwind by late afternoon. It may be the hardest paddling you do all day.

The California Highway 1 bridge pilings are one of the few potential hazards to careless paddlers. The hazard occurs only when the tidal current is strong or the wind strongly opposes the current. Keep your boat in line with the current through the bridge. Then head to the north side and the launch area. Take care not to be swept through the narrow harbor mouth into the swells of open Monterey Bay. Paddling upstream is difficult, and many large boats use that passage. The sandy beaches outside the harbor require a surf landing.

Access: Moss Landing Harbor District Launch Ramp is on the west side of CA 1, just north of the Elkhorn Slough bridge and the huge power plant, behind Little Baja, and next to Monterey Bay Kayak shop. MBK rents boats and leads tours of Elkhorn Slough. Fee parking for ramp users.

Kirby Park has parking, boat ramp, and dock at the east end of the slough. From CA 1 northbound, turn east onto Dolan Road at Moss Landing Power plant. After 3.5 miles turn left at Elkhorn Road, then go 4.5 curvy miles (pass the Elkhorn Slough National Estuarine Research Reserve Visitor Center) to Kirby Park. Look for a small sign on the left.

From CA 1 southbound: Turn east at Salinas Road and go 1.4 miles to Werner Road. Turn right onto Werner, then right again (south) on Elkhorn Road, and bear right once more to stay on Elkhorn Road. Go about 2.4 miles paralleling the slough to Kirby Park. From U.S. Highway 101: Go west on CA 156 toward Castroville. Then turn north onto Castroville Road, bear right (east) onto Dolan Road, then turn left (north) at Elkhorn Road, and go about 4.5 curvy miles to Kirby Park.

Shuttle: Optional. From Moss Landing to Kirby Park is 8 miles, or about 20 minutes.

For more information: (See Appendix B for phone numbers, websites, and street addresses.) Visit the Elkhorn Slough Foundation website for an excellent overview of the slough and the National Estuarine Research Reserve Foundation programs, or call them for more specific information. For rentals and guided tours, telephone Monterey Bay Kayaks or visit their website.

▦ Chesbro Reservoir

Character: Chesbro is a small, placid lake in the western foothills of the Santa Clara Valley.
Size: 1.1 miles long, 0.1 mile wide, 2.6 miles of shoreline.
Elevation: 525 feet.
Class: Flatwater lake.
Skill level: Beginner.
Best season: Spring, summer, and autumn.
Craft: Canoes and kayaks.
Hazards: No unusual hazards.
Maps: USGS 7.5 Mt. Madonna.

Overview: Santa Clara County manages the 650-acre Chesbro Reservoir for recreation and to help recharge the groundwater supplies of the Santa Clara Valley. Fishing for largemouth bass, catfish, and crappie is popular. The park limits water activities to 8:00 A.M. to 30 minutes before sunset and prohibits swimming and gasoline engines. A boat-launch ramp and parking area are near the lake's east end.

Hills surrounding the lake support grasslands, hardwood habitats, chaparral, and ranchettes.

Summer days are warmer than most of the San Francisco Bay Area, but not as toasty as the Central Valley.

The paddling: Easy access from the southern Santa Clara Valley suburbs makes Chesbro a pleasant choice for a peaceful paddle or to practice technique. Due to the shallow depth, the water gets warm in the summer but also recedes after prolonged dry winters.

Avoid landing on the private lands bordering the western third of the south shore. Public lands include all the area between the water and Oak Glen Avenue and the eastern two thirds of the southern shore closest to the dam.

Access: From Morgan Hill, exit U.S. Highway 101 at Tennant Avenue. Go west on Tennant for 1 mile. Turn right onto Monterey for 1 block, then west on Edmonston Avenue for 1.8 miles to Oak Glen Avenue. Turn right (north) on Oak Glen Avenue for 1.6 miles to the intersection with Llagas Creek Avenue. Turn right onto the combined Llagas Creek and Oak Glen Avenue. At 0.1 mile, turn left to follow Oak Glen up the hill by the dam. The parking area and launch ramp are just past the dam.

Shuttle: None.

For more information: (See Appendix B for phone numbers, websites, and street addresses.) Contact the Santa Clara County Parks and Recreation Department for current use fees by telephone or check the Chesbro Reservoir County Park web page.

Chesbro Reservoir

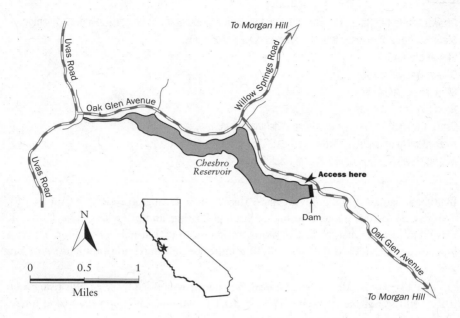

⁴ Lexington Reservoir

Character: In the Santa Cruz Mountains, this lake is popular for rowing, paddling, and fishing.
Size: Length 2.2 miles, width 0.2 mile, shoreline 7.2 miles.
Elevation: 645 feet.
Class: Flatwater lake.
Skill level: Beginner.
Best season: All year.
Craft: Canoes, kayaks, sailboats, and fishing boats.
Hazards: No unusual hazards.
Maps: USGS 7.5 Los Gatos, Castle Rock Ridge.

Overview: Santa Clara County manages the 960-acre Lexington Reservoir County Park. This day-use park is popular for hiking, fishing, boating, and picnicking. The "Fish Sniffer Online" reports that the lake supports black bass, trout, bluegill, and crappie. The park limits water activities to 8:00 A.M. to 30 minutes before sunset and prohibits swimming and gasoline engines.

The lake sits astride the San Andreas Rift Zone surrounded by steep hills rising more than 1,000 feet above the water. These Santa Cruz mountains support redwood forests, chaparral, grasslands, hardwoods, and mixed conifer habitats.

Summer days are comfortable although fog often swirls atop the mountain ridges to the west. Bring a jacket and your wallet for the day-use fee.

The paddling: Proximity to the South Bay and public access make this a favorite place for South Bay paddling clubs and kayaking shops to train beginners. Several rowing clubs take advantage of the lake's 2-mile straight midline for rowing practice.

A few landing spots are scattered along the western (freeway) side of the lake, but the eastern shoreline tends to be very steep. Several short side canyons are interesting to explore at higher water levels.

Access: From southbound California Highway 17, exit at Bear Creek Road, cross the highway, and reenter CA 17 northbound. Exit at Alma Bridge Road and go east on Alma Bridge Road 0.3 mile to the dam. Cross the dam to the launching area. From northbound CA 17, exit directly to Alma Bridge Road.

Shuttle: None.

For more information: (See Appendix B for phone numbers, websites, and street addresses.) Contact the Santa Clara County for current use fees by telephone or check the Lexington Reservoir County Park Internet site.

Lexington Reservoir

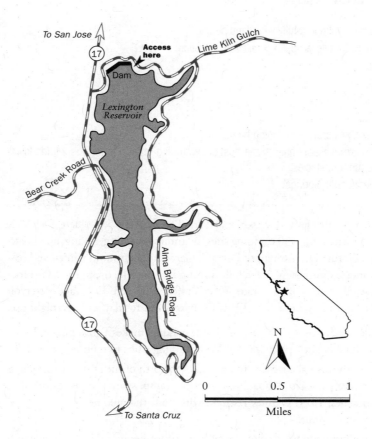

5 Lake Del Valle

Character: Long, narrow lake in a hilly woodland setting.
Size: 4.8 miles long, 0.25 mile wide, 14.6 miles of shoreline.
Elevation: 700 feet.
Class: Flatwater lake.
Skill level: Beginner.
Best season: All year.
Craft: Canoes, kayaks, sail craft, and fishing boats.
Hazards: Lifeguards are available only at the posted swimming areas. During the winter, lower water levels expose more obstacles.
Maps: USGS 7.5 Mendenhall Springs.

Overview: Operated by the East Bay Regional Park District, the 5,000-acre Del Valle Regional Park offers picnicking, 150 camping sites, swimming, boating, hiking, and horseback riding. The California Department of Fish and Game stocks trout in winter, and bass fishing is excellent in the summer. Wooded hills surrounding the lake rise to the 2,000-foot elevation. Constructed as part of the State Water Project, 700-acre Del Valle Reservoir stores water for the South Bay Aqueduct. EBRPD charges fees for day and overnight use.

The paddling: Wide, sandy East Beach, with its ample parking, makes a great put-in. Excellent facilities make this a favorite place for Bay Area paddling clubs to train new members.

Long and skinny, the several coves are fun to explore. North of the ramp, swimming is permitted anywhere the park allows boats. South of the ramp, swimming is restricted to designated swim beaches. EBRPD rules restrict boats from the area near the dam and impose a 10-m.p.h. speed limit.

Blustery summer afternoon winds blow from the northwest end of the lake. The winds that make good windsurfing also make tough upwind paddling. Winter water levels drop enough to expose the bottom at the southeast end and along parts of the lake's east side.

Access: From California 84 in Livermore, go south on Livermore Avenue, which becomes Tesla Road. Turn south on Mines Road, then bear right onto Del Valle Road to the Del Valle Regional Park. Driving distance from Livermore is about 7 miles.

Shuttle: None.

For more information: (See Appendix B for phone numbers, websites, and street addresses.) You can obtain camping reservations and group-use information from the East Bay Regional Park District by phone or by visiting their website.

Lake Del Valle

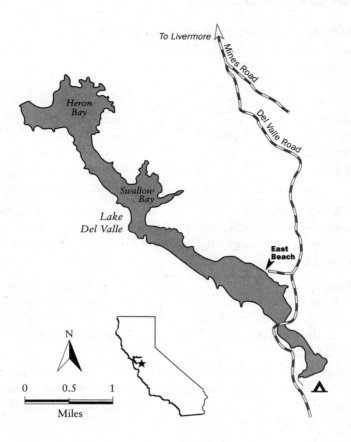

 Lafayette Reservoir

Character: Nestled in the East Bay hills, this lake is popular for paddling, fishing, and relaxing.
Size: Length 0.6 mile, width 0.7 mile, shoreline 2.6 miles.
Elevation: 456 feet, 126 surface acres.
Class: Flatwater lake.
Skill level: Beginner.
Best season: All year.
Craft: Canoes, kayaks, and other car-top boats.
Hazards: No unusual hazards.
Maps: USGS 7.5 Briones Valley.

Overview: East Bay Municipal Utility District owns and operates this popular day-use area for jogging, fishing, boating, and picnicking. You can rent rowboats and pedal boats at the lake. Because the reservoir holds emergency drinking water supplies, EBMUD prohibits swimming and gasoline engines.

The paddling: Good facilities make this a favorite place for Bay Area paddling clubs to train new members. The road from the dam leads to the rental boat docks, concession building, and rest rooms. Nearby is another small dock for launching canoes and other small, private boats. After unloading your gear, move your vehicle to the parking area on the dam or above the visitor center.

The surrounding hills climb 560 feet above the lake. Grasslands and a verdant mix of coastal trees disguise the proximity of urban development. Irregular in shape, the shoreline is long enough for the energetic paddler to get a good workout. Located between the ocean and the Central Valley, the climate is delightful year-round, not too hot in the summer nor too cold in the winter.

Access: Exit California 24 in Lafayette. The park entrance is south of Mount Diablo Boulevard, 0.8 mile east of Acalanes Road and 0.8 mile west of Happy Valley Road. The boat launch area is down the hill below the west end of the dam. EBMUD charges day-use and boat-launching fees.

Shuttle: None.

For more information: (See Appendix B for phone numbers, websites, and street addresses.) Contact the East Bay Municipal Utility District for current use fees by telephone or check their Internet site.

Lafayette Reservoir

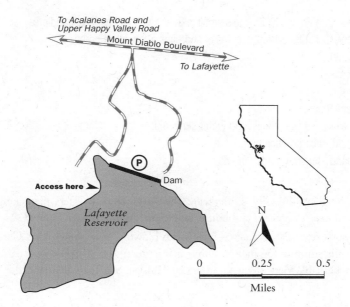

▨ 7 Berkeley Aquatic Park

Character: Beside San Francisco Bay, this small lake is handy to East Bay paddlers.
Size: 1.0 mile long, 0.1 mile wide, 2.1 miles of shoreline, 68 surface acres.
Elevation: Sea level.
Class: Flatwater lake.
Skill level: Beginner.
Best season: Year-round.
Craft: Canoes, kayaks, rowing shells, and water ski boats.
Hazards: Water ski clubs practice here.
Maps: AAA Oakland, Berkeley, and Alameda.

Overview: Operated by the City of Berkeley, the 100-acre park offers picnicking, rest rooms, Frisbee course, a water ski clubhouse, and launch ramp.

Only 150 yards from San Francisco Bay, winds blowing from the Golden Gate keep the park cool while summer fog makes sunburns infrequent. Look to the west past Interstate 80 for a remarkable view of the Golden Gate Bridge, San Francisco, and the Marin Headlands.

The paddling: Local paddlers and rowers use this long, straight lake for competitive practice. The narrow surface is far calmer than the choppy bay waters west of the freeway. Even if the city permitted swimming, typical Berkeley weather keeps the water cool, and it seldom looks clear enough to invite a dip.

Although surrounded by city, the park is an aquatic oasis for egrets, herons, and gulls.

Access: Bolivar Drive: From University Avenue in Berkeley go south on Sixth Street to Addison or Bancroft Way. Turn west and follow Bancroft or Addison to the park.

South end Bolivar Drive: From Ashby Avenue turn north onto Bay Street, then west onto Bolivar. Optionally, from Ashby Avenue take the Interstate 80 northbound ramp and exit onto Bolivar before reaching the freeway.

Shuttle: None.

For more information: (See Appendix B for phone numbers, websites, and street addresses.) Contact the City of Berkeley Recreation Office by phone.

Berkeley Aquatic Park and East San Francisco Bay—Emeryville to Berkeley

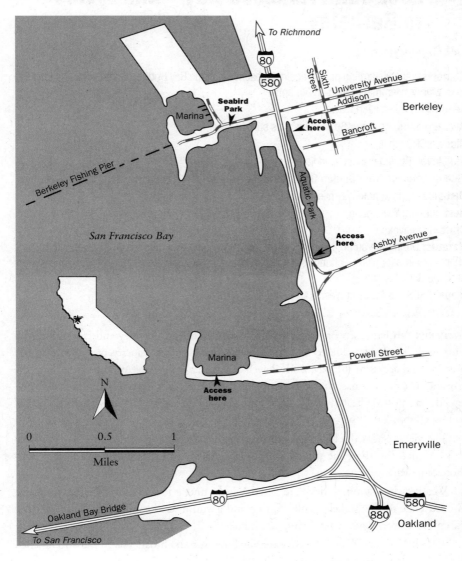

To Richmond

Sixth Street

University Avenue

Addison

Berkeley

Access here

Bancroft

Seabird Park

Marina

Aquatic Park

Berkeley Fishing Pier

Access here

Ashby Avenue

San Francisco Bay

N

Powell Street

0   0.5   1

Miles

Marina

Access here

Emeryville

Oakland Bay Bridge

To San Francisco

Oakland

East San Francisco Bay—Emeryville to Berkeley

(see map on page 31)

Character: An exhilarating paddle against a backdrop of the Bay Bridge, Alcatraz, and the East Bay Hills. Marine Mammal Protection Act applies.

Length: 1.8 miles each way.

Average paddling time: 60 minutes plus surfing time.

Class: SCRS I to II.

Skill level: Beginner to intermediate.

Tide differences from Golden Gate: Berkeley: high tides: +21 minutes; low tides: +38 minutes.

Distance: Approximately 2 miles.

Best season: Year-round.

Craft: Sea kayaks.

Hazards: During the summer, strong winds push the cold San Francisco Bay waves into a steep chop. Powerboats ply the channels leading to the marinas. Beware of fast-moving wind surfers near the Berkeley side.

Maps: USGS 7.5 Oakland West, AAA Berkeley and Oakland.

Overview: San Francisco Bay between University Avenue in Berkeley and Powell Street in Emeryville is popular due to its proximity to Berkeley, the paucity of other East Bay beaches, and access to the Bay. Both Powell Street and University Avenue extend into the Bay and support marinas, charter boats, restaurants, and commercial buildings. The Berkeley side has more dedicated public space for parks, a beach, a small craft wharf, and the Cal Sailing Club.

The views across the bay are a prime attraction. According to the East Bay Regional Park District, this shoreline will be a component of the future Oakland-Richmond Eastshore State Park.

Weatherwise, summer days are often windy under low clouds blowing from the Golden Gate to the Berkeley Hills. Spring and autumn yield some of the sunniest days. Except on stormy days, winter winds are milder.

Check National Weather Service marine forecast radio broadcasts from San Francisco or check their Internet site (see Appendix A).

The paddling: Emeryville Marina is busy with large and small yachts and charter fishing craft. Launch from the floating low dock next to the launch ramp. Since the channel leading into the marina is narrow and the adjacent water is shallow at low tides, clear the channel as quickly as possible to allow powerboats to pass. Once outside the marina, the view of the Bay Bridge is awesome. If the summer wind machine is working, paddling in the waves will be a great workout.

A shallow reef lies between Emeryville and Berkeley. Minus tides expose it. Some adventurous paddlers have picnicked there. Expect to detour around it.

The Berkeley fishing pier used to extend 2.5 miles to the San Francisco County Line. Only a short section is now in repair and open to the public. At the base of the pier are restaurants with customers admiring your courage and abilities. Put on a good show for them and surf your way with the swells toward the Berkeley take-out.

Paddle south of the restaurants, avoiding the riprap shoreline, then turn north to reach quieter water and the beach take-out. Keep an eye out for the many fast-moving wind-surfers and sailboats nearby.

No matter which place you put in, the return paddle makes for a good workout in an exhilarating setting.

Access: Emeryville Marina is near the end of Powell Street west of the Watergate Build-ings. From Interstate 80, exit at Powell (if westbound, follow the frontage road to Powell). Go west on Powell past the Watergate Buildings to the marina. The marina has a popular public launching ramp and paved parking.

Seabird Park, Berkeley, is on the south side of University Avenue west of I-80. Bear left past Marina Boulevard. Launch from the beach on the seaward side of the Cal Sailing Club and wharf.

Shuttle: Optional. 3.5 miles (15 minutes).

For more information: (See Appendix B for phone numbers, websites, and street addresses.) Call the East Bay Regional Park District or check their Internet site.

9 San Leandro Bay

Character: Protected from the wind and waves, this shallow estuary and wildlife refuge is an escape from the industrial East Bay. Marine Mammal Protection Act applies.
Length: 2 miles.
Average run time: 2 to 4 hours.
Class: SCRS I, flatwater estuary.
Skill level: Beginner.
Tide differences from Golden Gate: San Leandro Channel: high tides: +42 minutes; low tides: +52 minutes.
Best season: Year-round.
Craft: Sea kayaks and canoes.
Hazards: Apart from the cold water traditional to San Francisco Bay, the greatest concerns for San Leandro Bay are the presence of power boats, water unfit for swimming, and the wide expanse of mud flats that emerge at low water.
Maps: USGS 7.5 San Leandro, Oakland East, AAA Oakland.

Overview: San Leandro Bay is a place of contrasts—an estuarine wildlife sanctuary bounded by the Oakland Alameda County Coliseum to the east and the Oakland International Airport to the west. Martin Luther King Jr. Regional Shoreline is a 1,220-acre park that helps to protect a remnant of what was once an extensive marshland. Across Airport Channel, 50-acre Arrowhead Marsh is part of the Western Hemisphere Shorebird Reserve Network.

The paddling: Carry your boat to the floating docks or ramp along Martin Luther King Jr. Regional Shoreline. Low tides are a major concern here. Low tides ground the docks and expose the San Leandro Bay mud flats. So time your paddling for incoming tides to maximize your time on the water.

From the beach cafe, paddle westward along the Airport Channel 0.5 miles to Arrowhead Marsh. You can observe birds wading or in their marsh habitat.

From the north end of Arrowhead Marsh you can continue to explore the Oakland side of the bay. Continue to paddle counterclockwise first toward the fishing pier, then to Garretson Point and the Damon Marsh shoreline. This route will lead to the deeper water channel near the Alameda Estuary that leads back to the Airport Channel. The circuit is about 4 miles depending on tide and wind conditions.

They prohibit motorized boats and jet skis within 100 feet of the marshes and bird sanctuary, but the motor craft do visit the deeper waters.

Access: You can reach Martin Luther King Jr. Regional Shoreline from the Interstate 880 Hegenberger Road Exit. After exiting, turn toward Oakland Airport. Turn right onto Doolittle Drive, which parallels the shoreline of San Leandro Bay. A sign reads: "Martin

San Leandro Bay

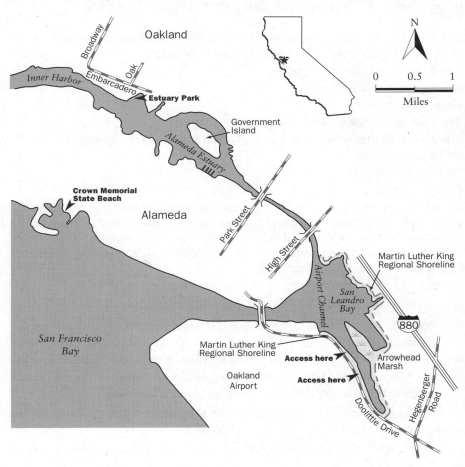

Luther King Jr. Regional Shoreline." After about a mile, look for the small boat dock. Another dock is found behind the closed Beach Cafe, 0.3 mile northward on Doolittle Drive toward Alameda Island. Both have public parking.

Shuttle: None.

For more information: (See Appendix B for phone numbers, websites, and street addresses.) Call the East Bay Regional Park District or check their Internet site.

San Francisco Bay—Angel Island

Character: This world class sea kayak tour visits some really expensive real estate and the largest island in San Francisco Bay. Marine Mammal Protection Act applies.
Length: 5.6 to 10.0 miles from Sausalito.
Average paddling time: 4 to 7 hours.
Class: SCRS II to III.
Skill level: Intermediate to expert.
Tide differences from Golden Gate: Sausalito Corps of Engineers Dock: high tides: +10 minutes; low tides: +21 minutes.
Best season: Year-round.
Craft: Sea kayaks.
Hazards: Sausalito is a busy nexus of marinas and pleasure craft. Beware of the considerable traffic and adhere to the "Navigation Rules of the Road." Raccoon Strait has strong currents and is a deep-water channel sometimes used by ocean-going cargo ships. Check the tide and current tables for your trip. Strong winds and steep waves may challenge your abilities along the San Francisco and Golden Gate sides of Angel Island.
Maps: USGS 7.5 San Francisco North, San Quentin, San Rafael.

Overview: The largest island in San Francisco Bay, Angel Island State Park has a rich history that includes Spanish ranchers, U.S. Army bases, "the Ellis Island of the West Coast," and Nike missile sites. World travelers visit by ferry boat from San Francisco, Vallejo, and Tiburon. Many paths and fire roads allow hiking and bicycle exploration of the beaches, historic barracks, and summit of 752-high Mount Caroline Livermore.

Raccoon Strait and the east sides of the island are usually protected from wind and waves. The west and south shores are exposed and rocky.

Angel Island State Park has several walk-in campgrounds, including one for kayakers.

The paddling: Consider the wind and current in planning this tour. Slack tide is best. A flood tide makes it easier to get to the island and an ebb tide eases the return trip. The current that accompanies exceptionally high tides or minus tides may be stronger than your paddling ability. If the prevailing westerly wind is strong, the paddling will be wetter and more tiring if you decide to circumnavigate the island.

Most folks put in at Schoonmaker Point or Horseshoe Bay in Sausalito, cross through the pleasure-boat traffic on Richardson Bay, then round Peninsula Point to Tiburon. From Tiburon paddle 0.6 mile across busy Raccoon Strait to Angel Island. Sheltered Ayala Cove is the busy landing for ferry boats and is an anchorage for pleasure craft staying overnight. Continue clockwise for more sheltered and quieter beaches at China Cove or Quarry Beach (0.7 mile and 1.9 miles, respectively, from Ayala Cove).

If you choose to continue paddling from Quarry Beach past Point Blunt, you will encounter all the force of wind and waves that the bay offers that day. The rocky shoreline

San Francisco Bay—Angel Island

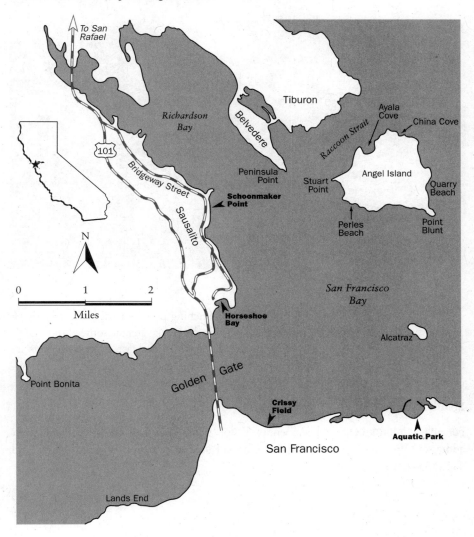

To San Rafael

Richardson Bay

Tiburon

Belvedere

Ayala Cove

China Cove

Raccoon Strait

Angel Island

101

Bridgeway Street

Peninsula Point

Stuart Point

Quarry Beach

Sausalito

Schoonmaker Point

Perles Beach

Point Blunt

N

San Francisco Bay

0   1   2

Miles

Horseshoe Bay

Alcatraz

Point Bonita

Golden Gate

Crissy Field

Aquatic Park

San Francisco

Lands End

to Perles Beach and Stuart Point (2.6 miles from Quarry Beach) offers little shelter. You will also experience one of the greatest views in the world, the Golden Gate and San Francisco. Calm or windy, it is an exhilarating tour.

Access: Schoonmaker Point Beach and Marina from U.S. Highway 101: Exit south, looking for signs to the "Bay Model." At the light, turn left on Libertyship Way and follow it all the way to Schoonmaker Marina and beach next to Sea Trek. Unload at the sandy beach, then find a legal parking space. This is a protected starting point to cruise Richardson Bay.

San Francisco from the Golden Gate.

East Fork Baker—Horseshoe Bay can be a launching point for trips into the bay or around the Marine Headlands. Immediately outside the breakwater are some of the wildest sea conditions on the West Coast. Steep waves, strong winds, and fast, swirling currents are the norm. Check your tide tables and weather before you paddle here. Adding to the confusion are many pleasure craft and large ocean-going vessels transiting the Golden Gate.

Shuttle: None.

For more information: (See Appendix B for phone numbers, websites, and street addresses.) Visit the Angel Island and California Parks websites. For ferry information, call 415–435–1915.

11 China Camp Shoreline

Character: Bordered by oak-studded hillsides, this bird-filled marshland opens to the broad expanse of San Pablo Bay. Marine Mammal Protection Act applies.
Length: 4.25 miles to China Camp, 5.0 miles to McNears Beach.
Average paddling time: 3 to 4 hours.
Class: SCRS I to III.
Skill level: Beginner with experience to intermediate.
Tide differences from Golden Gate: Gallinas Creek: high tides: +1 hour, 11 minutes; low tides: +1 hour, 30 minutes. Pt. San Pedro high tides: +59 minutes; low tides: +1 hour, 1 minute.
Favorable tides: Start at high tide at McInnis Park or low tide at China Camp.
Best season: Year-round.
Craft: Canoes, sea kayaks, sailboats, and motorboats.
Hazards: Summertime winds, particularly in the afternoon, blow away from the shore. Some powerboats share the channel to Gallinas Creek. When they occur, northerly winds blow across a wide fetch of San Pablo Bay, creating large waves. As the tide ebbs, stay in the Gallinas Creek channel to avoid being stranded on the mud flats.
Maps: USGS 7.5 Petaluma Point, Novato, San Quentin.

Overview: Popular John F. McInnis County Park provides a great beginning or end for a paddling tour of the marshlands of southwestern San Pablo Bay. The nearby hills of China Camp State Park offer scenic protection from the summer winds blowing in from the Golden Gate. At the end of the peninsula, the old fishing village of China Camp was once the site where hundreds of Chinese established a shrimp fishing village. Today only a few continue their shrimp fishing activities.

Back Ranch Meadows Campground, in the state park, offers walk-in campsites in the nearby hills. The trails are popular with mountain bike enthusiasts. Reservations are recommended on weekends and during the summer.

The paddling: At McInnis Park's small boat dock, Gallinas Slough is barely two kayak lengths wide. The bank on the park side is solid, but across the channel a wide expanse of marsh grasses extends to the south. Easy to paddle with the tide, the park is quickly left behind. Bright white egrets frequently catch the eye. Some seem almost tame, allowing paddlers to come within two boat lengths before taking flight. Less showy great blue herons stalk among the grasses.

The much wider South Fork joins the tide 0.6 mile from the put-in. Some utility lines stretch overhead, and a large sailboat may be moored near some long-established homes. An osprey rewarded our visual search of the marsh.

The marsh extends on both sides of the channel as broad San Pablo Bay comes into view. The breezes from the bay may feel gentle but look to the open water for the sight of whitecaps. Their presence may signal you to make a choice between wet, difficult paddling,

China Camp Shoreline

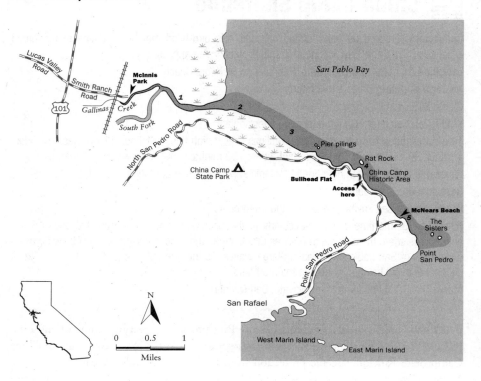

a return to the launch point, or a shortened tour with a take-out at Bullhead Flat. Invariably, the winds will get stronger as you continue toward China Camp.

The edge of the bay has three visual zones: 10 miles of open water to the north, the half-mile-wide swath of marsh grasses to the shore, and the 1,000-foot-high, oak-covered hills of China Camp State Park.

About 2.5 miles from McInnis Park, small hills emerge above the marsh. These are Turtle Back, Jake's Island, Bullet Hill, and Chicken Coop Hill. Just offshore are duck blinds, most frequently occupied by gulls and egrets. You can paddle right into the blinds. Other blinds lie hundreds of yards out in the shallow bay. Old pier pilings, called dolphins, remain at Buckeye Point. A few yards to the west is a narrow, sheltered beach suitable for lunch, if the tide is not too high.

Rounding Buckeye Point, the wind begins to exert its full force in your face. It may be hard work to paddle an open canoe, although comfortable for sea kayaks. The boat ramp at Bullhead Flat provides a take-out and put-in for a shorter trip. Continuing eastward, Rat Rock lies 80 yards from China Camp Point. Naked on the bottom and bushy on top, this small island offers fishing and tide pooling at a low tide.

Naked on the bottom and bushy on top, Rat Rock is close to China Camp Point. At low tide, the island is readily accessible by small boats for fishing and tide pooling.

Another 500 feet beyond are the sandy beach and pier of China Camp Village. The fishing pier and village cafe are open on weekends. A small museum describes the history of the Chinese fishermen at China Camp. Rest rooms and drinking water are also available.

McNears Beach is another 0.75 mile southeast of China Camp Village. It can be a pleasant paddle with great views of the Point Pinole Regional Shoreline across the bay. A popular beach with a 500-foot-long pier marks McNears. Land at the north end of the beach.

Access: John F. McInnis County Park: From U.S. Highway 101, exit at Lucas Valley Road, then turn east onto Smith Ranch Road. Go 0.7 mile to McInnis County Park. Cross the railroad tracks, pass under the park entrance arch, then turn right into a small parking lot. A small dock provides easy canoe and kayak access to the slough. If you passed all the sports fields and approached the golf course, you went too far.

China Camp State Park: From U.S. 101, exit at north San Pedro Road and follow the China Camp State Park signs 5.4 miles to China Camp Village. Turn left down the hill to beach parking. An alternative access point is Bullhead Flat 0.5 mile before the Village. The park requires a day-use fee.

McNears Beach Park: Continue past China Camp Village on San Pedro Road another 0.6 mile to the park entrance. Pay the day-use fee and follow the road to the beach parking area. OK for hand-launch boats. The 500-foot-long fishing pier is a major landmark.

China Camp Village now consists of a pier, shrimp drying sheds, a museum, beach, and snack store. Many Chinese fishermen once lived and worked here.

Shuttle: 8.4 miles, 20 minutes.

For more information: (See Appendix B for phone numbers, websites, and street addresses.) China Camp State Park may be contacted by telephone or on the Internet. Marin County Department of Parks, Open Space, and Cultural Services provides information about McInnis Park and McNears Beach via telephone or on the Internet.

12 Drakes Estero

Character: Point Reyes National Seashore surrounds this protected multi-fingered bay that is a wildlife watcher's dream. Marine Mammal Protection Act applies.

Class: SCRS I to II.

Skill level: Beginner.

Marine weather: 162.40 MHz or check the National Weather Service Marine Weather internet site. See Appendix A.

Tide differences from Golden Gate: Point Reyes: high tides: –50 minutes; low tides: –26 minutes. (Because of the narrow opening, the tides inside Drakes Estero can be hours out of phase with the Point Reyes tides.)

Best season: July 1 through February 28 each year.

Craft: Open canoes and sea kayaks.

Hazards: During ebb tides, beware that the current exiting Drakes Estero may be strong enough to carry boaters into the surf zone at the narrow entrance. Prevailing northwesterly winds may make paddling back to Schooners Bay difficult. Point Reyes water is cold and the weather is often cool enough to require warm jackets, even in summer! Since much of Drakes Estero is very shallow, avoid being stranded on the expansive mud flats at low tides. Thick fog (Point Reyes Lighthouse has the reputation of being the foggiest place in North America) may reduce visibility dramatically and make navigation difficult. Check marine weather forecasts for fog and wind before starting.

Maps: Point Reyes National Seashore, USGS 7.5 Drakes Bay.

Paddling distances:

Johnson's to mouth of Home Bay	1.7 miles	30 minutes–1 hour
Home Bay mouth to Drakes Cove	2.2 miles	45 minutes–1.5 hours
Drakes Cove to Drakes Head	1.4 miles	30 minutes–1 hour
Johnson's to Bull Point	1.7 miles	30 minutes–1 hour
Bull Point to Creamery Bay landing	0.7 miles	15 minutes–0.5 hour

Note that paddling times will double or triple with adverse winds or tides.

Overview: Miwok Indians once occupied Drakes Estero. They used boats of bundled rushes to navigate the calmer waters. In 1579 an English navigator, Sir Francis Drake, stopped for a month to clean the bottom of his *Golden Hinde*. Drake's crew complained of the cold and foggy days. The next visitor was Sebastian Rodriguez Cereno, en route to Acapulco from the Philippines. Heavy winds drove him to seek shelter at Drakes Bay on November 6, 1595, and later destroyed the ship. Cereno and remaining crew safely sailed the ship's small launch to Acapulco. Hoping to recover the wreck, explorer Don Sebastian Vizcaíno arrived on January 6, 1603, the day of the Three Holy Kings. Vizcaíno named the place "Puerto de Los Reyes" and the cape "Punta de Los Reyes" in honor of the three kings of Cologne.

Drakes Estero and Tomales Bay

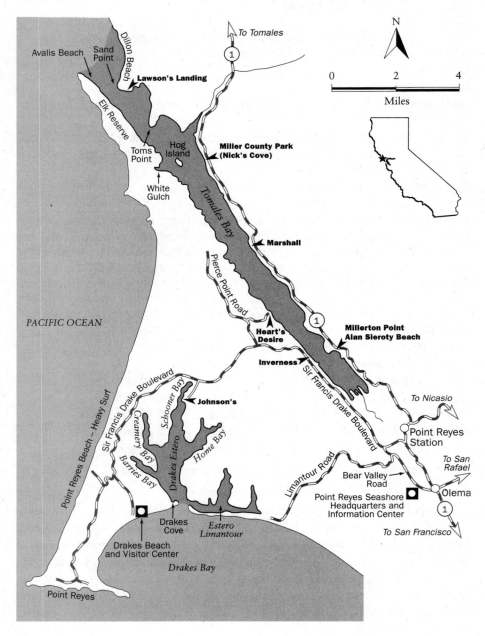

To Tomales

Avalis Beach
Sand Point
Dillon Beach
Lawson's Landing

Elk Reserve

Toms Point
Hog Island
Miller County Park (Nick's Cove)

White Gulch

Tomales Bay

Pierce Point Road

Marshall

PACIFIC OCEAN

Heart's Desire

Millerton Point
Alan Sieroty Beach

Inverness

Sir Francis Drake Boulevard

To Nicasio

Sir Francis Drake Boulevard

Schooner Bay
Johnson's

Creamery Bay

Home Bay

Barries Bay

Drakes Estero

Point Reyes Beach – Heavy Surf

Point Reyes Station

Limantour Road

Bear Valley Road

Point Reyes Seashore Headquarters and Information Center

To San Rafael

Olema

Drakes Cove
Estero Limantour

Drakes Beach and Visitor Center

To San Francisco

Drakes Bay

Point Reyes

N

0   2   4
Miles

During the 1800s, schooners landed at Creamery Bay, Schooner Bay, and Home Bay to transport the highly prized Point Reyes butter and pork to San Francisco. The agricultural era faded with the threat of residential development and creation of P.R.N.S. to preserve the peninsula for the public.

No public facilities exist at Drakes Estero. The closest public facilities are at the Bear Valley Visitor Center or the Ken Patrick Visitor Center (open weekends only) at Drakes Beach.

Wildlife abounds here. The park service reports that Drakes Estero offers the best birding opportunities during the fall migration and winter layover. You can see the largest harbor seal breeding colony in Point Reyes (and 20 percent of California's mainland harbor seal population) at Drakes Estero. To protect the seal population, Drakes Estero is closed to boaters for the seal pupping season, March 1 to June 30. The P.R.N.S. advises that "Harbor seals are extremely sensitive to human disturbance. Harbor seals and other pinnipeds need to haul out for several hours every day to rest. Give them a berth of at least 300 feet when the seals are on land and 50 feet in the water."

P.R.N.S. permits no camping within Drakes Estero.

The paddling: Start at Johnson's with high tide so you have ample depth in the estero, can float out with the ebb, and return with the incoming tide. Note the high white cliffs south of Johnson's in Schooner Bay. They are good landmarks when you return.

Oyster racks speckle the estero. Lattice-like wood structures, they stand several feet above the bottom. Cross members support wires holding oysters below the water surface even at low tide. Clear water in the estero provides the clean environment the oysters need. Near the long structures, a tall post usually protrudes at high tide when the racks submerge. Remember that the oyster racks are in deeper water, enough to float a kayak at low tide. At high tide the tall posts make the racks easier to avoid.

From Schooners Bay you have the choice of heading south to Home Bay, or west to the landing on Creamery Bay.

An old schooner landing sits at the end of Home Bay. At low tide, scores of gulls, cormorants, egrets, and American white pelicans may inhabit the sandbar. Large rafts of the pelicans float in Home Bay. Most of the north end is very shallow. The large grove of overgrown Christmas trees is reputed to host several owls. Contrasting sharply with the surrounding brown hills, the dark green pines make a distinctive landmark.

Paddle south across Home Bay to the low bluffs on the east side of the estero. Hikers often frequent the Sunset Beach trail paralleling this shoreline. Paddle close to the shore until it turns eastward and becomes mud flats.

Expect to encounter harmless bat rays and leopard sharks in the shallows. Rays may suddenly splash their "wings" if surprised. Look for the ends of their wings moving like two parallel dorsal fins. To find paddling depth in the shallows, look for long sea grass. It likes deeper water than the algae that cover mud only a few inches deep.

The low water route to Drakes Cove continues southwest to the far side of the estero. Then follow the steep bluffs seaward.

Sandy beaches are few in Drakes Estero, but Drakes Cove is one of them. Below the bluff just inside the estero is the cove where historians believe Sir Francis Drake landed the *Golden Hinde* for repairs. A large post and plaque commemorate the 1579 event.

A nearby grove of pines is home to egrets, great blue herons, and ravens in their respective breeding seasons. Near the pines is a dirt road and trail leading to the hilltop. On clear days, a spectacular view extends from Bolinas, along the P.R.N.S. surf line, to the distant ends of Schooner and Limantour Bays. The hilltop is also a good place to make a reality check on the weather and tides.

If fog is absent and the tide is not ebbing, you might paddle eastward from Drakes Cove to Estero Limantour. En route you will encounter waves that penetrate the mouth of the estero. Nearby sandbars are favorite places for seals to haul out. Some seals may surface near you for inspection. Soon Limantour Spit protects the estero from waves, and it is an easy paddle to the wind-protected beach at Drakes Head.

If you have timed the tour right, the incoming tide will assist your return paddle.

Much of the estero shoreline is muddy or covered with seaweed that the high tide floods. An exception is the landing site in Creamery Bay. Nearby bluffs protect the beach from the wind. The site has concrete pilings, footprints of wildlife visitors, litter from human visitors, and a small marsh.

Bring a map showing the location of the major mud flats. At low tide, paddle the channels between them. Along the cliffs, the water is usually deep enough for paddling.

Access: Johnson's Oyster Farm: From California Highway 1 take Bear Valley Road or Sir Francis Drake Boulevard to Inverness. Continue on Sir Francis Drake out of Inverness, up the hill, and toward the lighthouse. Go 2.8 miles past the junction with the Pierce Point Road and look for a narrow road on the left with a sign advertising Johnson's Oysters. Ask the workers at Johnson's where you should park to avoid hindering their commercial operations.

Limantour Beach is seldom used because of extensive mud flats if you miss the high tide. From CA 1, take Bear Valley Road west 2 miles to Limantour Road. Go up the hill, enjoy the view, and you'll end at beach-side parking. You can either carry to open water on Limantour Estero or, if you have the skills, try a surf launch into Drake's Bay. The mouth of Drakes Estero is almost 3 miles west of Limantour Beach.

Shuttle: None required.

For more information: (See Appendix B for phone numbers, websites, and street addresses.) To reserve space at the hike-in campsites, contact Point Reyes National Seashore by telephone Monday through Friday from 9:00 A.M. to 2:00 P.M. For other information including hiking, whale watching, and kayaking, telephone 415–663–1092 or view the Internet site at: www.nps.gov/pore.

This anchor and post recall the visit of Sir Francis Drake to the beaches separating Drakes Estero from Drakes Bay.

▚ 13 Tomales Bay

(see map on page 44)

Character: Point Reyes National Seashore borders this long sheltered bay with easy access, surf free beaches, and boat-in camping. Marine Mammal Protection Act applies.

Size: 12 miles long and 0.5 to 1.2 miles wide.

Class: SCRS I to II.

Skill level: Beginner to intermediate.

Marine Weather: 162.40 MHz or check the National Weather Service Marine Weather Internet site.

Tide differences from Golden Gate: Tomales Bay entrance: high tides: −12 minutes; low tides: +20 minutes. Inverness: high tides: +40 minutes; low tides: +1 hour, 24 minutes. Marshall: high tides: +38 minutes; low tides: +1 hour, 16 minutes.

Best season: Year-round.

Craft: Canoes, sea kayaks, sailboats, and motorboats.

Hazards: Although Inverness Ridge protects most of the bay from the Pacific swells, the mouth of Tomales Bay is exposed. Waves break on the rocky coast and across the extensive shallows off Dillon Beach. During ebb tides, be aware that the current exiting Tomales Bay may be strong enough to carry boaters into this broad surf zone. Tomales Bay water is cold and even summer weather deserves layered clothing. Prevailing northwesterly winds may make paddling toward the mouth of the bay difficult. Thick fog sometimes reduces visibility and makes navigation difficult. Check marine weather forecasts for fog and wind before starting.

Maps: Point Reyes National Seashore, USGS 7.5 Point Reyes NE, Tomales, Drakes Bay.

Approximate one-way paddling distances:

Millerton Point to Inverness	0.7 mile
Inverness to Heart's Desire	2.8 miles
Heart's Desire to Marshall Beach	2.4 miles
Marshall to Nick's Cove and Hog Island	3.4 miles
Nick's Cove to Lawson's Landing	3.7 miles
Nick's Cove to Avalis Beach	4.0 miles

Overview: Beautiful Tomales Bay is a great place to take the family and introduce newcomers to sea kayaking. Close to the San Francisco Bay area, Point Reyes is a popular retreat for beach walking, clamming, picnicking, and boating. The bucolic setting, small villages, and recreation opportunities were preserved from wanton development when Congress established the Point Reyes National Seashore (P.R.N.S.) in 1962.

Called an "Island in Time," Point Reyes is a tectonic island separated from the California coast by the San Andreas Rift Zone. Tomales Bay sits on top of the rift zone.

During 1846, Paul Revere's grandson visited Point Reyes. He reported many herds of hundreds of elk, many wild horses, mountain lions, antelope, wolf, coyote, black grouse, crested partridge, geese, blue cranes, wild pigeons, and turkey. Today, Tule elk have returned to Tomales Point north of Pelican Point. Tomales Bay is now part of the Gulf of the Farallones National Marine Sanctuary.

Ten miles of the western shore are public lands managed by the Tomales Bay State Park and the P.R.N.S. In contrast, the eastern shore is privately owned.

P.R.N.S. permits boat-in camping on beaches north of Indian Beach. As of November 1999, camping regulations require that all waste, including human waste, must be packed out. Campers must pay for camping permits in advance. At the same time they can get campfire permits. Carry water or be prepared to treat any water from park streams. Driftwood for fires is usually scarce, so bring your own fuel. Build fires below the high-tide line.

Point Reyes Station and Inverness have several excellent restaurants and some good motels. Olema has fine bed-and-breakfast accommodations for those wanting a more pampered life. Several kayaking outfitters lead trips to Tomales Bay.

Check National Weather Service broadcasts from San Francisco on 162.55 MHz or taped telephone recordings at: 831-656-1725 (Monterey).

The paddling: Paddlers can reach Tomales Bay from a half dozen points scattered along its 12-mile length. Paddling across the narrow bay is easy. In the summer, the wind predictably blows from the northwest and increases in the afternoon. Use the wind and tide to your advantage, by paddling northward in the morning, then return with the flood tide and the wind at your back.

The south end of the bay is shallow and interesting to explore from Inverness or Millerton Point at high tides. Many birds inhabit the area and harmless rays and leopard sharks swim in the shallows.

Paddling northward from Inverness, 8 miles of the west shore has a beach in almost every cove. Teachers, Shell, Heart's Desire, and Indian Beaches are in Tomales Bay State Park. Land at Indian Beach to see a Miwok Indian lodge replica, like those that used to exist along Tomales Bay.

On the east shore is the Marconi Conference Center, site of the 1913 trans-Pacific Marconi wireless station. If you stay at the center, plan to kayak Tomales Bay. Other historic sites include schooner landing wharves at Lairds Landing, Pierce's Wharf, and Paper Mill Creek.

Kilkenny, Marshall, Tomales, White Gulch, Blue Gum, and Avalis Beaches have space above high tides suitable for camping. Low tides expose narrower sandy areas suitable for lunch stops.

Tule elk roam the hills once used for cattle grazing. North of Pelican Point, look for antlered elk bulls on the skyline. At White Gulch we saw more than fifty elk. The elk cropped the grassy flat behind Avalis Beach like a park.

To protect the wildlife, P.R.N.S. has instituted the following wildlife protection closures: Pelican Point is closed for day and overnight use to provide a roosting place for pelicans; the east side of Hog Island is closed for overnight and day use to provide a haul-out for harbor seals; the west side of Hog Island remains open for day use; South Blue Gum

Beach is closed March 15 through June 30 to provide a safe haul-out for harbor seals during pupping season.

The P.R.N.S. advises that "Harbor seals are extremely sensitive to human disturbance. Harbor seals and other pinnipeds need to haul out for several hours every day to rest. Give them a berth of at least 300 feet when the seals are on land and 50 feet in the water." Never handle seal pups found anywhere.

To protect paddlers, P.R.N.S. advises that, in 1996, white sharks attacked two people at the mouth of Tomales Bay. Such a rare event is most likely to happen at seal haul-out areas, such as Tomales Bay north of Tom's Point.

From Miller County Park (Nick's Cove) it is an easy 0.75-mile paddle to Hog and Duck Islands. Both sprout a grove of trees above the high-tide lines. Larger Hog Island is open to day use. A sandbar on the northwest side provides an easy place to land. Low tides expose a narrow path between the islands. The sandbar on the east side is reserved for seals.

Continuing westward, a white cliff marks the cove at White Gulch and a nearby beach. The easiest paddle northward is along the west shore where the water is deeper and more sheltered from the wind. Pleasant, narrow, sandy beaches line the coast.

An exhilarating adventure is to ride the morning ebb out toward Avalis Beach. Other beaches line the route to match your comfort with the wind, waves, and current. Remember that only rocks line the coast north of Avalis Beach, and the narrow channel at Sand Point accelerates the current out to sea. Avoid the shallows and surf on the Dillon Beach side. In the afternoon, ride the flood into the bay and surf the waves with the wind at your back.

From Sand Point and Tom's Point, the shortest route is not always the quickest. The water south of both points is very shallow and the tide channels convoluted. Commercial metal shellfish cages line the shallow bottom to scrape your boat bottom between Tom's Point, Walker Creek, and Hog Island. Floating the main channel toward Hog Island is faster and easier.

For windy days with a high tide, explore the sheltered lower reaches of Walker Creek, paddling between Nick's Cove and the access near Camp Tomales along California Highway 1.

Access: Alan Sieroty Beach of Tomales Bay State Park lies on the east shore 4.3 miles north of Point Reyes Station. Look for the eucalyptus grove at Millerton Point. Carry your boat 100 yards to a sheltered beach at medium to high tides. This day-use park is a fee area.

Tamal Saka Tomales Bay Kayaking is sandwiched between California Highway 1 and the bay on the south end of Marshall and 9.4 miles north of Point Reyes Station. Tamal Saka provides kayak rental, instruction, and guided trips. Ask before parking there.

Miller County Park (Nick's Cove) on CA 1 is 13 miles north of Point Reyes Station and 4 miles south of Tomales. This park charges a daily fee (bring dollar bills for the machine) and permits overnight parking in the upper lot.

Kayakers and deep water sailors enjoy calm Tomales Bay.

Lawson's Landing: From CA 1 in Tomales go west on Dillon Beach Road for 4 miles to Dillon Beach. Lawson's Landing is at the end of the county road south of Dillon Beach. Lawson's charges launch and camping fees.

Heart's Desire Beach lies on the west shore, 4 miles north of Inverness on Pierce Point Road. This very popular day-use area in Tomales Bay State Park has rest rooms and drinking water but charges fees to park and launch at the beach.

The Golden Hinde Inn and Marina are on Sir Francis Drake Boulevard in Inverness about 4.6 miles from CA 1. They charge a fee for launching and overnight parking. The neighboring Blue Waters Kayaking rents kayaks and provides instruction and guided trips.

Shuttle: Optional.

For more information: (See Appendix B for phone numbers, websites, and street addresses.) For updates on kayaking, camping, hiking, and whale watching contact Point Reyes National Seashore by telephone or view their Internet site. You can make camping reservations at the Bear Valley Visitor Center or by telephoning Point Reyes National Seashore Campground Reservation up to three months in advance. Reservations are taken Monday through Friday from 9:00 A.M. to 2:00 P.M.

Call Tomales Bay State Park about access at Heart's Desire Beach or Millerton Point or visit the website. For a long list of restaurants, lodging places, and businesses in the Tomales Bay area, visit the Coastal Traveler website. Contact Lawson's Landing via phone or on the Internet about camping, launch, and charter trips.

14 Estero Americano

Character: Alive with birdlife, this placid waterway leads from serene pastures to a beach with thundering surf. Marine Mammal Protection Act applies.

Length: 5.6 miles.

Average run time: 2 to 6 hours.

Class: Flatwater.

Skill level: Beginner.

Optimal flow: Medium to high tides. Width of Estero Americano varies from two boat lengths to more than 0.5 mile when flooded.

Tide differences from Golden Gate: Bodega Harbor entrance: high tides: −38 minutes; low tides: −16 minutes.

Best season: Autumn through spring.

Craft: Canoes, kayaks, and inflatables.

Hazards: Getting stuck in the wrong channel at low tides can cause a serious delay in your trip. At the ocean end, land so the current will not pull you into the surf.

Maps: USGS 7.5 Valley Ford, Bodega Head.

Overview: Americano Creek offers a delightful smorgasbord of paddling environments, from rolling hills to a steep, fiord-like mouth, from a narrow creek to a wide estero, from warm sun to cold, windy fog.

Private lands border both sides of the estero and livestock graze on the hills, which turn wonderfully green in the winter. In their season, migratory waterfowl, shorebirds, eagles, and red-tailed hawks dwell here. Duck hunters seasonally enjoy hunting the waterfowl along this scenic treasure.

A local winter event is an informal fun race called the Cow Patty Pageant. Kayakers paddle from the bridge to the beach, and return. This is done at a low tide to add mud and humor to the challenge.

The broad, sandy beach at the mouth provides a great view extending from Bodega Head to Tomales Point. On the ocean side the surf pounds against huge rocks and headlands. A lonesome house on the northern headland overlooks the beach and the ocean. Informal beach camping is enjoyable when the wind is mild. No facilities exist here and campers should carry out all waste.

Summer days regularly bring in low clouds, cold fog, and winds strong enough to test any paddler's will. Late autumn, winter, and spring months offer sunny days warm enough to remove layers down to t-shirts.

Courtesy suggests that you do not undress in view of the neighbors' homes or the highway.

The paddling: Water levels and currents in the estero are subject to storms and tides. During the early winter, high winter surf reforms the sandbar blocking the estero's mouth and

Estero Americano

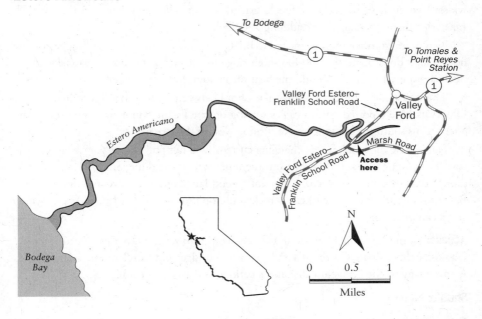

the water level rises. Then Estero Americano forms 0.5-mile-wide lagoons, similar to Elkhorn Slough or Drakes Estero. Paddling is a delight. You can explore the enlarged shoreline, enjoy eagles soaring, and watch the abundant waterfowl.

If winter rains raise the water level enough, the estero overflows the sandbar and washes a new channel. If mother nature has not cooperated, and if the water covers too much of their roads and pasture, the local farmers bulldoze the channel. Then the estero becomes subject to the ebb and flow of the tides and it is time to consult your tide book.

At the put-in, pasture lands border the well-defined channel. The channel quickly turns north in a long loop that returns 0.2 mile from the starting point. Your view at first depends on water level. You may look above the scene in full view of your paddling partners; float at eye level with the grass catching only glimpses of paddle blades; or descend into the channel isolated from all except the channel ahead.

Where the channel turns west again, the estero widens, your view expands, and some bay trees mark the south hillside.

Three miles from the bridge, the estero widens into the first broad bay. At low tides this is as far as you can easily paddle since the wide bays divide into shallow channels. If you choose the wrong channel, the water turns to deep, sticky mud that you have to push or wade through, a very unpleasant and exhausting experience. At high tides or if the estuary mouth is blocked, the water backs up to form wide bays and pools that are havens for waterfowl. Bring your favorite field guide to help identify the various birds.

When the water is high, the lagoons expand and submerge adjacent pastures. The widest lagoons have barbed wire fences extending from the north shore to the channel. Beware of them, particularly if paddling at twilight.

Two miles from the mouth, the estero briefly narrows again. Farm buildings and a few houses look down from the 500-foot-high ridge to the north. The lower waterside bluffs offer pleasant viewpoints. Around the next turn another wide bay opens.

The west end of this bay narrows like a fiord between 500- and 600-foot-high ridges. Observers have reported golden eagles soaring on the Pacific winds over the ridges. The estero turns south for 0.5 mile before turning west to the beach.

Land along the beach where changing currents will not pull you or your boat into the surf. Then enjoy the surfside view from the other side of the dune. Since the surf usually dumps directly onto the beach, this is not a good launching site to venture into Bodega Bay. At the south end of the beach, a rocky outcrop provides shelter from westerly winds and a campfire site.

Access: From California Highway 1 at Valley Ford turn south onto Valley Ford Estero—Franklin School Road. Go about 1 mile, cross the bridge, and turn left onto Marsh Road. A paved lane by the bridge usually allows parking and an easy put-in.

Shuttle: None.

For more information: (See Appendix B for phone numbers, websites, and street addresses.) Telephone the kayaking outfitters serving Tomales Bay to learn if the sandbar is closed.

⟨15⟩ Lake Sonoma

Character: A picturesque, narrow, fingered lake featuring fine fishing, low speed zones, and boat-in camping in the heart of wine country.

Size: 7 miles of lake with restricted speeds, 0.1 to 0.5 mile wide.

Elevation: 490 feet.

Average paddling time: 2 hours to several days.

Class: Flatwater lake.

Skill level: Beginner.

Best season: Spring, summer, and autumn.

Craft: Canoes, kayaks, sailboats, and motorboats.

Hazards: Outside the restricted speed zones, water skiing and fast motor boats are popular. Underwater dead trees commonly reach to the water surface along the narrow lake fingers.

Maps: Corps of Engineers Lake Sonoma Park; Fish.N. Map Co. L.Sonoma.

Overview: Warm Springs Dam impounds the canyons of Dry Creek, Warm Springs Creek, Yorty Creek, and Cherry Creek to form 2,700-acre Lake Sonoma. These narrow fingers have no-ski and 5-m.p.h. zones desirable for paddle craft. Avoid the southern portions during water ski seasons.

Thirty boat-in campsites are situated along the lake's low-speed reaches. Rustler Camp on Yorty Creek is closest to the put-in. Cherry Creek finger hosts the Thumb Camp and Skunk Camp. Amenities include picnic tables, fire pits, chemical toilets, and tent pads—but bring your own drinking water. Reserve your campsite in advance.

Lake Sonoma summers are hot with temperatures averaging in the high 90s F. Winter days can be cool, foggy, and wet.

Submerged trees still stand in the upper reaches of the lake to provide habitat for fish. As a result, the lake holds largemouth bass, Sacramento perch, channel catfish, and sunfish.

The paddling: Yorty Creek boat ramp provides an easy put-in for canoes and kayaks. In summer, water warm enough to swim in adds to the attraction. An easy 0.8-mile paddle brings you to the Brush Creek and Dry Creek fingers. From here it is fun to explore and fish the different reaches.

Brush Creek finger is short. Dry Creek finger extends 3 miles to the north and west. Hilltops reach 800 feet above the lake surface. The 0.5-mile-broad confluence with Cherry Creek is most apt to be affected by blowing winds.

Cherry Creek finger stretches 2 miles around a long horseshoe bend to Thumb Camp and Skunk Camp. Power boaters also use these camps. At the northernmost arc of the horseshoe bend, a cool, narrow, tree-shrouded ravine invites exploration until fallen trees block your paddling.

The Corps normally reduces winter water levels to provide storage space for flood control.

Lake Sonoma

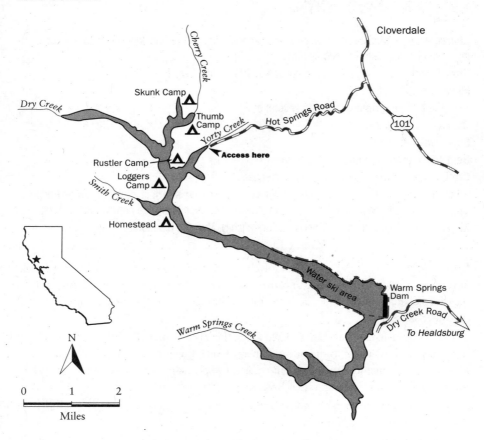

Access: Yorty Creek Recreation Area has a wide, sandy swimming beach, picnic pavilions, and a launch ramp for cartop boats. From Cloverdale Boulevard in Cloverdale, turn west near the fire station onto Comazzi Road. Go about 0.1 mile and turn onto Hot Springs Road. Follow Hot Springs Road for 4.5 narrow (five steep hairpin turns) miles to the recreation area. Enjoy the sight of the magnificent old oaks profiled along the ridge leading down to the lake.

Because many powerboats use the ramp at Lake Sonoma Resort, and nearby portions of the lake are popular for water skiing, the ramps near the dam are not recommended for paddlecraft. Reach these ramps from Dry Creek Road in Healdsburg.

Shuttle: None.

This Marin resident likes to relax on summer Sunday mornings by paddling on Lake Sonoma.

For more information: (See Appendix B for phone numbers, websites, and street addresses.) Call the U.S. Army Corps of Engineers or view their Internet site, where you may also obtain current lake levels. Make camping reservations by contacting the National Recreation Reservation Service.

16 Navarro River

Character: A wilderness canoe run through redwood forests.

Length: 19.4 miles.

Average run time: 7 to 10 hours, often paddled in two days.

Class: I with frequent trees and brush.

Skill level: Beginner with whitewater experience.

Optimal flow: 400 to 1,000 cfs (Navarro River near Navarro gauge).

Average gradient: 8 feet per mile.

Best season: Winter and early spring during receding storm flows.

Craft: Open canoes, kayaks, and inflatables.

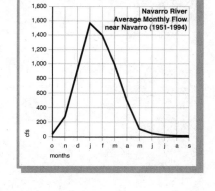

Hazards: Between Hendy Woods and Dimmick Campground, the steep canyon slopes are prone to landslides during prolonged winter rainstorms. The landslides regularly contribute rocks and trees, creating new rapids and snag hazards. Brush lines many parts of the river. Occasionally landslides create temporary dams across the river. Be sure to ask the rangers at Hendy Woods State Park if recent storms have caused unusual changes in the river.

Maps: USGS 7.5 Elk, Navarro, Cold Spring, Philo.

Overview: From the orchards and vineyards of the Anderson Valley, the Navarro River courses through remote, richly forested canyons to the North Fork confluence at Paul Dimmick Campground. Navarro River Redwoods State Park protects the rest of the river corridor to the ocean. Steelhead fishing is popular in the fall.

Only the tidal section is boatable after the rainy season that usually ends by mid-spring. If the winter has been wet and storms persist, then the river may be runable into late April. At 300 cfs, expect to walk your boat through the shallows. At lower flows, maneuvering around the brush becomes more difficult.

Rich riverside forests effectively screen from view the timber harvesting that continues on the slopes above. During the late 1800s, a railroad paralleled the river, lumber mills dotted the estuary, and lumber schooners loaded cargo in the estuary.

When the river is runable, Hendy Woods State Park and Paul Dimmick Campground are apt to be damp and cool. Summer weather at the campgrounds is warmer and less foggy than the sea coast. Hendy Woods contains a year-round campground and a grove of magnificent redwood trees.

When not flooded by winter storms, Dimmick Campground is open. The toilets are open in winter and summer, but the tables are removed for flood season. Dimmick's piped water is from the river and marked "Unsafe Drinking Water," so be prepared to treat it or bring your own drinking water.

Navarro River

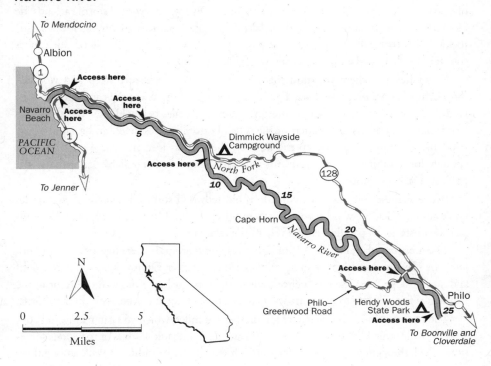

To Mendocino

Albion

1

Access here

Access here

Navarro Beach

Access here

PACIFIC OCEAN

1

5

To Jenner

Access here

Dimmick Wayside Campground

North Fork

128

10

15

Cape Horn

Navarro River

20

N

0   2.5   5
Miles

Access here

Philo–Greenwood Road

Hendy Woods State Park

Access here

Philo

25

To Boonville and Cloverdale

The paddling: The easiest put-in is at the Hendy Woods State Park picnic area where the parking lot is close to the river. Fast-flowing water soon requires adroit paddling skills to avoid the steep-cut left bank. Apple orchards line the right bank. A mile downstream, the high concrete bridge for the Philo-Greenwood Road crosses the river. The gravel bar under the bridge has been a popular put-in. It also serves as a take-out for paddlers who find their skills outmatched by the river.

Beyond the bridge 1.5 miles, the river leaves Anderson Valley and enters the remote canyon. For the first few miles the river drops 17 feet per mile. Steep slopes rise 800 feet to Greenwood Ridge. Although a new generation of redwood trees and Douglas fir have regrown this century, tributary names such as Skid Gulch and Floodgate Creek reflect times when lumbermen denuded the hills and floated or hauled the logs to mills along the river estuary. Obscure remnants of old logging roads and railroads still parallel the river.

The most difficult obstacles are brush and fallen trees in the channel. Their location changes from year to year and the paddler must stay alert. One example of the caution required is found about 2 miles below the bridge. When we floated it, dense brush lined both sides of the narrow channel, and a tree lay diagonally across the river. Two canoes in our party capsized. Some paddlers lined their gear-laden boats past this section.

During the major floods of 1997 and 1998, large landslides contributed huge amounts of gravel, rocks, and debris to the river channel. During one winter storm, a landslide blocked the river, creating a 2-mile-long lake behind it. What remains are shallow, Class II rocky rapids that will change with the passing years. At 300 cfs, we walked our canoes through the shallows below the second landslide.

Campsites are where you find them. Since the banks are very steep and wooded, most campsites are on gravel bars. The higher the water, the fewer the campsites. A large landslide on the left identifies a picturesque campsite 7 miles below Hendy Woods. Landmarks here are house-size boulders at the slide's bottom, a deep pool, and a rapid as the river turns sharply right. A steep tributary on the left has formed a large gravel bar flat enough for camping. Three more miles downstream, another reliable campsite is the peninsula at Cape Horn.

Between these campsites, a tremendous old redwood stump lies in the river. Guidebook author Dick Schwind reported it here 30 years ago. Other fallen trees and stumps provide obstacles to paddlers all the way to the take-out.

The most popular take-out is Paul Dimmick Campground where the wide North Fork joins the Navarro. No other tributary this large joins the river. Dimmick is on the river right and a mild slope from the confluence leads to the cars. At higher flows the current in the Navarro is fast. Be sure to recognize the take-out by looking at it when you do the shuttle.

The river continues this character for another 4.4 miles, which you can paddle in about 2 hours. California Highway 128 closely follows the right bank. Groves of redwoods sometimes block the sight and sound of the traffic. It is well worth landing to walk among these redwood groves. Large second-growth trees circle the stumps of their ancestors. The root systems of the original redwood sent sprouts to form clones of the original tree. Mud stains high on the tree trunks mark flood heights that at one time even covered the highway.

The stream gradient steepens to 8 feet per mile between the North Fork confluence and the gauging station. Below river mile 5, the tidal influence becomes noticeable. Views expand as the channel width doubles. A cable stretched high above the river marks the flow gauging station. The staging markers may be visible in the sand along the right bank.

Past Dimmick 4.5 miles is a short take-out. It occurs just upstream of where the river bends to the left and the road clings to the right bank (CA 128 mile marker 4.0).

If you continue downstream, a majestic stand of second-growth redwoods quickly separates the river from the road. Screened from the road by the forest giants, the wonderful deep pool and sandy beach offer another take-out at one of the nicest spots below Dimmick.

Access: Hendy Woods State Park is in the Anderson Valley. From Boonville, follow CA 128 for 8 miles to the Philo-Greenwood Road. Turn left. The park is 0.5 mile south on Philo-Greenwood Road. A choice of put-ins exists. One is the gravel bar under the Philo-Greenwood Road bridge. Recent floods have eroded and dramatically steepened the poison oak-streaked trail just downstream of the bridge. The second put-in is much easier and has ample parking at the picnic site in the state park. The park charges user fees.

Fallen trees require experienced paddlers to pay attention at every turn in the river.

Paul Dimmick Campground is on CA 128, 8 miles east of CA 1 and 14 miles west of Hendy Woods State Park. Parking is available immediately above the confluence of the North Fork and the main stem of the Navarro. A short slope leads to the water.

At CA 128 road mile marker 3.66, roadside parking is close to a 100-yard-long trail leading to a deep pool that is a local summer swimming spot. At CA 128 road mile marker 4.0, a roadside turnout named Hollow Log is closer to the river.

Shuttle: Hendy Woods to Dimmick: 14 miles (20 minutes). Dimmick to CA 128 mile marker 3.66: 4 miles (ten minutes).

For more information: (See Appendix B for phone numbers, websites, and street addresses.) In recent years, the Hendy Woods State Park rangers have been paddlers themselves and may have important information about river levels and the effect of recent storms. Call them for assistance.

17 Navarro River Estuary

(see map on page 59)

Character: A gentle float between the beach and the redwoods.
Length: Up to 5 miles.
Average run time: 2 to 4 hours.
Class: Tidal flatwater.
Skill level: Beginner.
Tide differences from Golden Gate: Navarro Beach high tides: –31 minutes; low tides: –19 minutes.
Best season: Year-round except during floods.
Craft: Open canoes, kayaks, dories, and sea kayaks.
Hazards: For much of the year and especially at high winter flows, the river surges directly into the breaking Pacific surf.
Maps: USGS 7.5 Albion, Elk.

Overview: Navarro River Redwoods State Park protects the river corridor between Paul Dimmick Campground and the ocean. Steelhead fishing is popular in the fall. Only the tidal section is normally boatable after early spring.

State park rangers offer guided summer canoe trips on the estuary. Look for notices in the campgrounds.

Navarro Beach has a small, no-frills campground, no drinking water, and a smorgasbord of natural delights. One May evening I looked over the high tide to see a huge dorsal fin less than 25 yards away. It charged the beach through the surf, then slid back to deeper water. Again it rushed toward the beach, paused just beyond the wave break, then ebbed to the sea. The next morning, 20 seals had hauled out onto the sand near the mouth. A park ranger told me that gray whales and calves also frequented the cove during much of the winter and spring.

The paddling: Like other tidal waters, the easiest way to explore this waterway is to go upstream with the incoming tide, then follow the ebb downstream. The channel is wider, slower, and deeper than the upper reaches.

The mile of estuary between the beach and the California Highway 1 bridge is more than 100 yards wide. Steep hillsides form the north bank and a broad terrace lines the south bank.

Upstream of the bridge, CA 128's presence along the north bank does not seem to deter the wildlife. I have listened to loons on the river, paddled next to seals, and gazed up at ospreys. The channel narrows dramatically. Two miles from the bridge, redwoods occupy the river terraces.

In the late 1800s, railroads paralleled the river and lumber mills dotted the estuary. To keep the mouth of the river open for lumber schooners, seamen built a breakwater from the big pointed rock (Pinnacle Rock) to the bluff. Today, the beach provides campsites and a great place to watch whales and seals.

A very different activity existed one hundred years ago. Lumber mills lined the river and schooners sailed in from the ocean. Now only the dilapidated Navarro River Hotel remains on the road to Navarro Beach.

Access: Two easy put-ins are available for this reach. Both allow floats along the full length of the estuary. From the CA 1 bridge, go upstream on CA 128 for 0.2 mile. A long, wide shoulder is next to a crude, unpaved boat ramp. The site is useful to hand-launch boats. The bank is only 5 feet high and the water level rises and falls with the tides.

Navarro River Redwoods Beach has lots of parking in a spectacular setting. At the south end of the CA 1 bridge turn west and go 0.7 mile along the south side of the river to the beach. Floating over sandbars is easier than slogging through silty sand, so use this location only at higher tides.

Shuttle: Optional. 1 mile (five minutes).

For more information: (See Appendix B for phone numbers, websites, and street addresses.) To learn if Navarro Beach Campground, Paul Dimmick Campground, and Hendy Woods campgrounds are open, call Hendy Woods State Park. More general information about these two parks is available on their Internet sites.

18 Albion River

Character: A magically beautiful escape along a gentle coastal stream snuggled between lush fir hillsides. Marine Mammal Protection Act applies.
Length: 5 miles.
Average run time: 4 to 5 hours.
Class: Flatwater.
Skill level: Beginner.
Tide differences from Golden Gate: high tides: –31 minutes; low tides: –19 minutes.
Best season: Spring and autumn.
Craft: Canoes, kayaks, and inflatable kayaks.
Hazards: Give right of way to occasional large fishing boats near the boat ramps and in Albion Cove. Consult tide tables to go with the flow and avoid being left high and dry.
Maps: USGS 7.5 Elk, Albion.

Overview: From the California Highway 1 bridge, the view upstream into the hills entices one to trace the Albion River. Access is easy from the wide Albion Flat under the bridge. This privately operated campground has hot showers, a small marina for fishing boats, a boat ramp, and a sandy beach facing seaward to Albion Cove. They charge a use fee.

Summer mornings are often foggy. During summer afternoons strong winds blow upstream from the ocean to make downstream paddling difficult. Spring and autumn have brighter, calmer days.

Exploring the ocean waters of Albion Cove can be enticing but requires negotiating the fast water in the narrow channel under the south end of the bridge. See chapter 20 about paddling Albion Cove.

The paddling: The campground's boat ramp is an easy put-in. Larger fishing boats heading for the ocean also use it, so clear the narrow channel by the ramp soon after launching.

The Albion River is smooth, without rocks, and easy to paddle upstream with slack water or an incoming tide. At low tides, shallow mud bars can slow the inattentive paddler. A second small commercial marina and boat ramp is found about 0.3 mile upstream. The marina is quickly left behind and the dense fir forest comes down to the water.

Several curious features characterize the Albion. About 1.25 miles from the bridge, a floating assemblage of boats, floats, and a house intercept the broad river. This is the shaky habitation of Dan and his dogs. Along the north bank, a narrow woods road is intermittently visible. Occasionally, low marshy grasses extend from the hillsides to the water. The Albion gently flows through a forested scene reminiscent of British Columbia.

A charming floating cottage heralds the entrance to The Lagoon at 2.3 miles. The cottage is an escapist dream, complete with fishing, forests, peace, and solitude. Please respect it as private property. Behind the cottage, a breach through an old levee provides an entrance to the lagoon. Once a pond for storing logs, the picturesque crescent encloses a

Albion River

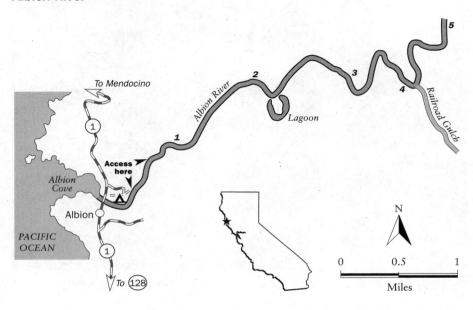

small, steep island. Over the years, sediment has filled much of the lagoon bottom with soft mud, making landing difficult.

Another mile upstream, we encountered an energetic young man constructing another floating cottage. His ideal was to build with only hand tools, use all secondhand materials, and haul everything to the site in his small skiff. Such a dream fit wonderfully in that marvelously beautiful setting. His only fear was that timber companies would return to scar the landscape by logging the trees along the river.

Along the channel, weather-sculpted old gray pilings recall past days of logging by rail. Soon the river becomes narrower, and snags lay in the channel to block passage at low water. The depth of the water and your energy level determine how far upstream you will navigate. Just remember that an ebbing tide can leave you with shallow water and a slow return trip.

Access: Albion River Campground is under the CA 1 bridge 6 miles south of Mendocino and 3.5 miles north of the junction of CA 1 and CA 128. Turn east from CA 1, 50 feet north of the Albion bridge. Descend steeply into the campground below the bridge, between the river and Albion Cove. A boat ramp is available for a fee, or you can park close to the water under the bridge and carry your boat to the channel. Alternatively, at the bottom of the hill follow the road upstream 0.25 mile to another marina.

An escapist's dream, this floating cottage harmonizes perfectly with the beautiful Albion River near Mendocino.

Shuttle: None.

For more information: (See Appendix B for phone numbers, websites, and street addresses.) The Fort Bragg–Mendocino Coast Chamber of Commerce provides camping, lodging, dining, and recreation information. Contact them via phone or e-mail, or view their Internet site. Call the Albion River Campground and Fishing Village for camping reservations and fishing reports.

⊞ 19 Big River

Character: This easy paddle close to Mendocino, follows a tidal estuary into a placid, intimate stream bordered by North Coast forests. Marine Mammal Protection Act applies.

Length: 8 miles.

Skill level: Beginner.

Average run time: 4 to 6 hours.

Tide differences from Golden Gate: Mendocino Bay high tides: −38 minutes; low tides: −21 minutes.

Best season: Spring and autumn.

Craft: Canoes, kayaks, and inflatables on the river.

Hazards: Consult tide tables to go with the flow and avoid being left high and dry.

Maps: USGS 7.5 Mendocino, Mathison Peak.

Overview: The town of Mendocino and the Mendocino Bay area have long been retreats for artists and tourists. Before the artists and tourists this was the home of loggers and Indians. As you cruise the Big River, picture what the river must have been like when lumber mills lined the lower river. Logs floated downriver to the mills, and coastal lumber schooners waited in Mendocino Bay. The river has visually recovered from many of those activities.

American Indians from interior valleys and mountains visited the mouth of Big River for one or two weeks in summer. They gathered sea delights such as abalone, mussels, clams, and fish.

The paddling: The Big River can be paddled year-round. However, during much of the summer, strong afternoon winds blow upstream from the ocean. The winds make the return paddle difficult. So, spring and autumn are favored paddling seasons. Then the Big River is a delight to paddle upstream during slack water or an incoming tide.

The put-in is easy. If you have your own boat, use the broad, unpaved parking lot just upstream of the CA 1 bridge on the Mendocino side of the river. Rental outrigger craft are available on the opposite side of the river almost underneath the bridge.

For 3 miles the river is a wide estuary with flat shoreline leading to hills that rise 500 feet. Paddling is easy with occasional mud flats supporting kelp-like aquatic growth. Along the broad banks, pilings are historic remnants from lumber mills. Ducks, geese, and other birds are plentiful and sometimes sea lions enjoy lunch in the estuary.

Beyond 3 miles, the hills form steep banks down to the river, and the trees grow to the water's edge. Gradually, big leaf maple, tan oak, and fir replace the alder. As the tidal influx slackens, the clearer water reveals a sandy river bottom. Farther upstream, gravel replaces sand, but large rocks are absent. Were the rocks removed in the days when they floated logs to the mills?

Big River

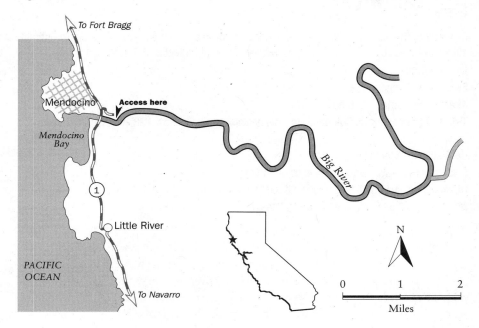

Occasional large stumps and logs lie buried in the river bottom. Note the pontoon craft bearing winches tied to the riverbank. Some sunken redwood stumps, abandoned years ago, are now highly prized for their color and grain. New treasure seekers use the pontoon craft to recover these prizes.

Comfortable lunch spots are few due to thick vegetation and steep banks. On one outing with an incoming tide, we found our cramped sandbar shrinking about our feet. An alternative is to tie the boats along the north bank. Then climb through the brush screening a narrow dirt road that closely follows the river.

From miles 3 to 8 the river becomes intimate as it carves lazy loops through growing forested hills. How far you can travel depends upon how much water is in the river and your ambition. Eventually the banks close to less than 20 feet apart and tidal signs vanish. Summer flows become too thin to float the boats. Just remember that an ebbing tide can leave you with shallow water and a tough return trip.

Access: Immediately south of Mendocino, CA 1 crosses the Big River. From the north end of the bridge turn east to the broad parking area and gravel launch ramp. A locked gate blocks entry to a dirt road that follows the river.

The Big River near Mendocino offers delightful paddling.

Shuttle: None.

For more information: (See Appendix B for phone numbers, websites, and street addresses.) Contact the Fort Bragg–Mendocino Coast Chamber of Commerce about dining, campgrounds, hotels, and outfitters by telephone or Internet. Call for reservations on the wildly scenic Skunk Train between Willets and Fort Bragg. Catch a Canoe and Bicycles Too rents out rigger-adapted canoes near the bridge.

![20] Mendocino Coast

Character: A sea kayaking kaleidoscope of rock gardens, sea caves, and open ocean. Marine Mammal Protection Act applies.

Class: SCRS III to V.

Skill level: Intermediate to advanced.

Marine Weather: Eureka radio 162.40 MHz or telephone 707–443–7062.

Sea conditions and wave heights: NOAA Point Arena buoy.

Tide differences from Golden Gate: Mendocino Bay high tides: –38 minutes; low tides: –21 minutes.

Best season: Spring, summer, and autumn.

Craft: Sea kayaks.

Hazards: The California Department of Boating and Waterways advises that this "…coastline offers a variety of weather hazards—storms, dense fog, heavy surf, and very often rough seas." Pacific Ocean water temperatures in the Mendocino area seldom rise above 55 degrees F, even in summer. The presence of rock gardens, surf, occasional rogue waves, and caves add hazards (see the safety section in this guide). Even in the calmest of weather, rogue waves may quickly disrupt your paddling pleasure. Sea kayakers venturing into these waters should paddle in teams and be able to perform self-rescues.

Maps: USGS 7.5 Albion, Mendocino.

Overview: Weather and sea conditions permitting, this is a spectacular area to paddle. Spring has wildflowers. Summer gives a cool respite from inland heat, and fall offers warmer days with less chance of fog. Moviemakers use the scenic coast, state parks, and community of Mendocino for various films. Many tourists visit this New England-style town with its rock-bound shoreline, clean air, wind-swept seas, and forested mainland.

Accommodations are numerous and popular. Van Damme, Russian Gulch, and Mackerricher State Parks provide nearby camping. Several excellent hotels and restaurants serve coastal visitors between Albion and Fort Bragg. Make summer reservations in advance.

Commercial outfitters frequently rent open kayaks from Van Damme Beach.

The rocky coast, sea stacks, and sea caves are exciting to explore. It is necessary to paddle with experienced teams, wear helmets and wet suits and do it during calm weather conditions. Check National Weather Service broadcasts from Eureka. If the sea conditions are unfavorable, then explore the neighboring Albion or Big Rivers described in the two preceding trips.

Since prevailing summer winds blow from the northwest, it is usually easiest to paddle from north to south so that the wind and swells help your passage. Your time to paddle from place to place can vary greatly depending on sea conditions and how much exploring you do.

The following tale from the Mendocino Historical Society provides a vivid picture of changeable sea conditions.

Mendocino Coast

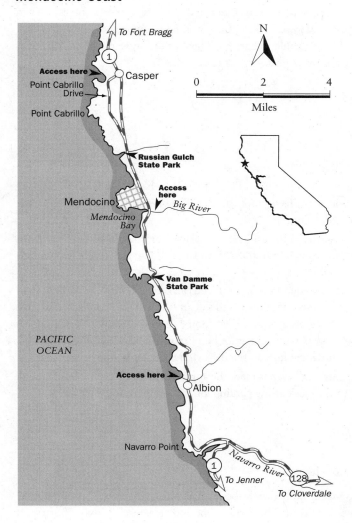

"Three vessels were in Mendocino Harbor being loaded with lumber on a pleasant sunny day. Suddenly, big rollers came in, breaking from point to point across the harbor. The first heavy roller dashed two of these little vessels against the rocks. The surge carried one wrecked vessel across the harbor to the mouth of a big blowhole. When it first hit the mouth of the blowhole, the main mast was broken 'like a pipestem.' The receding wave carried it back to the same place where it had been and the boat righted itself. A second big wave came and carried the boat again to the same blowhole. This time all the superstructure was carried away. Six sailors had dived into the sea, hoping that they could either swim or be saved by the men dashing from the lumberyard down to the beach. One young man started to jump overboard, but he held onto the deck and just froze there. He just could not let go. Then a third wave came and carried it into the blowhole. It was never heard from since."

The paddling:
Albion to Van Damme
Length: 4.5 miles.
Average run time: 2 to 4 hours.

At Albion Campground, you have a choice of launching into the Albion River or carrying across the beach and launching directly into the bay. The current under the high trestle bridge may influence your decision.

Because the Albion River provides a protected marina, commercial and charter boats frequent the serpentine channel in and out of Albion Cove. If you stay to the rocky north side, you should miss the traffic.

If skills, equipment, and sea conditions permit, you can probably visit the narrow channels, arches, and caves that connect with the north side of Albion Head. Farther north, the ocean has carved arches and sea caves on this coast. Some caves have multiple openings. A few tunnel into sunlit chambers with miniature beaches surrounded by cliffs. These are sinkholes. Other caves twist dangerously in the dark while echoing to the ocean surge.

Several large sea stacks or small islands mark the approach to Van Damme Beach. Look for the hills descending to the creek at the parking lot and campground.

Van Damme to Mendocino
Length: 3.5 miles.
Average run time: 2 to 4 hours.

Beachside parking is available immediately beside California Highway 1 opposite the entrance to Van Damme State Park. The carry to the surf-free beach is only 50 yards. If you do not have a boat, an outfitter in the parking lot will rent you a sit-on-top kayak or even lead a guided tour.

The north side of the cove is often relatively calm. Towering sea stacks, shore cliffs, and clear tidal pools perk your enthusiasm. Sometimes seals swim up to investigate you. One passage leads to another, each teasing you with how far it goes. Eventually rocks and ledges block your way. Then the choice is to retreat a short distance and punch through the surf, or retreat to the cove and paddle seaward to round the northerly headlands.

Exploring sea stacks near Van Damme.

Note the buoy that marks the entrance to the cove. If you are traveling in a southerly direction, the buoy locates the passage to the beach. Avoid the deepwater reefs and waves that break in the outer cove. If fog rolls in, the buoy and beach will be difficult to find without negotiating the breakers.

Spectacular headlands and shoreline continue to Mendocino Bay. Its broad opening is unmistakable. You can paddle through the kelp beds with some work, but beware the rock gardens when the surf is breaking nearby.

Aim for the CA 1 bridge in the northeast corner of the bay. The bridge marks the Big River and the beach take-out. Plan your arrival for an incoming tide to make the short upriver paddle easier. Another choice is to continue to Russian Gulch.

Mendocino to Russian Gulch
Length: 3.5 miles.
Average run time: 2 to 4 hours.

The Big River put-in is calm water. Paddling seaward you soon encounter the surf as swells cross the bar at the river's mouth. You can examine the situation from the Mendocino Bay end of the put-in.

The north side of the bay is under the cliffs of the Mendocino Headlands State Park. At lower tides a sandy beach extends along part of this shore. Do not sit too close to the cliffs since rockfall is common.

Paddling westward, you can look up at the tourists exploring the headlands and marveling at the roar and bellow of the sea caves below. Some of these caverns are very large with several openings. During calmer conditions sea kayakers paddle through them.

These caves connect with a series of rock channels, arches, and other caves that provide an inside passage to the west of Agate Beach. From there, it is a brief paddle to the rock gardens approaching Russian Gulch.

You'll recognize Russian Gulch by the arched concrete bridge high over the creek. Land at the beach under the bridge.

Russian Gulch to Caspar

Length: 4 miles.

Average run time: 2 to 3 hours.

Russian Gulch State Park offers a protected beach, beach-side parking, and a cold freshwater shower for rinsing the salt from your body and gear. Coin-operated hot showers get lots of use in the campground.

The narrow mouth of Russian Gulch gradually opens to a wider cove. A small sea cave on the north side is easy to reach and explore.

Round the rocky headland and head northwest. If the ocean conditions are worse than you expected, you can retreat to the cove. If conditions are gentle, you may be comfortable exploring passages between the rocks and looking for arches and more caves.

If conditions let you stay inside, a series of channels, arches, and sea caves may be accessible that provide an inside passage to Caspar Anchorage. Don't be surprised if you encounter sea lions expressing their territorial presence over the narrow passageways.

If you go outside, the view of the coast is great with the sight of the rock-studded shoreline leading to Cabrillo Lighthouse. Floating kelp seems to have expanded in El Niño years. Going over acres of kelp is like paddling over inflated bicycle tubes. You may seek corridors between the floating mats. Reefs near the southern approach to Caspar Anchorage warrant a detour seaward before heading into the cove.

Wide Caspar Cove is delightfully well protected from the prevailing summer winds. Look for the beach at the southeast end. As you approach the shore you can usually choose between a calm-water or a surf landing. Caspar is an uncrowded and pleasant place to practice surfing.

As you enjoy the quiet cove and beautiful Caspar, think of how it seemed when George Hee landed here in 1854. He came from China in a sampan about 8 feet high and 30 feet long. He and his crew rowed and sailed for 18 months, living on an eight months' supply of rice, dried fish, and vegetables. Of seven sampans that set out to look for gold, two reached California, one in Monterey and the other in Caspar. Then they walked to Mendocino. (Information from *Mendocino County Remembered—An Oral History*, by Bruce Levene et al., The Mendocino County Historical Society, 1976.)

Access: Albion River Campground is under the CA 1 bridge 6 miles south of Mendocino and 3.5 miles north of the junction of CA 1 and CA 128. Turn east from CA 1, 50 feet north of the Albion bridge. Descend steeply into the private campground below the bridge between the river and Albion Cove. Launch from a protected beach under the bridge.

Van Damme State Park: Beachside parking and launching on CA 1 is 2.5 miles south of Mendocino. At the entrance to the park with its campgrounds, the cove is a favorite dive spot for abalone fishing.

Mendocino: 0.3 mile south of Mendocino, CA 1 crosses the Big River. From the north end of the bridge turn east to the broad parking area and gravel launch ramp. Follow the river through the surf into Mendocino Bay.

Russian Gulch State Park: Exit CA 1 at the Russian Gulch State Park about 1.8 miles north of Mendocino and head toward the sea. Turn left to the park kiosk (user fee), go down the hill, and turn right toward the beach.

Caspar Beach: From Fort Bragg, follow CA 1 until you cross Caspar Creek. From the bridge turn west 0.7 mile to the beach and RV campground. From Mendocino, turn off at the Russian Gulch State Park exit sign, then immediately turn right, following Point Cabrillo Drive north 2.5 miles to Caspar Beach. The nearest rest rooms are 0.5 mile away in the Caspar Beach RV Campground, at the south end of the beach and across the road. Caspar Headlands State Reserve includes the north promontory of the cove and the north end of the beach.

Shuttle: Albion to Van Damme: 5 miles (15 minutes). Van Damme to Mendocino: 2.5 miles (10 minutes). Mendocino to Russian Gulch: 2.5 miles (10 minutes). Russian Gulch to Caspar: 2.7 miles (10 minutes).

For more information: (See Appendix B for phone numbers, websites, and street addresses.) Contact state parks for camping reservations or contact ReserveAmerica. To learn of other conditions at the Mendocino area state parks, contact the Mendocino Coast State Parks. Obtain other travel information from the Fort Bragg–Mendocino Coast Chamber of Commerce via phone or Internet.

South Fork Eel River—Leggett to Redway

Character: This Wild and Scenic River boasts salmon and steelhead fishing, magnificent redwood groves, and fine paddling.

Length: 24 miles.

Class: I to III.

Skill level: Intermediate.

Optimal flow: 500 cfs to 1,000 cfs (South Fork Eel River at Leggett gauge).

Water source: Rainy season runoff.

Best season: Spring.

Craft: Whitewater canoes, kayaks, rafts, and dories.

Hazards: During rainy season, flows can rise dramatically in a short time. Several low-water bridges require portages.

Maps: USGS 7.5 Leggett, Noble Butte, Piercy, Garberville.

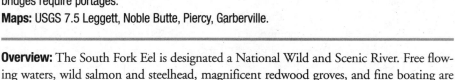

Overview: The South Fork Eel is designated a National Wild and Scenic River. Free flowing waters, wild salmon and steelhead, magnificent redwood groves, and fine boating are prime attractions. Following the rains, many small waterfalls appear along the river.

Without reservoirs, the flows rise with the winter rains and shrink in summer. Winter flows average more than 2,000 cfs, and late summer flows dwindle to 55 cfs or less. The water level is more desirable a few days after storms when the water clears. Anyone planning a trip on the Eel should be ready for rain.

This reach is the southern entry to the majestic stands of redwood trees preserved in state parks along the Avenue of the Giants.

As the watershed was subjected to road building and timber harvesting, salmon populations in the South Fork Eel River declined drastically. The 1930s fish counts at Benbow Dam showed that approximately 20,000 Chinook salmon and 15,000 to 17,000 coho salmon annually returned to the river. Recent estimates suggest that about 1,000 adult coho salmon return to the watershed. The National Marine Fisheries Service recently listed the coho salmon in the Eel River Basin as a threatened species under the Endangered Species Act. Federal, state, and local groups are working to restore fish habitat.

When the South Fork Eel is running clear, the water is an inviting, translucent blue-green hue. Under those conditions, steelhead fishing is popular, producing fish from 8 to 16 pounds. Other fish recorded in the river include Chinook salmon, coho salmon, coastal cutthroat trout, chum salmon, green sturgeon, Pacific lamprey, and American shad.

Rainy season camping is available at Humboldt Redwoods State Park, Standish Hickey State Park, Richardson Grove State Park, Benbow Lake State Recreation Area, and several private campgrounds.

South Fork Eel River—Leggett to Redway

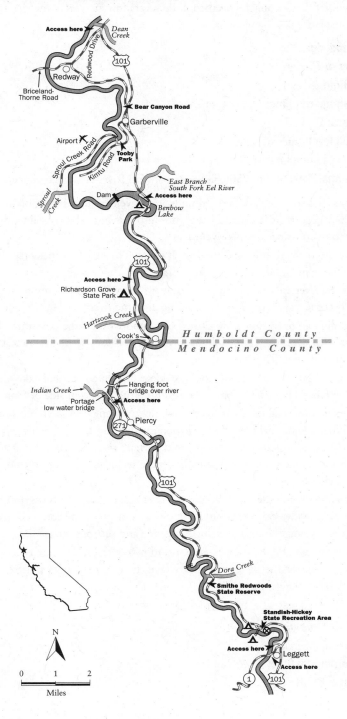

Dean Creek

Access here

Redwood Drive

101

Redway

Briceland-
Thorne Road

Bear Canyon Road

Garberville

Airport

Tooby Park

Sproul Creek Road

Kimtu Road

East Branch
South Fork Eel River

Dam

Access here

Sproul Creek

Benbow Lake

101

Access here

Richardson Grove
State Park

Hartsook Creek

Humboldt County
Mendocino County

Cook's

Indian Creek

Hanging foot
bridge over river

Portage
low water bridge

Access here

271

Piercy

101

Dora Creek

Smithe Redwoods
State Reserve

Standish-Hickey
State Recreation Area

Access here

Leggett

Access here

1   101

N

0   1   2

Miles

Below Leggett, the river has cut a deep, narrow canyon. Many landslides line the river. Since winter flows scour the riverbed, little vegetation survives in the channel, and only an occasional stump or log remains.

The paddling:

Leggett to Piercy

Length: 14 miles.

Average run time: 4 to 6 hours.

Class: II to III.

Skill level: Intermediate.

Average gradient: 16 feet per mile.

Optimal flow: 500 to 750 cfs (South Fork Eel River at Leggett gauge).

Standish Hickey State Park campgrounds are convenient to this portion of the South Fork Eel. From Leggett or Standish Hickey, put into this beautiful river lined with forests in a narrow canyon rising to expansive ridges.

At Leggett the river is pool and run. It changes to a Class II rocky rapid at the summer road crossing in Standish Hickey State Park.

As the river cuts deeper into the canyon, the walls become more impressive. Rocky rapids become the norm. You can view much of the river from U.S. Highway 101.

Paddling an open canoe, we carried one rapid with a large hole at the bottom. A tall, black tree trunk on the right bank marks it. You can easily see the tree and rapid from U.S. 101 at mile marker 95.

Smithe Redwoods State Reserve provides another put-in and take-out only 3 miles below Standish Hickey. The Smithe access is on the upstream side of Dora Creek.

At 400 cfs, several rapids are so shallow that you might walk your canoe. One narrow, more difficult rapid includes brush, a log on the right bank, another log mid-channel, shallow rocks guarding a favorable route, and current washing into a boulder. Higher flows make the river more bouncy, sometimes more technical, and more enjoyable in a good whitewater boat.

Two miles above the Piercy access, the river makes a hairpin turns under two U.S. 101 bridges. The wider canyon affords longer views of green hillsides and wildflowers. The geology also changes into interesting sandstone and siltstone strata.

After the bridges, the river veers westward past a "resort" that appears to have seen better days. Look for the Piercy take-out where the channel angles northeast and CA 271 drops closer to the water.

Piercy to Benbow

Length: 11 miles.

Average run time: 3 to 5 hours.

Class: I to II.

Skill level: Intermediate.

Average gradient: 12 feet per mile.

Optimal flow: 500 to 1,000 cfs (South Fork Eel River at Leggett gauge).

This reach starts busily. Near Indian Creek and only 0.4 mile below the put-in, carry around a low-water bridge. Just downstream a hanging footbridge crosses above the river. Rounding the bend toward U.S. 101 is a rocky chute. The next mile relaxes a bit. As the river veers away from U.S. 101 you encounter several shallow rapids.

Passing a few houses once known as "Cook's," the river swings east under bridges for CA 271 and U.S. 101. A terrace topped with redwoods sits on the left above the easy channel. Gravel bars and a rock quarry border the right side. As you round the long loop toward the highway, rocky ledges border the left side.

Below Hartsook Creek, Richardson Grove State Park borders both sides of the river. The impressive trees here include the ninth tallest coastal redwood. The park includes campgrounds, hiking trails through the redwoods, and river access across broad gravel bars.

Twice more U.S. 101 crosses the river. The second crossing is close to the upstream end of Benbow Lake. The campgrounds are on the left, and the picnic area and river access are on river right.

Benbow to Redway

Length: 11 miles.

Average run time: 3 to 5 hours.

Class: I to II.

Skill level: Beginner with moving-water experience.

Average gradient: 8 feet per mile.

Optimal flow: 450 to 1,000 cfs (South Fork Eel River at Leggett gauge).

Benbow Lake provides an easy put-in and an easy paddle to the dam. If the dam is closed, the lake is flatwater. If the dam is open, there is a moving river. Next to the Benbow Inn, the East Branch adds significant flows.

As the river swings west you can see Benbow Dam. Approach it with caution. Constructed in 1928 to provide electrical power for the community, Benbow Dam forms Benbow Lake. In recent years the Benbow Dam gates have been open during the rainy season to allow the migration and spawning of anadromous fish. If you can clearly see a continuous flow of smooth water flowing through and beyond wide-open gates, no portage is necessary. Otherwise, portage on river left starting well upstream from the structure.

Beyond the dam, the river sweeps in a wide loop away from the highways and settlements. This section is one of the prettiest parts of the river above Redway. Rich forests cover the slopes. Sproul Creek, with good habitat conditions, is an important coho salmon spawning stream.

As you slide over easy gravel-bar riffles, the current carries you quickly. Only an occasional rock or stump demands much maneuvering.

After running due north, the river turns abruptly east, then north again. Kimtu Road parallels the right bank. Sproul Creek Road and the Garberville airport parallel the left bank. Downstream of the airport, the Sproul Creek Road bridge marks the Tooby Park take-out. Land at the bridge on the right.

Downstream 2.3 miles, portage the low-water bridge at Bear Canyon Road. This rough bridge and accompanying gravel bar form a put-in and take-out between Garberville and Redway.

As far as flows go, 400 cfs at Leggett (or 1,000 cfs at Miranda) will suffice near Redway, but more water is better. At 400 cfs, sharp-eyed paddlers can find the deeper channels around gravel bars with little scrapping and no carries. There are only a couple of rocks and stumps adjacent to the banks.

At this flow, the current moves steadily for an easy Class I paddle. The scenery is appealing, although Redwood Drive is perched 100 feet above the right bank and many Redway cottages are tucked under the trees. A loon sang to us from the river before diving and disappearing. Deep pools and some smooth, moss-covered rocky ledges drop into the water. Rope swings show the popularity of some pools for summer swimming. In contrast, the wide, brush-free gravel bars suggest the bed-scouring capacity of winter storm flows. The lush riverside foliage includes redwood, alder, Douglas fir, and laurel trees.

Next to Redwood Creek, the Briceland-Thorne bridge crosses the river. It marks the upstream portion of Humboldt Redwoods State Park. Two miles downstream is the take-out at Dean Creek Resort on the right bank.

Access: Leggett: At the east end of the California Highway 1 bridge, climb down a steep slope through the redwoods. A rope may be handy to control the boats down the slope.

Leggett: Where CA 1 meets U.S. 101, a gravel road runs north from a wide gravel area. Follow the increasingly steep, unpaved road down to a gravel bar. Four-wheel drive is recommended to come back up the hill.

Standish Hickey State Park: 1.5 miles north of Leggett on U.S. 101. They gate the road to the river during the rainy season, so carry 0.4 mile to the river.

Smithe Redwoods State Reserve: 4 miles north of Leggett turn into the reserve from U.S. 101.

Piercy: Exit U.S. 101 at Piercy onto CA 271 heading north. Follow CA 271 parallel to U.S. 101 and the river for 0.7 mile. Park next to a gravel road and carry 300 yards to the nearby river. Inspect the take-out so you will recognize it from the river.

Richardson Grove State Park: Off U.S. 101, 7 miles south of Garberville.

Benbow Park: Exit U.S. 101 at Benbow. Go west to Benbow Lake picnic area with its rest rooms, paved parking, and grassy lawns.

Much of the South Fork Eel River is visible from U.S. 101.

Tooby Park: From U.S. 101, exit at Garberville onto Redwood Drive. Turn west onto Sproul Creek Road, going under U.S. 101, then bending south. Follow to the junction of Kimtu Road and Tooby Park next to the Sproul Creek Road bridge.

Bear Canyon Road near Garberville: From Garberville go north on Redwood Drive, cross U.S. 101, and pass Alderpoint Road. From Redwood Drive turn left onto Bear Canyon Road, past the Pacific Gas & Electric service center, down the steep, paved road to the gravel bar and low-water bridge.

Dean Creek Resort: From U.S. 101, exit onto Redwood Drive north of Garberville/ Redwood. Go south on Redwood Drive 0.2 mile to the resort. This commercial RV park and campground has easy access to the river.

Shuttle: Leggett to Piercy: 10 miles (20 minutes). Piercy to Benbow: 10 miles (15 minutes). Benbow to Garberville/Redway: 6 miles (15 minutes).

For more information: (See Appendix B for phone numbers, websites, and street addresses.) To learn the status of area state parks, call the North Coast Redwoods District Headquarters or visit their website. For other lodging in the Eel River area, contact the Humboldt Lodging Guide on the Internet.

South Fork Eel River—Sylvandale to Weott

Character: Lined with majestic redwood groves, this broad, powerful river invites early-season paddlers with basic moving-water skills.

Length: 24 miles.

Class: I to II.

Average run time: From a few hours to three days.

Skill level: Beginner to intermediate.

Water source: Rainy season runoff.

Optimal flow: 900 cfs to 2,500 cfs at "South Fork Eel River at Miranda" gauge.

Average gradient: 6 feet per mile.

Best season: Spring.

Craft: Canoes, kayaks, inflatable kayaks, rafts, and dories.

Hazards: During rainy season, flows can rise dramatically in a short time. Dress for cool weather and cold water. Several rapids require fast-water skills.

Maps: USGS 7.5 Garberville, Miranda, Myers Flat, Weott.

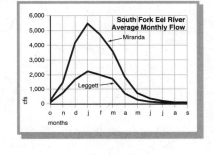

Overview: Humboldt Redwoods State Park contains most of the lower portions of the South Fork Eel. Magnificent redwood groves, with some trees thousands of years old, border this National Wild and Scenic River. Much of the channel is wide with immense gravel bars. These would be ripe for camping except that they are in the state park where camping and campfires are limited to designated campgrounds. Fishing is popular for wild salmon and steelhead. Park rangers lead canoe trips in April and May.

Without reservoirs, the flows rise with the rains in winter and go down in summer. Winter flows average more than 5,500 cfs and late summer flows dwindle to 60 cfs or less. Flow volumes at Miranda are usually 2.5 to 3.5 times greater than flows at Leggett. Winter and spring water levels are more desirable after storms when the water clears. Anybody taking a trip on the Eel should be ready for rain.

River access is generally easy from the many facilities in the park and the riverside communities. U.S. Highway 101 follows the west bank, and the scenic Avenue of the Giants parallels the right bank.

Rainy season camping is available at Humboldt Redwoods State Park, Richardson Grove State Park, Benbow Lake State Recreation Area, and several private campgrounds.

Wind can be a serious nuisance to Eel River paddlers. When the weather warms up inland, the fog comes to the coast. Then the prevailing northwest winds blow up the river canyons from the cool coast to the warm interior. Start early in the day as the winds strengthen later in the afternoon. Since inflatable boats perform poorly in strong wind, use hard-shell craft here.

Eel River and South Fork Eel River—Sylvandale to Weott

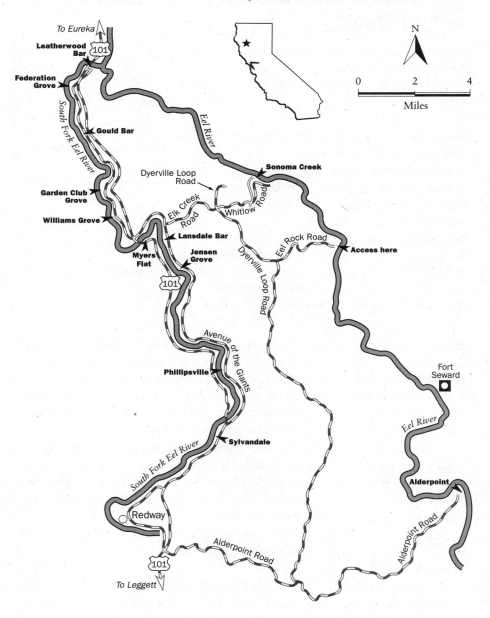

To Eureka

Leatherwood Bar

101

Federation Grove

South Fork Eel River

Gould Bar

Eel River

Garden Club Grove

Williams Grove

Dyerville Loop Road

Elk Creek Road

Whitlow Road

Sonoma Creek

Lansdale Bar

Myers Flat

Jensen Grove

101

Dyerville Loop Road

Eel Rock Road

Access here

Avenue of the Giants

Phillipsville

Fort Seward

Eel River

South Fork Eel River

Sylvandale

Alderpoint

Redway

101

Alderpoint Road

Alderpoint Road

To Leggett

N

0   2   4
Miles

The paddling: Only 0.5 mile below the Hooker Road put-in, U.S. 101 crosses the river again. The bridge is also the site of the USGS gauge known as South Fork Eel River at Miranda.

After 2 miles, the broad river terrace of Phillipsville appears on river right. Access is on river right.

Sliding quickly through broad gravel bars, the river turns west as it approaches the Fish Creek confluence on river right. Then the hills close in as the river again turns northward to Miranda.

Approaching Miranda, you pass under a bridge and the channel widens into giant gravel bars. These continue to the Jensen Grove at Dry Creek.

The riverside land downstream is mostly in the Humboldt Redwoods State Park. Enjoy the views of the redwoods that the park preserves. Better yet, take the time to walk slowly through these forest giants. You will long remember that experience.

After passing Dry Creek, the riverbed braids before again narrowing where U.S. 101 cuts away from the river across the base of Eagle Point. The absence of vehicle noise is welcome. Look for additional riffles as the river rounds the horseshoe bend. Twists and turns provide an isolated feeling between the 200-foot-high slopes, beaches, and redwood forests. They also protect you from much of the upstream wind.

The next landmark is the U.S. 101 bridge near Myers Flat. This is the last bridge before the bridges at the main Eel confluence. Myers Flat has an access site. The next access site is at Williams Grove, 2 miles downstream. Look for the summer road crossing there.

Additional summer bridges cross the river at several access points: Garden Club Grove, Robinson Creek, and Bull Creek (Federation Grove). These are underwater at boatable flows and may cause some bouncy riffles. They also mark the access points.

The final take-out on the South Fork Eel is Leatherwood Bar at the last U.S. 101 bridge. Take out on the right.

Access: Sylvandale: Exit U.S. 101 3.1 miles north of Redway. Go upstream along Hooker Creek Road adjacent to the river. Access is at river mile 24.4.

Phillipsville: From Avenue of the Giants in Phillipsville, follow Phillipsville Road as it loops west to the river. Access is at river mile 21.

Jensen Grove: North of Miranda on Avenue of the Giants the road closely parallels the river 0.2 mile north of Jensen Grove. Access is at river mile 15.

Lansdale Bar: A side road from Avenue of the Giants provides access 0.7 mile south of Elk Creek Road at river mile 13.5.

Myers Flat: U.S. 101 and Avenue of the Giants intersect here. Access is at river mile 10.

Williams Grove: 1 mile north of Myers Flat, turn from Avenue of the Giants into Williams Grove. Go toward the river. Access is at river mile 8.1.

Garden Club Grove: 2.3 miles north of Myers Flat on Avenue of the Giants turn into the Garden Club Grove picnic area. Access is at river mile 6.5.

Cruising near Redway on a Memorial Day weekend.

Gould Bar: Exit U.S. 101 at Weott, then go west to Avenue of the Giants. Turn south on Avenue of the Giants for 0.5 mile to side road leading toward the river. Access is at River mile 3.0.

Federation Grove: 2 miles north of Weott turn from Avenue of the Giants into the California Women's Clubs Federation Grove picnic area. Access is at river mile 1.6.

Leatherwood Bar: Dyerville Road, Avenue of the Giants, and U.S. 101 come together at the South Fork Eel River confluence with the main Eel River. From Dyerville Road a side road slopes down to the river near the U.S. 101 bridge. Access is at river mile 0.4.

Shuttle: Driving distances are slightly shorter than river distances. Speeds along Avenue of the Giants are 20 to 30 miles per hour.

For more information: (See Appendix B for phone numbers, websites, and street addresses.) To determine the status of Humboldt or other area state parks, call the North Coast Redwoods District Headquarters or visit their website. To learn the schedule of ranger-guided canoe trips, visit Humboldt Redwoods State Park on-line. For other lodging in the Eel River area, contact the Humboldt Lodging Guide on the Internet.

⬛23 Eel River

(see map on page 84)

Character: Magnificent Wild and Scenic River with fine canoe camping.

Class: I+.

Skill level: Beginner with experience.

Water source: Rainy season runoff.

Best season: Spring.

Craft: Whitewater canoes, kayaks, inflatable kayaks, rafts, and dories.

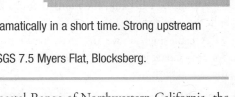

Hazards: During rainy season, flows can rise dramatically in a short time. Strong upstream winds may battle boaters.

Maps: Six Rivers National Forest, Garberville, USGS 7.5 Myers Flat, Blocksberg.

Overview: Draining much of the remote Coastal Range of Northwestern California, the Eel is a big river in a 2,000-foot-deep canyon. The segment described here is a brief sample of the Eel River below Fort Seward.

The untamed Eel is a river of extreme flows. Winter flows average more than 13,000 cfs, and floods max out at 560,000 cfs. Late summer flows dwindle to 55 cfs or less. The paddlers' trick is to be there in the spring when the river is dropping and the weather is dry. Very flashy, Eel River flows sometimes jump 10,000 cfs in a day. Rain is always a possibility.

As you traverse the length of the canyon, the remains of Northwestern Pacific Railroad hide behind redwood trees, dart through tunnels, and lay under landslides. The railroad is the only path attempted along the unstable terrain. The few roads that lead to the river are long and mountainous.

Prevalent northwest winds sometimes blow strongly up the canyon. Warm weather in the Central Valley accelerates the winds. Strong winds and flows below 1,000 cfs result in dreary paddling and may be too strong for rafts to make downstream progress.

The paddling:

Eel Rock to Whitlow (Sequoia)

   Length: 5 miles.

   Average run time: 2 to 4 hours.

   Class: I+.

   Skill level: Beginner with experience.

   Optimal flow: 1,000 to 4,000 cfs (Eel River at Fort Seward gauge).

   Average gradient: 4 feet per mile.

Soon after the put-in, some large rocks with sharp eddy lines may require some forceful paddling to avoid upsets. Above 3,000 cfs the current is fast and makes for swift downstream progress.

The channel is more than 100 yards wide with gravel bars extending 200 yards beyond the water's edge before meeting the canyon slopes. The gravel bars make great campsites. Sometimes the wildlife will come to you. We saw fresh bear tracks emerging from the river when we floated this stretch.

Expansive views open to the forested western slopes and the grass-covered ridges to the east. Some ridges descend as cliffs directly to the water. High-water marks on the cliffs and trees are 20 feet above desirable paddling stages. At high water, the river extends from bank to bank in a wide, powerful torrent.

Along the left bank, the railroad enters a tunnel at a huge jointed rock face that has split into the river.

A cable high above the river marks the approach to Whitlow. At the next bend, Sonoma Creek joins on the left. This is the take-out. Two houses sit far across the Eel on the opposite shore.

Access: Eel Rock: From U.S. Highway 101 at Myers Flat, exit to Avenue of the Giants. Follow Avenue of the Giants 1.8 miles to Elk Creek Road and turn east. After another 2.8 miles turn north on the Dyerville Loop Road. Follow it 3.0 sinuous miles, then turn east on Eel Rock Road. Go 4.3 miles down a steep mountain road to the community called Eel Rock, next to the railroad. A gated unpaved road leads 0.25 mile to the river.

Whitlow: From Eel Rock go back to the intersection of Eel Rock Road and Dyerville Loop Road. Turn east on Elk Creek Road which becomes Whitlow Road. Go another 3 miles to the flat called Whitlow. At the corner where the road flattens and turns right, look for a parking space. A foot trail follows the railroad downstream to a trestle, then turns downhill to the mouth of Sonoma Creek. Carry distance is about 0.25 mile. Note the two houses (one yellow) across the Eel River.

Shuttle: Eel Rock to Whitlow: 10.3 miles (45 minutes).

For more information: (See Appendix B for phone numbers, websites, and street addresses.) For lodging in the Eel River area, contact the Humboldt Lodging Guide on the Internet.

24 Trinity River—Lewiston to Junction City

Character: Reliable flows, pretty mountain scenery, and gravel bar rapids attract paddlers to this Trinity River reach.

Length: 33 miles.

Class: I to II.

Skill level: Beginner with experience negotiating brush and rocks.

Optimal flow: 450 to 1,000 cfs (Lewiston or Douglas City gauges).

Water source: Clair Engle Lake and Lewiston Lake.

Average gradient: 12 feet per mile.

Best season: Summer and autumn.

Craft: Whitewater canoes, kayaks, inflatables, and rafts.

Hazards: Brush along the stream banks and fallen trees are the primary concerns to the paddler. If implemented, new release schedules may dramatically increase late spring and early summer flows to the river.

Maps: BLM 1/100,000 Redding, Shasta-Trinity National Forest, USGS 7.5 Lewiston, Weaverville, Junction City.

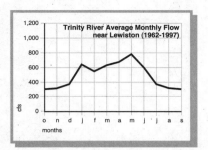

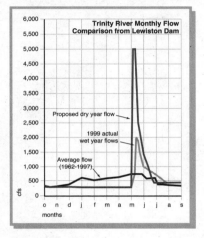

Overview: Near the fishing resort town of Lewiston, the Trinity River emerges clear and cold from Clair Engle Lake and Lewiston Lake into a mountain valley. Soon the valley narrows and the Trinity looks like other famous fly-fishing streams from an Orvis catalog. Below Douglas City, the river changes to a broad canyon surrounded by mountains. Boating difficulty remains consistent with Class I and II rapids, gravel bars, brush hazards, and fallen trees.

Trinity County has an abundance of camping places. Steel Bridge, Douglas City, and Junction City campgrounds are on the river. Downstream of Steiner Flat, you can choose your own unimproved site on public land, but please respect private property.

When the Trinity River Division of the Central Valley Project was completed in 1960, the Bureau of Reclamation diverted up to 90 percent of the Trinity's water to the Central Valley. The result was a devastating decline in the steelhead and salmon fisheries. With major flood flows subdued by reservoirs, the streambed changed. Clair Engle Lake captured new gravel from the mountains. Sediment accumulated in the gravel bars instead of

POST outdoor club members enjoy the Trinity.

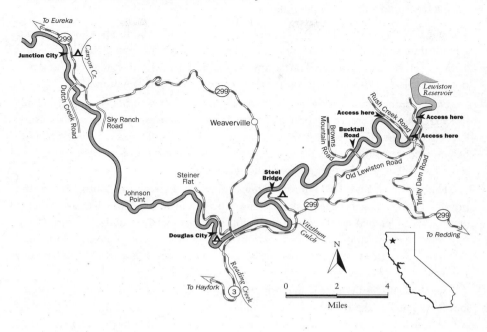

being washed higher onto the river banks. Brush emerged and stayed on the gravel bars without storm flows to uproot it. Two decades of studies have sought solutions to the problems.

Various experimental flow schedules will affect boating on the Trinity. From May through September, Lewiston Lake flow releases will increase. During wet years release peaks may reach 8,000 cfs. Even during dry years, release peaks may reach 5,000 cfs, compared with a peak of 2,000 cfs in May 1999 (a wet year). Later summer flows have exceeded 1000 cfs for several weeks. Fish habitat improvements may add cobbles and remove brush in the next few years. The resulting changes to the riverbed should be noticeable to paddlers, and the increased pulses of water will be noticeable along the 110-mile length of the river.

The paddling:

Lewiston to Steel Bridge Campground

Length: 12 miles.

Elevation: 1,800 feet.

Average run time: 4 to 6 hours.

Class: II.

Skill level: Advanced beginner.

Optimal flow: 500 to 1,000 cfs (Lewiston or Douglas City gauges).

Average gradient: 13 feet per mile.

The put-in at the weir is only 1.0 mile below the Lewiston dam and fish hatchery. The cold water dumps over the weir into a brief eddy that exits into a brief rapid above and below Trinity Dam Boulevard bridge. The narrow channel and frequent riffles require your attention. The splashy riffles continue over the spawning gravels near Lewiston.

Downstream 0.8 mile is the newly restored, one-lane Lewiston bridge, originally built in 1903. The north end of the bridge has a great put-in. Between Lewiston and the Rush Creek access, the Trinity is a drift boater's dream. These 2.1 miles mix calm water and riffles, great for paddling and fly fishing. The Rush Creek access is on river right, at the bottom of the hill where the river and road diverge.

The mouth of Rush Creek forms the next riffle as the river turns south again to the private river crossing between Salt Flat and Goose Ranch. This area has several large gravel bars, riffles, and brush. In the next 2 miles the river follows a long "U" turn to the northwest into a steep bank. Then the narrow channel turns south to the Bear Mountain Road bridge with its parking area, fishing access, and take-out. It is all readily visible from the river.

Below the bridge 0.1 mile is an abrupt right turn into a local fishing hole. Bear Mountain Road parallels the right bank for 1.1 miles before climbing up Trinity House Gulch. A few houses and summer camps are scattered along the 6 miles from Bucktail to Steel Bridge.

Below Poker Bar, starting near Limekiln and China Gulches, the BLM manages the land the next 2 miles to Steel Bridge Campground. Approaching Steel Bridge Campground, the channel slants left around a gravel bar. The campground is slightly downstream on the left bank and is screened by trees. This is a good reason to look over the take-out when you set up the shuttle so you don't miss it. There is no bridge at the campground. Only an abutment remains below the day-use area.

Steel Bridge Campground to Douglas City Campground

Length: 6.7 miles.

Elevation: 1,673 feet.

Average run time: 2 to 4 hours.

Class: II.

Skill level: Beginner with fast-water experience.

Optimal flow: 450 to 1,000 cfs (Douglas City gauge).

Average gradient: 5 feet per mile.

Put-ins are easy at both the Steel Bridge campground and day-use area. The Trinity runs swiftly over a gravel-lined bed through this area. Tall trees shade much of the river's width and help to keep the clear water cold. At many river bends, trees have fallen into the river, creating hazards. About 1.5 miles below the put-in, the channel next to Steel Bridge Road is so tree choked that it is impassable, so use the right channel. A short distance beyond this point, some large midstream rocks are easy to paddle around at low flows but can provide turbulent, swirling currents at high flows. This section of the Trinity reminded me of Vermont because of its clear water, green hills, and small houses scattered along the left bank. Some houses have wide lawns next to their own fly-fishing paradise.

Below Vitzthum Gulch, California Highway 299 joins the river. A small gravel bar on the left bank presents a lunch spot away from the houses, out of sight from the highway, and on public land.

Near the CA 299 bridge at Douglas City the channel broadens with gravel bar riffles and more tree hazards. The left bank below the bridge is the site of Reading Bar, named after Major Reading, who discovered gold here.

A trailer park on the right bank signals your approach to a rapid with a little more spice, perhaps Class II. As the river starts a long "U" turn, it bends abruptly to the west. Gravel piles line the right banks. In river center there is a large rock, and logs totally block the right side. The next flood or high-water release may move the logs.

Continuing to curve north, the river encounters another riffle marked by bedrock rising from the right bank. In the late 1990s, the rapid was a mild chute at 450 cfs, but years earlier it was a more difficult challenge.

Below the rapid 50 yards is the take-out at the BLM's Douglas City Campground. The picnic area and parking are on river right.

Douglas City Campground to Junction City
Length: 14.5 miles.
Elevation: 1,640 feet.
Average run time: 4 to 7 hours.
Class: II.
Skill level: Beginner with experience.
Optimal flow: 450 to 1,000 cfs (Lewiston or Douglas City gauges).
Average gradient: 16 feet per mile.

The take-out for the previous run is the put-in for this run. Here the river begins to change character. The channel has cut deeper into the canyon and bedrock layers begin to appear. Other folks visit this very scenic section to fish or pan for gold. Most of the land between Douglas City Campground and Steiner Flat is public land managed by the BLM.

From Douglas City Campground the river turns west and then south. Several exposed ledges appear on river left. Although the river seems remote from civilization, Steiner Flat Road unobtrusively hugs the right slope. Above the road, steep forested slopes drop down from high ridges.

Gravel bar rapids occur less frequently on this stretch, with deeper cut channels between rocks and high-cut banks taking their place. Fallen trees are still a challenge to avoid. Some rapids above Steiner Flat are more technical than the rapids above Douglas City.

When we floated this stretch, two capsizes occurred at a simple-looking rapid that directed water from a gravel bar into a cut left bank. A fallen tree along the left bank and a stump in the fast water demanded careful boat control, which not everyone displayed. Be careful through here.

Near Steiner Flat, several houses are visible, including some that look new and well appointed. This remote community at the end of Steiner Flat Road seems neatly nestled into the canyon above the Wild and Scenic Trinity River.

Look for another bouncy Class II rapid below Steiner Flat. A mile below Steiner Flat, a gravel bar on the right provides a welcome campsite. Well above summer flow level, the camping area used to be sandy, but floods recently turned it to gravel. Emerging from the gravel is an old steel structure that only a few years ago was in a channel. These changes, plus debris high in the neighboring trees, evidence the magnitude of the 1997 and 1998 floods. From here to Junction City the river is less difficult and you can make faster time. Wide gravel bars, suitable for camping, alternate from one side of the river to the other. The ridges are still steep and high but are more set back from the river.

Near Johnson Point a large landslide—a remnant of hydraulic mining—scars a steep hillside on river left. Soon the river makes two sharp turns. Between the turns a gravel bar sends the flow into a high-cut bank on river right. Beware of the nasty snag blocking the right side of the channel!

Starting near Johnson's Point, the land ownership is a mixture of private, Forest Service, and BLM all the way to CA 299. Since the gravel and sand flats look ripe for camping, check with the Weaverville Ranger Station. Seemingly incongruous among the long gravel and cobble bars is a huge house with spacious lawns less than 0.5 mile below Johnson's Point.

At Bell Gulch the river turns northeast to expose the first water level views of the 8,000-foot Trinity Alps mountains, almost 20 miles away. A few more riffles, easy rapids, and avoidable snags speckle the river as it flows in a valley once exploited by hydraulic mining and gold dredges. From a canoeist's view, emerging trees and brush hint that the scars are beginning to heal.

Two roads, well set back from the river, parallel the last few miles—Sky Ranch Road on the east side and Dutch Creek Road on the west. Both join CA 299 in Junction City. CA 299 rejoins the Trinity River near Oregon Creek. About 4 miles up the creek, hillsides exposed by the famous La Grange hydraulic gold mine are slowly healing.

The next obvious landmark is the mouth of Canyon Creek, which has high gravel mounds. During spring and early summer, Canyon Creek contributes a lot of snowmelt from the Trinity Alps to the river. Soon after Canyon Creek you encounter the Dutch Creek Road bridge, almost 2 miles from the take-out.

Through this section, the river flows immediately next to the CA 299. Then the Trinity swings south and forms a large loop back toward the highway. The gravel bar inside this loop (river right) is the take-out. If you paddled next to CA 299 again, you went too far. Go back upstream to the gravel bar.

Access: Lewiston Gauge and weir are just 0.1 mile upstream from Trinity Dam Boulevard bridge. A gravel area just below the weir offers a short, steep gravel ramp for boat launching. Trinity Dam Boulevard exits north from CA 299 about 27 miles west of Redding.

Old Lewiston bridge connects Deadwood Road in Lewiston with Rush Creek Road along the north bank. The large gravel bar access is at the north end of the one-lane bridge.

Rush Creek (Hog Hole) fishing access is west of both Trinity Dam Boulevard bridge and the old Lewiston bridge. Go to the north side of the river and turn west onto Rush Creek Road. The graded gravel parking area is about 2.1 miles from Trinity Dam Boulevard bridge.

Bucktail Hole fishing access: From CA 299 go north on Old Lewiston Road for 3 miles to Browns Mountain Road. Turn onto Browns Mountain Road for 0.3 mile. Next to the bridge are easy parking and river access. Here the clear river is small, intimate, and very attractive. Upstream, the channel meanders into a cliff.

Steel Bridge Campground occupies the end of Steel Bridge Road about 2 miles from CA 299. The turnoff from CA 299 is 3 miles east of Douglas City. You can easily launch your boats from the campsites. The Steel Bridge day use area provides riverside parking on a wide gravel bar 0.2 mile downstream of Steel Bridge Campground.

Douglas City Campground and day-use area is on Steiner Flat Road 0.5 mile downstream of Douglas City and CA 299. This fee area is open May 1 to November 1.

Steiner Flat is public land with primitive camping at the end of Steiner Flat Road. Continue west and downstream along Steiner Flat Road from Douglas City and Douglas City Campground. The area is open year-round, weather permitting.

Junction City access is on the opposite side of CA 299 from Junction City Campground, about 1 mile west of the Canyon Creek bridge. An unmarked gravel road is 50 feet east of the campground entrance and leads to a large gravel bar with ample parking. Typical take-out is on the west side of the bar. The fee campground provides potable water, toilets, tables, and campsites from May 1 to November 1.

Shuttle: Lewiston to Steel Bridge Campground: 15 miles (30 minutes). Steel Bridge Campground to Douglas City Campground: 6 miles (20 minutes). Douglas City Campground to Junction City Campground: 17 miles (30 minutes).

For more information: (See Appendix B for phone numbers, websites, and street addresses.) Camping information and maps may be obtained from the Bureau of Land Management, Redding Field Office, and the Weaverville Ranger District of the Shasta Trinity National Forest. You may obtain more lists of Trinity County recreation resources and accommodations from the Trinity County Visitor Guide. The Bureau of Reclamation may post the annual streamflow schedule on the Internet.

25 Trinity River—Junction City to Cedar Flat

Character: This mountain river has lots of easily accessible whitewater for intermediate and advanced skill levels.

Length: 23 miles.

Class: II to IV.

Skill level: Intermediate to advanced.

Optimal flow: 400 to 1,500 cfs (Trinity River near Burnt Ranch gauge).

Water source: Snowmelt in spring and early summer, and releases from Lewiston Lake mid-summer through mid-October.

Average gradient: 16 feet per mile.

Best season: Spring through early autumn.

Craft: Whitewater canoes, kayaks, inflatables, and rafts.

Hazards: Several rapids are severe enough to warrant scouting and, at some flows, portaging. Be prepared for high water and very cold snowmelt in spring.

Maps: Shasta-Trinity National Forest, USGS 7.5 Junction City, Dedrick, Hayfork Bally, Big Bar, Del Loma, Ironside Mt.

Overview: The Wild and Scenic Trinity River provides whitewater boating excitement for boaters with prior whitewater experience. The steep whitewater on the Pigeon Point to Big Flat run is a favorite commercial run for outfitters using rafts and inflatable kayaks. Most of the rapids have pools at the bottom. Downstream reaches are popular for training and overnight runs. Many larger rapids are visible from the road for easy scouting.

Throughout the reach, California Highway 299 parallels the north side of the river with many access points on national forest lands. You can camp along the river. Most folks stay at established campgrounds and take day trips.

The paddling:

Junction City to Pigeon Point

    Length: 6.1 miles.

    Average run time: 2 to 4 hours.

    Class: I to II.

    Skill level: Beginner.

    Average gradient: 4 feet per mile.

The put-in is the same as the take-out for Trip 24 (Lewiston to Junction City). Like the last mile of that run, the river starts swiftly as it heads into a left turn along the road. For the next 2.5 miles, wide gravel bars alternate along the banks, remnants of gold-dredging days. By late summer the wide riffles become shallow between deeper pools.

Trinity River—Junction City to Cedar Flat

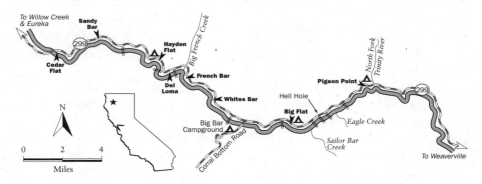

Below Coopers Bar the river turns west again, leaves the dredge tailings behind, and enters a much narrower channel. Downstream 1.5 miles, a steeper riffle drops you into the North Fork Trinity River confluence in sight of the bridge. This major tributary contributes high flows during spring runoff.

The bridge over the North Fork is a difficult take-out. Go about 0.5 mile downstream to a much easier take-out and better parking at Pigeon Point. You can see this popular access on river right with a campground in the trees beyond. Land quickly since the river runs fast here.

Pigeon Point to Big Flat

Length: 5.5 miles.

Average run time: 3 to 5 hours.

Class: III to IV.

Skill level: Intermediate to expert.

Average gradient: 21 feet per mile.

From Pigeon Point the canyon becomes prettier. Enjoy the scenery when you can because exciting whitewater will soon take all of your attention. If you are not ready to navigate steep, complicated, rock-filled rapids that are dangerous to swim, then enjoy this stretch of river from the road. There are plenty of milder miles in downstream reaches.

The Trinity runs fast at the put-in and you can quickly sense that the river is getting steeper. Bedrock instead of gravel creates the rapids. Ledges drop down to the water and steep banks guard both sides. At first some short riffles alternate with calmer sections. Then about 1.2 miles from Pigeon Point there is a significant drop, soon followed by more brisk rapids. Approaching Eagle Creek (2 miles from Pigeon Point), you will encounter a significant steep drop quickly followed by two more spicy rapids.

Hell Hole rapid was once known as Malcolm's Delight. From a broad pool, the channel turns to the right, with shallow rocks on the right and bedrock ledges on the left. This Class III or IV rapid (depending on water level) runs to the left, goes over a couple of ledges, then drops vertically into a pool. Choose your route with care since some rocks are close to the surface at summer flows. Easy to scout from either bank, the easier portage is on the right.

Below Hell Hole, an easier section contains a couple of larger rocks before and in the middle of a riffle. The fun is not over yet. Almost at the confluence with Sailor Bar Creek is Sailor Rapid, once known as Triple Drop. A half-mile beyond that is Pin Ball, an extended rapid with rocks in the middle, lots of choices to make, and splashy waves. Pin Ball demands respect and good paddle strokes to enjoy the pool at the bottom.

Opposite the Fishtale Inn is the long and complicated Fishtale rapid, Class III.

Wilderness Adventures guides are found in Big Flat near the RV park. They will provide river access for their customers. In the river just beyond are some big boulders for a slalom course that at high water can make bouncy rapids with strong hydraulics. Gigantic boulders in the river and a huge rock outcropping on river right mark the Big Flat river access. The take-out is about 100 yards from the paved road, toilets, and parking.

Big Flat to Hayden Flat

Length: 10.5 miles.

Average run time: 3 to 6 hours. This stretch is sometimes combined with the Hayden Flat to Cedar Flat reach for a two-day trip.

Class: II.

Skill level: Intermediate.

Average gradient: 16 feet per mile.

This section is much easier than the Pigeon Point run. Just out of sight from the put-in is a rapid that has waves and requires maneuvering, but a long, calm stretch follows.

About 0.8 mile from Big Flat, the Skunk Point Picnic Area provides a potty break for those willing to climb the steep sand path to the parking area. The river below stays slow with a few big rocks.

The Corral Bottom Road bridge connects to Big Bar Campground on the south side of the river. On the north side is the Big Bar Ranger Station. The banks are high and steep and offer only poor river access. Enjoy the rocky rapid as you leave Big Bar. Below Denny Creek 0.5 mile are some more rocky rapids with bouncy waves at the bottom. After another 0.25 mile, a gravel-bar rapid narrows the river with big boulders in the channel and on both sides.

Where the road climbs higher above the river, look for the Whites Bar river access. Named Little Prairie, this pretty section of river has rapids scattered frequently along the next 1.3 miles. At 0.1 mile below Rock Bar Creek is a long rapid with big rocks in the center, some big waves, and holes. Then the Trinity turns north and then east as it approaches

Hell Hole Falls (at 450 cfs) tests many paddlers on the Trinity River's popular Pigeon Point run.

French Bar and the French Bar river access. Look for two picturesque rocks in the river, a wide gravel bar, and a retaining wall. Across from the take-out is a tunnel gold miners dug to divert the river through the promontory. French Bar is an easy put-in and take-out.

More rapids are found both upstream and downstream of Big French Creek. A long flat section, then another strong rapid come just upstream of the Del Loma access road. The area has several sandy beaches and swimming holes where the river sweeps in a long arc from southwest to northeast. Expect some more rapids near the tiny community of Del Loma.

The highway and river rejoin here and turn southwest again, eventually coming to the picturesque Hayden Flat river access. The campground is across CA 299 from the river.

Hayden Flat to Cedar Flat
Length: 7 miles.
Average run time: 3 to 5 hours.
Class: II to III.
Skill level: Intermediate.
Average gradient: 15 feet per mile.

Visit the rocks above the river in the evening or early morning. You will treat yourself to a wonderful, peaceful view of the river. However, the pace soon changes to rapids alternating with pools. Below Little Swede Creek is a rock garden with a modest drop. At Schneider's Bar, a ledge extends diagonally across the river with hard-to-see slots and some boulders. This rapid has been dubbed Picket Fence.

On the highway side, steep rocks lead up from the river. The south side has small sandy flats for camping. The highway is far enough above the river to be out of mind. One mile below Schneider's Bar, the river takes two quick turns, first south then west. The Sandy Bar river access is the broad gravel bar at the second turn. There are riffles about the bar.

Approaching Don Juan Point, the rapids continue. A ledge extends upstream into the pool and starts a non-trivial rapid that includes a pour-over, a snaggle tooth, and waves that could swamp an open boat. Flows above 500 cfs may cover more of the rocks and make it easier. This is a bouncy ride for inflatables and rafters wearing helmets. It is a test of skills for canoeists in open boats.

Just around the sharp bend of Don Juan Point is the final Class III rapid of the run. A mile downstream is the stream flow gauge known as Trinity River near Burnt Ranch. Downstream 700 feet, the CA 299 bridge crosses the Trinity at Cedar Flat.

Take out on the right just upstream of the Cedar Flat bridge. An obvious sign at the take-out reads, "Caution: Extremely Difficult Rapids. Experts Only 1.5 Miles Below This Point." This sign refers to the Class V Burnt Ranch Gorge that is beyond the scope of this guidebook.

Access: The Junction City access is on the opposite side of CA 299 from Junction City Campground, about 1 mile west of the Canyon Creek bridge. An unmarked gravel road is 50 feet east of the campground entrance and leads to a large gravel bar with ample parking. The typical take-out is on the west side of the bar.

Pigeon Point Campground: CA 299 mile marker 36.5, paved road, heavily used in summer by rafters.

Big Flat: CA 299 mile marker 30.4, paved parking, toilet, paved road.

Whites Bar River Access: CA 299 mile marker 26.5.

French Bar River Access: CA 299 mile marker 23.61, marked by a retaining wall down to the river made of native rock and concrete, gravel road to parking area, wide gravel bar, easy put-in and take-out, two picturesque rocks in the river.

Del Loma Access: CA 299 mile marker 22.6, dirt road to river, sandy beach, and gravel bar for an easy put-in and take-out.

Hayden Flat: CA 299 mile marker 20.57, across from Hayden Flat Campground.

Sandy Bar River Access: CA 299 mile marker 17.06, broad gravel bar, nearby riffles but quiet downstream.

The Cedar Flat Access at the CA 299 bridge (14 miles east of Salyer) provides a take-out with parking and rest room.

Shuttles: Junction City to Pigeon Point: 5.3 miles (10 minutes). Pigeon Point to Big Flat: 6 miles (10 minutes). Big Flat to Hayden Campground: 10 miles (20 minutes). Hayden Campground to Cedar Flat: 6 miles (10 minutes).

For more information: (See Appendix B for phone numbers, websites, and street addresses.) Check the Internet for the Trinity County Visitors Guide for RV Parks and Campgrounds. For activities on the Shasta Trinity National Forest, see their website or call them.

26 Trinity River—Hawkins Bar to Willow Creek

Character: Forgiving rapids that subside into fast water in richly forested canyons.

Length: 15 miles.

Class: II.

Skill level: Beginners with whitewater experience.

Water source: Snowmelt in spring, Lewiston releases and South Fork flows in summer.

Best season: Spring and summer.

Craft: Whitewater canoes, kayaks, inflatables, and rafts.

Hazards: The Trinity has the typical hazards of whitewater streams.

Maps: Six Rivers National Forest, USGS 7.5 Hennessey Peak, Salyer, Willow Creek.

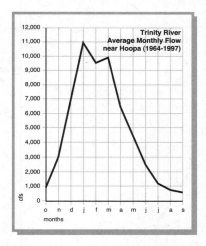

Overview: A highway sign greets visitors, "Welcome to Willow Creek—River Fun in the Mountain Sun." You too will enjoy this river. These two canyons provide whitewater fun that changes into fast riffles in a much bigger, richly forested section below the South Fork confluence. With the highway several hundred feet above the water, the river seems remote.

Most of the flow at Hawkins Bar comes from the major tributaries between Junction City and Hawkins Bar. Late summer is the exception when Lewiston releases sustain the flows. Below Salyer, spring and early summer flows are greatly augmented by the South Fork Trinity River.

The paddling:

Hawkins Bar to near Salyer

Length: 6 miles.

Average run time: 2 to 4 hours.

Class: II.

Skill level: Advanced beginner.

Average gradient: 12 feet per mile.

Optimal flow: 700 to 2,000 cfs (Trinity River near Burnt Ranch gauge station).

The paddling starts with fast, rocky water, and you get to use your whitewater skills in a hurry. A mile below the put-in, the river turns north into a 2-mile-long horseshoe bend. Trinity Village is spread on the gentler slopes where the bend begins. The water slows into long pools between rapids.

Past some houses on the left, the river turns west into a rocky rapid. Even at 500 cfs, some rapids have large enough waves that open whitewater canoes need to bail. Fortunately,

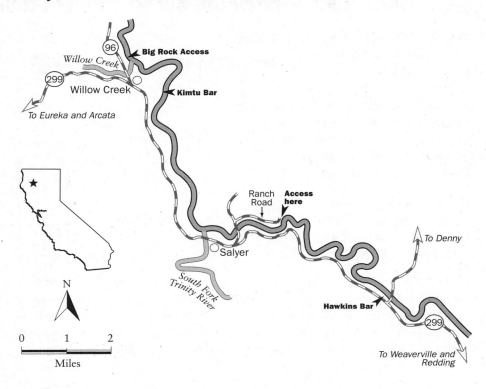

pools follow most rapids. Another horseshoe turn brings you to a promontory with a secluded beach on river left. A steep path leads from here to the highway. In the next 1.5 miles, the river flows under two bridges without access to California Highway 299. Another mile downstream is the take-out.

The easiest take-out near Salyer is at the northern apex of a hairpin "U" turn around a rocky promontory on the left. On the right side are a large lagoon and a sandbar. Higher water may submerge the sand bar. Land on the sandbar and carry up through the blackberries to the vehicles.

Salyer to Willow Creek

Length: 8 to 9 miles.

Average run time: 2 to 5 hours.

Class: II.

Skill level: Beginner with experience.

Average gradient: 9 feet per mile.

Optimal flow: 1,200 to 2,000 cfs (Trinity River at Hoopa gauge).

Trinity River below Hawkins Bar.

From the previous take-out near Salyer, the Trinity continues with few riffles to the South Fork Trinity River confluence. The Salyer bridge crosses high overhead 1.4 miles below the put-in and 1.2 miles above the South Fork confluence. Between Salyer and the South Fork, the gravel bars broaden.

From under a high bridge, the South Fork Trinity River substantially adds to the flows in the main channel. Near the confluence, the channel widens markedly with large, flat-topped gravel bars. At higher flows, water courses over many gravel bars, making the river easier to float. A few houses at the confluence are close to water level, but most buildings are much higher above flood level. California Highway 299 parallels the river 100 to 200 feet up the west side of the canyon. On the east side, Campbell Ridge Road follows the canyon for much of the distance between the South Fork confluence and Willow Creek.

Kimtu Bar access is in a calm reach on river left. Opposite Kimtu, a small canyon road comes plainly into view. This popular day-use area has a wide gravel bar and a rich conifer forest on river left. Below Kimtu Bar, the river makes a long turn to the west and flows under River Road bridge about 0.5 mile above the Big Rock Trinity River access. The river turns right at the Willow Creek confluence amid large gravel bars. Look for the large gravel piles on the left, then work your way through the gravel bars to the crude boat ramp at the Big Rock Trinity River access.

Access: Hawkins Bar: From CA 299 opposite the Hawkins Bar Store, turn north, and then immediately left down a steep dirt road leading 0.4 mile to the river. At the bottom a sign reads "Hawkins Bar—Day Use Only." Accompanying the sign are a toilet, ample

A well-equipped member of the Six Rivers Paddling Club.

parking, and a 75-yard walk over cobbles to the water. The access road is 0.1 mile west of the Denny Road.

Near Salyer: From CA 299 go north across the high bridge, then bear right onto Ranch Road, past the cemetery, past the end of the county road. A sign reads "River Access Parking" and a gate blocks the road. Between some roadside boulders, a well-worn path leads through an acre of blackberries down a short but steep slope to a sand bar. Inspect this take-out when you do the shuttle so you will recognize it from the river.

Kimtu Bar day-use area and campground have a large gravel beach, easy access, picnic tables, and a partly paved road. From CA 299 entering Willow Creek, turn east on Country Club Road. Follow Country Club Road to Kimtu Road, then go to the day-use area at the end.

Big Rock Trinity River access in Willow Creek is accessible from CA 96 only 0.1 mile north of the junction of CA 299. A paved road leads 0.2 mile behind a large gravel operation with large sorting piles and active haul road. A picnic table and gravel launch ramp lead to the water and wide gravel bars.

Shuttle: Hawkins Bar to near Salyer: 6 miles (20 minutes). Salyer to Willow Creek: 8 miles (20 minutes).

For more information: (See Appendix B for phone numbers, websites, and street addresses.) For campground availability, contact the Six Rivers National Forest Lower Trinity Ranger Station via phone. To engage shuttle service, contact the Bigfoot Rafting Company or see their Internet site.

27 Sacramento River—Redding to Balls Ferry

Character: With dependable flows, this big, fast river is extremely popular for boating, fishing, and rafting as it flows through the expanse of the upper Sacramento Valley.

Length: 22 miles.

Average run time: 5 to 7 hours.

Class: I.

Skill level: Beginner with moving water experience.

Optimal flow: 5,000 to 12,000 cfs (Bend Bridge gauge).

Average gradient: 6 feet per mile.

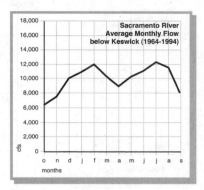

Best season: Spring, summer, and autumn.

Craft: Canoes, kayaks, dories, rafts, and shallow-draft power boats.

Hazards: The Sacramento River—the longest river in California—deserves respect. The summer currents are strong, so stay with your boat in case of an upset. Eddies like the one below Tobiason Rapid are strong enough to thwart a swimmer getting to shore. Each year new snags and shifting shoals reshape the river channel. Avoid winter flood flows as they often contain trees and other dangerous debris.

Maps: USGS 7.5 Redding, Cottonwood, Balls Ferry, BLM Red Bluff CA.

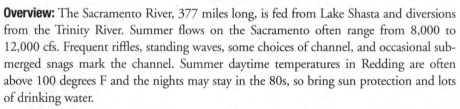

Overview: The Sacramento River, 377 miles long, is fed from Lake Shasta and diversions from the Trinity River. Summer flows on the Sacramento often range from 8,000 to 12,000 cfs. Frequent riffles, standing waves, some choices of channel, and occasional submerged snags mark the channel. Summer daytime temperatures in Redding are often above 100 degrees F and the nights may stay in the 80s, so bring sun protection and lots of drinking water.

Where the banks are low, a wide panorama reveals 14,400-foot Mt. Shasta dominating the northern horizon, 10,000-foot Lassen Peak crowning the Sierras, and splendid views of the 7,000-foot coastal range summits.

Many people share the Sacramento River. Dory fishermen row and motor the river during fishing season. Often friendly, they wave and greet paddlers. The Sacramento is also a great place for wildlife watching. On one trip several great blue herons played follow the leader. Above Anderson, four river otters provided entertainment diving and splashing. Their slide down the riverbank was plainly visible. Overhead, an osprey greeted another osprey carrying a fish to its nest. Close to the right shore a huge nest is perched on the side of a wood-processing plant tower. From September through May, the salmon repeat their spawning spectacle.

The paddling: At Posse Park, the long riffle immediately below the put-in requires some attention. Make an extended ferry toward the opposite bank to avoid shallow rocks. A

Sacramento River—Redding to Balls Ferry

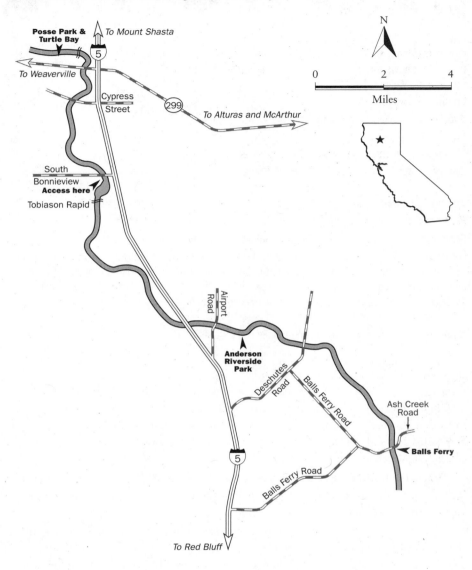

short distance downstream, a submerged rock mid-river produces waves large enough to swamp a heavily loaded canoe.

Between Redding and Anderson, the river races at 4 or 5 m.p.h. down a 15-feet-per-mile gradient. Strong eddies and wave trains evidence the strength of 10,000 cfs flowing more than 100 yards wide. High cliffs line the river left for the next 2 miles, then shrink to river level past the Cypress Street bridge. Impressive homes with large yards line the right bank—these must be cool, refreshing sites during the hot Redding summers. Farther downstream, many houses are set well back from the river's edge and the opposite shore is low enough for the winter high water to flood the land and not the buildings. On a recent trip, we were pleased to see river otters playing near here.

Downstream of the golf course, the left bank of the river again rises to a high bluff with a large building and nearby driving range. Below it, a large eddy swirls against the cliff and gravel bar on river right.

The South Bonnieview Road boat ramp is tucked against the right-downstream side of the bridge. Just downstream, the river divides around a large island. Most of the river flows left to Tobiason Rapid, a series of bouncy, jumbled waves. The right channel around the island starts calmly, descends through a minor riffle, then joins more smooth water. At the lower end of the island, the channel turns abruptly left into a jet on a bouncy collision course with the main current. Together, the rapid and jet form a fast oval-shaped eddy, more like a whirlpool. The jet turns the eddy, swirling to the main current where it abruptly turns 90 degrees. The eddy then flows slightly downstream and closer to shore. About 15 yards from shore, water wells up from the bottom, forcing the current upstream and back into the jet. Paddlers who upset their boat can circle a long time in this mid-river merry-go-round.

Downstream, the riffles become easier and the waves smaller as the gradient eases to 6 feet per mile. The views expand to include the Coast Range mountains. More homes with sumptuous yards border the river. It was a bucolic scene when we floated past, with little kids playing on the banks and teenage rafters exploring a huge snag, stranded mid-river.

The Anderson Riverside Park boat ramp is on the right bank, downstream of the Inter-state 5 bridge. Below I–5, Airport Road crosses on a smaller bridge. On its girders are painted the words, "Rafters take out ½ mile." After you pass more homes, the park comes into view just before the river sweeps left. Watch carefully between the trees for a narrow slough cut into the bank. The boat ramp is 20 yards up the slough. If you miss the ramp, the park extends downstream, but the bank is steep.

Below Anderson the Sacramento winds around the islands upstream of Stillwater Creek, then passes under the Deschutes Road bridge. Cow Creek soon joins on the left. Large gravel bars spread along the right bank opposite a low-cut bank.

Balls Ferry Fishing Access ramp rises steeply up the left bank immediately downstream of the Ash Creek Road bridge. It should end a long and pleasant day.

Access: Posse Park: From I-5 in Redding go west on CA 299, cross the Sacramento River bridge, then immediately exit at Convention Center/Turtle Park. Follow the road north (upstream) between the convention center and the riverside park to parking lots and con-crete boat ramp behind the rodeo arena. The parking area road is gated at night.

South Bonnieview Road connects CA 273 and Churn Creek Road from the I-5 exit south of Redding. The paved boat ramp is on the west side of the river and downstream of the bridge. A short slough separates the ramp from the river.

Three brothers enjoy an autumn day salmon fishing below Redding.

To reach Anderson Riverside Park, follow I–5 south to Anderson. Take the North Street exit, go south, parallel to I–5 for 0.3 mile, then turn east on Balls Ferry Road. Follow Balls Ferry Road 0.5 mile, turn left on Stingy Lane for 0.25 mile, then right on Rupert Road 0.3 mile to the Anderson Riverside Park. On your left, close to the park entrance, is a parking lot for the boat ramp. Popular for community sports as well as river access, the park has flush toilets and a pay phone.

Balls Ferry: From the I–5 Cottonwood exit (Gas Point Road), go east 0.9 mile on Fourth Street to Balls Ferry Road, then take Balls Ferry Road left (parallel to the railroad tracks) 3.5 miles to the intersection with Ash Creek Road. Follow Ash Creek Road 1.2 miles across the bridge to the access and boat ramp downstream of the bridge. Alternatively, from Anderson take the I–5 exit to Balls Ferry Road east, or the Deschutes Road exit east 2.0 miles where it intersects Balls Ferry Road and then turns southeast. Follow Balls Ferry Road 3.0 miles to Ash Creek Road and the bridge.

Shuttle: 20 miles (35 minutes).

For more information: (See Appendix B for phone numbers, websites, and street addresses.) Regarding accommodations and outfitters, call the Shasta Cascade Wonderland Association.

28 Sacramento River—Balls Ferry to Red Bluff

Character: Through this section the Sacramento cuts deep into lava flows down Chinese Rapid and scenic Iron Canyon.

Length: 33 miles.

Average run time: 9 to 12 hours; often done over 2 days.

Class: I to II.

Skill level: Beginner with experience in fast water.

Optimal flow: 6,000 to 12,000 cfs (Bend Bridge gauge).

Average gradient: 3 feet per mile.

Best season: Spring, summer, and autumn.

Craft: Canoes, kayaks, dories, rafts, and shallow-draft power boats.

Hazards: The strong currents accelerate through bedrock rapids instead of the gravel bar variety upstream. Beware of jet skis and water skiers on Lake Red Bluff. Even in summer the water stays cold.

Maps: BLM Red Bluff CA, USGS 7.5 Balls Ferry, Bend, Red Bluff East.

Overview: The deceptively calm surface cloaks the river's strength. The BLM manages 7 miles of land between Balls Ferry and Red Bluff. Permitted activities include hiking, picnicking, camping, and wildlife watching. The Sacramento is famous for great salmon, steelhead, and trout fishing. Other local wildlife include river otters, ringtail cats, blacktail deer, red-tailed hawks, osprey, and bobcats.

According to the BLM, the mouth of Inks Creek and 0.75 mile above and below the mouth are closed to camping. From mid-May to mid-September, the closed gates of Red Bluff Diversion Dam form Lake Red Bluff.

The paddling: Fifty yards below the Balls Ferry boat ramp, a riffle stretches across the channel, stranding logs at the center. Beyond, the Sacramento River continues its fast flow in the wide, tree-lined channel. Two miles downstream, where the channel narrows a little, the Reading Island Recreation Area (a historical site) occupies the terrace along a cut right bank. This BLM site provides day-use facilities and group camping by permit. Hundreds of oaks have been planted to restore the once dense riparian habitat. The best landing spot is at the downstream confluence with little Anderson Creek.

The state manages the land along the right bank between Reading Island and the mouth of Cottonwood Creek. It is open to camping. Additionally, a large gravel bar sits opposite the mouth of Cottonwood Creek. The river bank beyond the gravel bar is private land.

Enjoy the view upstream where snow-capped, 14,450-foot Mt. Shasta gleams 70 miles to the north. Below Cottonwood Creek, the lava beds intermittently emerge to obscure the view. Two miles farther, Battle Creek joins the Sacramento from the slopes of Lassen Peak.

Sacramento River—Balls Ferry to Red Bluff

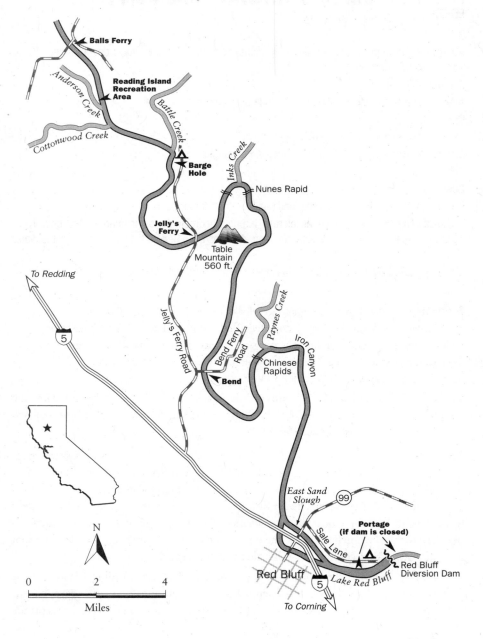

In 1998, Battle Creek gained the distinction of having diversion dams removed to help restore salmon spawning. A mile below Battle Creek, the huge gravel bars of Barge Hole occupy river left. This BLM land is open to camping and access. Where the river again turns to the south, the BLM manages more land for camping on river left.

Jelly's Ferry bridge is the next put-in and take-out site. From there, look to the east to see 10,457-foot Lassen Peak about 35 miles away.

Below Jelly's Ferry the river landscape changes. First turning north, then turning south, the river has cut through the lava that makes Table Mountain. Sheer canyon walls, oak sloops, and riverside terraces replace farmlands. The speed and waves of Jelly's Ferry Rapid add excitement to boating.

Inks Creek meets the canyon at the apex of the northerly turn. The area is interesting to explore but the BLM prohibits camping within 0.75 mile of the mouth of Inks Creek. Just below the creek is Nunes Rapid. The BLM manages lands along the left bank from Inks Creek to a mile below the point where "the rock wall" descends to the river from Table Mountain.

Passing Lookout Mountain, Bend Bridge comes into view. A good access ramp, parking, and rest room are on river left. As the channel loops to the east, then north around the flat farmlands of Bend, you can build your anticipation for Chinese Rapids and Iron Canyon.

As the channel bends northward, the mini-beaches between the rock outcroppings on the left are private lands, but the river right is BLM land. The channel narrows as it approaches Chinese Rapids. The 0.5-mile-long rapid consists of haystacks in a generally clear channel that curves to the right in the bottom half where you encounter strong eddy lines. Boulders, sand, and bedrock alternate along both banks. Just when you think you have reached the rapid's end, lava boulders block the channel's left half. The wide sluice on the right is clear and bouncy.

Paynes Creek enters on the left with its wetland reserve. Here impressive Iron Canyon begins. The river turns sharply south and the sheer canyon walls rise 300 feet. After 2 miles the wall on river left turns to rolling hillsides and the river flows in an almost straight line to Red Bluff. Ida Adobe State Historic Park overlooks the river from the picturesque bluff just upstream from Dibble Creek.

Immediately upstream of the first Interstate 5 bridge, the left channel feeds East Sand Slough. From mid-May to mid-September, Lake Red Bluff floods the sandy channel. East Sand Slough has calm water for conservative paddlers to reach the ramp upstream of the diversion dam. In the summer, beware of jet skis and water skiers using this area. If you follow the main channel, cut to the left bank after passing the islands.

To continue downriver, portage your gear 0.5 mile over paved roads and grassy parks to the ramp below the dam. From mid-September through mid-May the dam gates are open to allow fish migration. When the gates are completely open, the dam is navigable, other conditions permitting. For descriptions of the next reach, see the next chapter.

Chinese Rapid is an exciting part of the Sacramento River between Balls Ferry and Red Bluff. Motor boats can go upstream against the fast current.

Access: Balls Ferry: From the I–5 Cottonwood exit (Gas Point Road), go east 0.9 miles on Fourth Street to Balls Ferry Road, then take Balls Ferry Road left (parallel to the railroad tracks) 3.5 miles to the intersection with Ash Creek Road. Follow Ash Creek Road 1.2 miles across the bridge to the access and boat ramp downstream of the bridge. Alternatively, from Anderson take the I–5 exit to Balls Ferry Road east, or the Deschutes Road exit east 2.0 miles where it intersects Balls Ferry Road and then turns southeast. Follow Balls Ferry Road 3.0 miles to Ash Creek Road and the bridge.

Historical Reading Island is 5.4 miles east of Cottonwood at the end of Adobe Road. Adobe Road meets Balls Ferry Road 0.1 mile east of the point where the road and railroad separate, and 1.4 miles west of the Ash Creek Road junction. The concrete boat ramp is unusable to all but the most determined paddlers due to dense aquatic vegetation and shallow water in the slough leading to the river. The downstream tip of the island offers a fair landing site but is 0.5 mile from the parking area.

Barge Hole Fishing Access is an unimproved, unmarked road and large gravel bar suitable for hand launching and camping. From Jelly's Ferry bridge, continue another 2.4 miles along Jelly's Ferry Road up and down the hill until the road comes close to the river. Look for a dirt road toward the river. Expect to walk or use four-wheel drive on the gravel bars.

Jelly's Ferry bridge can be reached from the south by continuing 4.5 miles on Jelly's Ferry Road past the Bend Ferry Road junction. This BLM day-use area provides access for hand-launch watercraft.

Bend Bridge can be reached from I–5 north of Red Bluff by exiting at Jelly's Ferry Road. Follow Jelly's Ferry Road northeast 2.7 miles to Bend Ferry Road, then 0.3 miles to the bridge and the launching ramp.

Red Bluff River Park is on the west bank of the river. From the intersection of CA 36 and Main Street, go south on Main Street a few blocks. Turn left on either Sycamore or directly into the park by the Chamber of Commerce building. The park provides day-use facilities and a concrete launch ramp.

Lake Red Bluff Recreation Area is adjacent the Red Bluff Diversion Dam on the east side of the Sacramento River. From I–5, take the Red Bluff exit for CA 36. Go east on CA 36, then turn right onto Sale Lane by the stoplight and fast-food places. Follow Sale Lane south 2 miles to the Lake Red Bluff launching ramp and parking. Go another 0.5 mile to the launch ramp below the Salmon Plaza and diversion dam.

Shuttle: Balls Ferry to Red Bluff Diversion Dam: 25 miles (40 minutes).

For more information: (See Appendix B for phone numbers, websites, and street addresses.) About camping along BLM lands, contact the BLM Redding office via telephone number or Internet. For other accommodations and outfitters, call the Shasta Cascade Wonderland Association.

Sacramento River—Red Bluff to Woodson Bridge

Character: Swift currents and wide horizons make this an attractive float trip.

Length: 25 miles.

Average run time: About 6 to 8 hours.

Class: I.

Skill level: Beginner.

Optimal flow: 5,000 to 12,000 cfs (Woodson Bridge gauge).

Water source: Lake Shasta and the Trinity River Diversion.

Average gradient: 3 feet per mile.

Best season: Spring, summer, and autumn.

Craft: Canoes, kayaks, dories, rafts, and shallow-draft power boats.

Hazards: The summer current is strong, so stay with your boat in case of an upset. Outboard motorboats frequently travel the deeper channels. Each year new snags and shifting shoals remake the river channel. Avoid winter flood flows as they often contain floating trees and other debris.

Maps: BLM Red Bluff CA, USGS 7.5 Red Bluff East, Gerber, Los Molinos, Vina.

Overview: Along this stretch of river, wide channels and low banks allow expansive views of Mt. Shasta, the Trinity Alps, and Lassen Peak. Winter flows from the Sacramento's many tributaries move the channel frequently, creating new oxbows and cutoffs. A floatable channel one year may be a sandbar the next year.

Several units of the Sacramento National Wildlife Refuge protect and restore 9 miles of waterfowl and fish habitats along the west bank between Craig Creek and the mouth of Elder Creek. Easy-to-see summer species include osprey, turkey vultures, red-tailed hawks, and some bald eagles. Look for some of them perched on the tall cottonwood snags or oaks along the banks.

Woodson Bridge State Recreation Area is a 142-acre oak woodland park nestled along the Sacramento River. Kopta Slough provides access to boat-in campsites. Adjacent to the park is a 328-acre riparian forest preserve. This jungle-like array of large valley oak, California black walnut, Oregon ash, black cottonwood, sycamore, and willow are a winter home to bald eagles and summer nest sites for yellow-billed cuckoos. Car camp on the east side of the river, 0.5 mile from the Tehama County River Park launch ramp.

Summer daytime temperatures often exceed 100 degrees F with only mild cooling at night, so bring lots of drinking water.

The paddling: Normal summer flows exceed 10,000 cfs and give a fast 4-mile-per-hour ride. Riffles add excitement at the bottom end of many gravel bars, particularly near Blackberry Island, Craig Creek, and Sacramento Bar.

Sacramento River—Red Bluff to Woodson Bridge

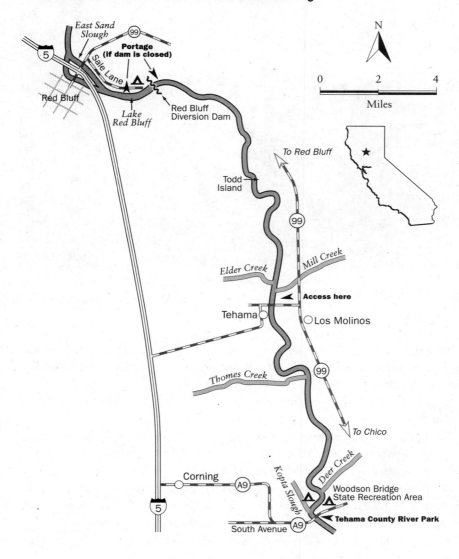

Todd Island is a very large gravel bar on the right side 5 miles below Red Bluff. A cut-off from the old river channel, the BLM manages the land. Todd Island is approximately the center of the 9 miles of the Sacramento National Wildlife Refuge along this stretch of river. More big gravel bars are found downstream at the mouth of Butler Slough and at Sacramento Bar. Depending on the channel-carving whims of recent floods, you can probably explore the side sloughs around the oxbows and gravel bars. Aerial photos and topographic maps show many old channels along these 6 river miles.

The gates of Red Bluff Dam are raised from mid-September to mid-May to allow fish passage. Fisheries biologists use the conical floating device to count fish.

Wide turns interspersed with riffles continue to the mouth of the North Fork of Mill Creek on the left bank and Elder Creek on the right bank. Here orchards and houses line the bank, the channel straightens, and the Tehama bridges come into view. Upstream of the bridges, look for the Mill Creek boat ramp on the left bank just below the mouth of Mill Creek.

Two miles below the Tehama bridges, and upstream of Thomes Creek, the river makes a long horseshoe bend with several gravel bars. Then it straightens before 2 more miles of bends, gravel bars, and shallow riffles around Copeland Bar.

Where the river turns abruptly south, China Creek and Deer Creek join with the Sacramento. Theodora Kroeber's book *Ishi in Two Worlds* made Deer Creek famous. It is the true story of Ishi, the last Yahi Indian, who emerged from the wilderness in 1911.

When you round the bend and see Woodson Bridge, you have choices. You can paddle up Kopta Slough (river right) to the boat-in campgrounds of Woodson Bridge State Recreation Area, or you can head to the opposite bank and the Tehama County River Park boat ramp. For information about going downstream, see the next chapter.

Access: Lake Red Bluff Recreation Area is adjacent to the Red Bluff Diversion Dam. From I–5, take the Red Bluff exit for California Highway 36. Go east on CA 36, then turn right onto Sale Lane by the stop light and fast food places. Follow Sale Lane south 2 miles to the Lake Red Bluff launching ramp and parking. Go another 0.5 mile to the launch ramp below the Salmon Plaza and diversion dam. From mid-September through mid-May the gates are open to allow fish migration. When the gates are completely open, the dam is navigable, other conditions permitting.

Mill Creek Access is 0.2 mile upstream of the Tehama Bridge. Aramayo Way connects the bridge to CA 99. Go north on CA 99 for 0.2 mile to the Tehama and Vina Road. Turn west on Tehama and Vina Road for 1.8 miles. Immediately past the ballpark, turn right to Mill Creek Park. If you go too far, the Tehama and Vina Roads will reconnect with Aramayo Way.

Tehama County River Park and Woodson Bridge State Recreation Area are 6 miles east of I–5 from the South Avenue exit (first exit south of Corning). Follow South Avenue and the signs to Woodson Bridge State Park. At the east end of the bridge, the county park with the launch ramp is immediately downstream of Tehama County Road A9. Woodson Bridge State Recreation Area campground is on the north side of A9 opposite the County Park. The bridge is 3.5 miles west of CA 99.

Shuttle: Red Bluff to Mill Creek: 15 miles (25 minutes). Mill Creek to Woodson Bridge: 13 miles (20 minutes).

For more information: (See Appendix B for phone numbers, websites, and street addresses.) Call Woodson Bridge State Recreation Area to arrange use of boat-in campsites. For camping information at the Red Bluff Diversion Dam, call the Forest Service Area Manager.

30 Sacramento River—Woodson Bridge to Colusa

Character: This popular river meanders through the heart of Northern California farmlands and close to wildlife refuges visited by 40 percent of the waterfowl in the Pacific Flyway.

Length: 74 miles.

Average run time: 2 or 3 days.

Class: I.

Skill level: Beginner.

Optimal flow: 5,000 to 12,000 cfs (Woodson Bridge or Colusa gauges).

Water source: Lake Shasta and the Trinity River Diversion.

Average gradient: 2 feet per mile.

Best season: Spring, summer, and autumn.

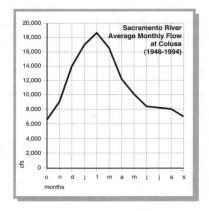

Craft: Canoes, kayaks, dories, rafts, and shallow-draft power boats.

Hazards: The hot summer days invite swimming, but be careful. The summer current is strong, so stay with your boat in case of an upset. Each year new snags and shifting shoals reform the river channel. Avoid winter flood flows, as the cold water often contains floating trees and other debris.

Maps: USGS 7.5 Vina, Foster Island, Glenn, Princeton, Moulton Weir, Colusa, Nord, Ord Ferry, Llano Seco, Butte City, Sanborn Slough, Meridian.

Overview: Bring your fishing rod, sun hat, bird book, binoculars, and lots of water. The mix of easy water, pastoral lands, riparian vegetation, beaches, and gravel bars make this a favorite summer float trip. Summer days can be very hot with only mild cooling at night. Many different kinds of watercraft use the river, and every spring hundreds of students from California State University in Chico ride their homemade "floats" near Chico landing. Several marinas sponsor fishing tournaments. Many shallow-draft power boats ply the waters as the summer temperatures rise.

The flood flows contributed by the Sacramento's many tributaries move the channel frequently, creating new oxbows and cutoffs. Aerial photos plainly show that a floatable channel one year may be a sandbar the next year. Deeply eroded banks topped by orchards with exposed irrigation pipe further evidence the power of winter flows. In the entire reach, we only saw one set of rocks. They once served as riprap.

Woodson Bridge State Recreation Area facilities are described in the preceding chapter. The state park's 328-acre riparian forest preserve is part of the multi-agency effort to preserve and restore riparian forests along the Sacramento River corridor. The U.S. Fish and Wildlife Service reports that "This riparian community is one of the most important wildlife

Sacramento River—Woodson Bridge to Colusa

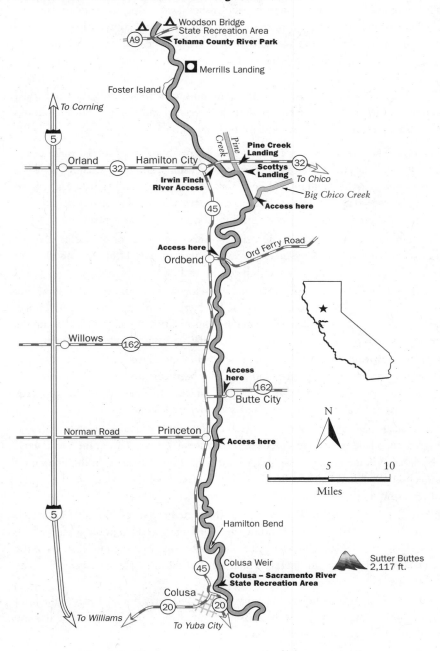

Woodson Bridge
State Recreation Area
Tehama County River Park
A9
Merrills Landing
Foster Island
To Corning
5
Orland
32
Hamilton City
Pine Creek
Pine Creek Landing
Scottys Landing
32
To Chico
Irwin Finch River Access
Big Chico Creek
45
Access here
Access here
Ordbend
Ord Ferry Road
Willows
162
Access here
162
Butte City
Norman Road
Princeton
Access here
5
Hamilton Bend
Colusa Weir
45
Colusa – Sacramento River State Recreation Area
Sutter Buttes 2,117 ft.
Colusa
20
20
To Williams
To Yuba City

N

0   5   10
Miles

habitats in California and North America. Riparian habitats along the Sacramento River are critically important for various threatened species, fisheries, migratory birds, plants, and the natural system of the river itself. There has been an 85 percent reduction of riparian vegetation throughout the Sacramento Valley and foothills region. The relatively small amount of riparian woodlands that remain provides a strikingly disproportionate amount of habitat value for wildlife."

Glenn and Butte County farms grow large amounts of rice. Following the rice harvest in late summer and autumn, the farmers burn the residual stubble. The burning creates lots of smoke, and some of it blows close to the river.

The paddling: The river continues its fast (4+ miles per hour) pace for 10 miles below Woodson Bridge. The pastoral setting invites floating, fishing, and bird watching. Look for osprey nests near Merrills Landing and Foster Island, and occasionally a bald eagle. Keep one eye on the river to avoid sandbars and snags. The reach is popular for Boy Scout canoe trips. Most of the power boats they encounter are considerate of the canoes.

More signs of man-made activity are visible on this long stretch of river. One example is near Snaden Island where a large dredge excavates sand and gravel from the mouth of an oxbow. You should be able to easily avoid the cables anchoring the dredge.

Near the Glenn-Tehama County line the river velocity begins to noticeably slow. Five miles downstream, houses are visible along the left bank upstream of the CA 32 bridge. On the downstream side of the bridge, Irwin Finch boat launching ramp is tucked into the right bank. This ramp is a popular put-in for short floats to Big Chico Creek Beach.

A mile downstream, both banks form great beaches and gravel bars. The 2-mile-long double oxbow once known as Jenny Lind Bend has been cut through to 0.5 mile. Now Pine Creek Landing is 0.25 mile up Pine Creek instead of being riverfront property. Scotty's Landing, a focal point for power boats, is now at the confluence.

Land management around the Pine Creek confluence has changed to restore flood-prone agricultural land to riparian forest. Eventually it will become part of the Sacramento River National Wildlife Refuge. The Sacramento River Project focuses on the restoration and protection of habitats between Red Bluff and Colusa. Look for changes in the vegetation patterns and different wildlife in future decades.

Only a couple miles below Pine Creek are the wide beaches of Bidwell Sacramento River State Park and the old Chico Landing site. The large gravel bar at the mouth of Big Chico Creek is a popular launching and take-out spot for many rafters and jet skis. For the next several miles, clear early summer days offer views of the distant snow-covered Cascade and Coast mountains.

The next landing is the Ordbend County Park at Ord Ferry bridge. It lies at the head of a short, murky slough on river right and upstream of the CA 45 bridge. The day-use area has shade that is welcome on a hot day.

For 20 miles, backwater sloughs and old oxbow lakes reflect the river's geomorphology. The channel is straighter these days, but what will happen without the winding miles to dissipate the energy of flood flows?

The next set of large irrigation pumps is near Sidds Landing. At Sidds Landing, California Highway 45 is visible along the right bank atop the flood control levee. The flood control levees on river left begin 2 miles downstream. That levee is initially unnoticeable since it is set back from the current channel. As you float along the river, note how the river carves its changing course within the 0.5-mile to 1-mile corridor between the levees.

Above Hartly Island, people fly-fishing line the long, sweeping gravel bar on river right in early summer. The osprey must agree with the fishing prospects, since a pair nests in a snag a short distance downstream. When you spot the Butte City bridge for CA 162, look on the left for the slough leading to the launching ramp. It is about 0.5 mile upstream from the bridge.

Between Packer Island and Princeton, you can see the first river views of the Sutter Buttes to the southeast. The 2,100-foot ancient volcanoes are landmarks for much of the southern Sacramento Valley. Soon afterward, tiny Princeton shows its rickety old cable ferry that carried vehicles across the river. Supposedly Caltrans still operates it upon request. In contrast, a gigantic new pumping plant sprawls along the left bank.

Boggs Bend still supports some impressive looking riparian forest. Three miles downstream, the low structure on the left bank, called Moulton Weir, permits some floodwaters to escape the river and flow to the Butte Sink.

Levees now redirect the river to a shorter course around Hamilton Bend. High flood flows sometimes leave high sandy beaches with pleasant views on the river right. The next major flood control structure is the Colusa Weir. Like the Moulton Weir, it is a low levee on the left bank that allows flood water to escape the river to a flood bypass. The most visible feature is the bridge structure supporting the River Road across the weir. The river's course may lead away from the weir so it is sometimes unobtrusive.

Twin water towers mark the town of Colusa. Paddle toward them until you come to a narrow slough on river right. This leads to the boat ramp at the Colusa-Sacramento River State Recreation Area. This fee area has all the amenities of good California state parks.

The river downstream of Colusa is less desirable for paddling because of increased motor boat traffic, levees that closely confine the river, little riparian vegetation, and few gravel or sand bars.

Access: State and local agencies have provided good public access facilities to the Sacramento River. Tehama County River Park is 5.9 miles east of I–5 from the South Avenue exit (first exit south of Corning). Follow South Avenue and the signs to Woodson Bridge State Recreation Area to the bridge over the Sacramento River. The county park is on the east side of the river immediately downstream of Tehama County Road A9.

The Irvine Finch River Access is 1 mile east of Hamilton City and about 8.9 miles west of Chico, on river right downstream of the CA 32 bridge over the Sacramento River. The site provides parking and a launch ramp.

Pine Creek Landing is a private launch site 0.25 miles up Pine Creek from the river. On River Road, it is 0.6 miles south of CA 32 and 2.3 miles east of Hamilton City.

Boy Scout troops enjoy overnight camping trips along the Sacramento River.

Scotty's Landing has a private campground, launch ramp, and over-the-counter food and beverage sales. Located at the mouth of Pine Creek, it is on River Road, 0.8 miles south of CA 32 and 2.3 miles east of Hamilton City.

Big Chico day-use area is also on River Road about 4.2 miles south of CA 32 and 1 mile northwest of the junction with Chico River Road. Suitable for hand-launch craft or four-wheel-drive towed boat trailers.

Ordbend County Park is 0.6 miles east of the intersection of CA 45 and County Road 32 in Ordbend. The parking area and concrete launch ramp are on the upstream side of CR 32 (Ord Ferry Road) bridge. Fees for boat launching.

Butte City County Park provides day-use facilities and a launch ramp into a short slough connecting to the river. The park is in Butte City about 0.5 miles north of the CA 162 bridge over the Sacramento River on the east bank. If you intend to take out here, and since the slough is obscure from the river, be sure to inspect this take-out before you put in.

Princeton is about 10 miles east of I–5 on CA 45. About 0.2 miles south of Norman Road and near the high school is a rough road to the river for hand-launching boats.

Colusa-Sacramento River State Recreation Area is close to the intersection of CA 20 and CA 45 in Colusa. From Market Street (CA 20 and 45), take Tenth Street north past Main Street into the park. Excellent facilities and a concrete launch ramp are at the end of a narrow slough leading 0.2 miles to the river.

Shuttle: Woodson Bridge to Colusa: 65 miles (1.5 hours).

For more information: (See Appendix B for phone numbers, websites, and street addresses.) To arrange use of boat-in campsites, call the Woodson Bridge State Recreation Area. For other state park camping reservations, contact ReserveAmerica. To learn current operations at Colusa-Sacramento River State Recreation Area, call them or look at their website.

31 Feather River—Oroville to Wildlife Refuge

Character: Reliable flows provide year-round easy paddling through the Oroville Wildlife Refuge.

Length: 9.5 miles.

Average run time: 3 to 5 hours.

Class: I with one II–.

Skill level: Beginner with moving-water experience.

Optimal flow: 1,500 to 4,000 cfs (Feather River near Gridley gauge).

Water source: Oroville Reservoir 400 cfs flow below Fish Barrier Dam.

Average gradient: 5 feet per mile.

Best season: Year-round.

Craft: Canoes, kayaks, inflatables, and dories.

Hazards: Releases above 5,000 cfs from Thermalito Afterbay require extreme caution, lining, or portaging to avoid the turbulent discharge.

Maps: USGS 7.5 Oroville, Palermo, Biggs.

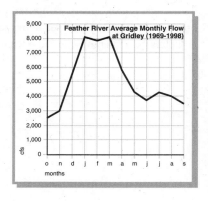

Overview: Oroville Dam generates hydropower and stores water for the State Water Project. Below the Feather River Fish Hatchery, the once mighty Feather River glides tamed and cold through the heart of Oroville. Except during floods, the SWP releases a steady flow of 400 cfs past the fish barrier dam into the Feather River channel. Downstream 7 miles, the bulk of the SWP water joins the river on its way to the Sacramento–San Joaquin Delta. From the delta, the pumps and aqueducts transport SWP water to farms of the San Joaquin Valley, the San Francisco Bay, the Central Coast, and Southern California.

Most of this low-flow stretch of river has only a few gravel bars and a couple of snags to challenge the paddler. Fly-fishing for steelhead is very popular in the low-flow section between Oroville and Thermalito. The most serious paddling concern on this easy run is the outflow from Thermalito Afterbay, an offstream reservoir connected by pumped storage facilities to Oroville Dam. Releases from the Afterbay to the river cause severe turbulence across the entire channel when the outflow exceeds 5,000 cfs. High releases may occur any time of year. Below Thermalito many powerboats ply the river when flows allow.

The 8,000-acre Oroville Wildlife Area borders 10 miles of the Feather River. The area allows primitive camping, boating, fishing, swimming, and in-season hunting. With a bird list of 178 species, the refuge is a favorite of bird watchers.

The paddling: Put in at the downstream end of Bedrock Park in Oroville. The river is smooth and wide, a good place for beginners and novices to practice their paddle strokes.

After flowing under the California Highway 70 bridge, the calm river swings south. The right bank rises 80 feet above the water. Several pleasant-looking homes adorn the

Feather River—Oroville to Wildlife Refuge

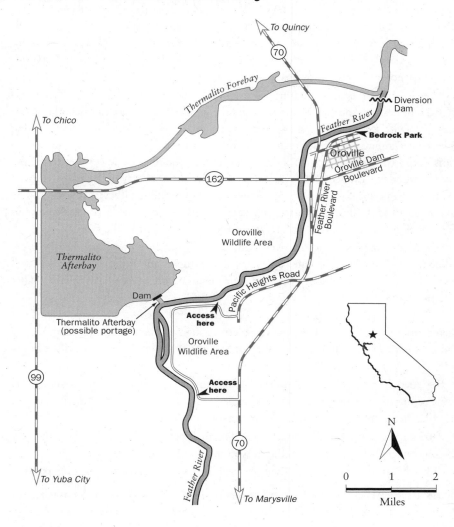

right shore above the Oroville Dam Boulevard bridge. Downstream of the bridge you encounter the first fast water, almost a riffle. Fast flows continue 1 mile to another riffle favored by fly-fishers. Just below, an RV Park (with a boat ramp) occupies the left bank. Oroville Wildlife Refuge manages the opposite side where the landscape is tall trees and dredge tailings from gold-mining and dam-building eras.

As the river turns west, you may spot the cranes of a gravel operation on the left. Soon some broken pilings and boulders cross the river. Take care to align your boat with the open channels. Several wide, shallow riffles and braided channels follow. One longer riffle has a reputation for changing from year to year. The river cuts abruptly left with trees and brush lining the left side. In the steepest drop of the reach, the current charges 150 bouncy yards around a gravel bar, past some strong eddies, and into a steep bank. Pools at the bottom provide easy recovery from an upset, while the right bank offers a portage for the cautious or inexperienced.

After you pass the large, rotating fish trap, focus on the discharge from Thermalito Afterbay. You can see the outlet structure and flow from 0.5 mile away. At discharges above 5,000 cfs, swift, exploding waves sweep across the entire river channel. The flow divides, much of it running swiftly upstream along the high levee on the river left. This action forms a huge eddy that returns to the turbulence along the right bank. If water covers the gravel bars and you can see lots of white from the outlet, stick closely to the left bank. Even next to the bank, the current is strong enough to make paddling difficult. You will not be the first to decide to line boats along the bank or portage along the levee top. If you can see exposed gravel bars on the left side, stay on the water and enjoy the ride.

If you carelessly floated to the river right, swept by fast current toward the discharge, paddle furiously for the boat ramp on the right bank upstream of the discharge. You will be safe there even if you cannot easily join your friends on the other side of the river. That requires going far upstream and crossing the river.

Below Thermalito Afterbay the flows usually match the size of the wide river. Even where islands divide the channel, flows are deep enough for the many motorboats during salmon season. The paddling is generally fast and easy with only a couple of riffles below 2,000 cfs.

Bounded on both sides by the wildlife refuge, this is a great place to bird watch. On a recent winter trip, we spotted osprey, bald eagles, red-tailed hawks, great American egrets, great blue heron, red-shouldered hawks and myriad ducks.

After the river turns right 2.5 miles below Thermalito, look for the take-out on the river left. You can probably see through the trees to spot your cars parked atop the high levee. Immediately upstream is a low spot with a small inlet and a culvert from wildlife ponds.

Access: Bedrock Park Oroville (river mile 66): From CA 70 take any of the 3 Oroville exits (Pacific Heights Road, Oroville Dam Road, or Montgomery Street) and turn east until you intersect Feather River Boulevard. Turn north and follow Feather River Boulevard until it ends at Bedrock Park. Use the lower parking area and paved bicycle trail to reach the river below the lagoon.

Thermalito Afterbay Outlet boat ramp (river mile 59): From CA 70 go west 1.8 miles on Oroville Dam Road (CA 62) to Larkin Road. Turn south and follow Larkin Road until the Thermalito Afterbay is on your right. Before you get to the discharge canal, look to the left for a gravel road access and launch ramp. Avoid using this put-in when the discharge is above 5,000 cfs, as the current is so strong that it will carry a paddler directly into the powerful discharge turbulence.

Anglers young and old catch big salmon at the Thermalito Afterbay discharge to the Feather River.

Vance Avenue to Oroville Wildlife Refuge (river mile 57.8): On the west side of the river, from Larkin Road 1.8 miles south of the Thermalito Afterbay Outlet, turn east on Vance Avenue. Go past the pavement to the levee top, jog right 100 yards, then bear left off the levee to river level. The unimproved site is suitable for trailer launch but is not marked from the river.

Oroville Wildlife Refuge (river mile 56.5): From Bedrock Park go 7 miles south on CA 70. Past a mobile home park and opposite a lumber barn, turn west on a dirt road with a large sign that reads "Oroville Wildlife Refuge." Go 1 mile to the high levee adjacent the gated haul road. Take out/put in at the low area near the culvert connecting the wildlife ponds with the river. Continuing to parallel the river north, the road leads to a popular fishing access opposite Thermalito Afterbay outlet. This is a steep but possible take-out. The dirt road continues east to connect with Pacific Heights Road which leads northeast and connects with CA 70. During floods, these roads may be impassable.

Palm Avenue to Oroville Wildlife Refuge (river mile 55.4): From Larkin Road on the west side of the river go 2.2 miles south of Vance Road or 0.5 mile south of East Biggs Highway. Turn east on Palm Avenue, go up on the levee and continue east into the Oroville Wildlife Refuge. On top of the tailings several dirt roads come together. Go north (upstream) 200 yards to an easy graded access to river.

Shuttle: 8 miles (15 minutes).

For more information: (See Appendix B for phone numbers, websites, and street addresses.) Call the Oroville State Wildlife Area for information about camping in the refuge. To identify commercial campgrounds and community facilities, telephone the Oroville Area Chamber of Commerce, or visit their website.

32 Yuba River

Character: A clear and dependable float for novices, the Yuba River scampers through immense dredge tailings of the Yuba Gold Fields.

Length: 17.9 miles.

Class: I to II.

Skill level: Beginner with fast-water experience to intermediate.

Water source: Bullards Bar Reservoir discharges and the South Fork Yuba River flow through Englebright Reservoir. Dependable flows all summer and autumn.

Best season: Summer and autumn.

Craft: Canoes, kayaks, and rafts.

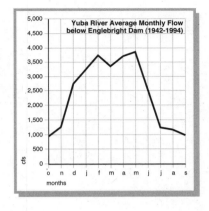

Hazards: Slopes of the tailings piles are unstable. If you try to climb them, rocks large and small will slide under your feet and bring you crashing down in a landslide. Daguerra Point Dam is a hazard to boaters at any flow. Portage the dam on river left.

Maps: USGS 7.5 Browns Valley, Yuba City.

Overview: Above Daguerra Dam, the landscape is typical California foothills: oak trees and grasslands. They are beautiful with wildflowers in the spring, but toast to California brown in the hot summers. Contrasting with the foothills are the mile-wide Yuba River Gold Fields. In years past, giant machines floated over the geologic river channel, dredging down to bedrock all the cobbles and gold. Mining companies kept the gold and left the endless rows of dredge tailings that line the river. Some mining continues today.

Below Daguerra Dam, orchards, farms, and homes eventually border the river. High levees protect the city of Marysville. Wildlife watchers will enjoy this river. Striped bass, steelhead, and shad spawn in the spring and salmon return in the fall. Overhead soar hawks and occasional ospreys, while turkey vultures and gulls line the banks. All wait for a fish dinner. A special treat in this part of the Central Valley is the annual migration of North American waterfowl. Hundreds of high-flying birds often fill late afternoon autumn and winter skies as they return to the wildlife refuges and grain fields in the Sacramento Valley.

Sustained summer flows are the result of two features. The Yuba County Water Agency delivers water for diversion at Daguerra Dam. YCWA also sells surplus water to other parts of the state. YCWA conveys water from New Bullards Bar, through Englebright Reservoir, and down the Yuba, Feather, and Sacramento Rivers to the Sacramento–San Joaquin Delta.

The paddling:

Parks Bar to Hallwood Boulevard

    Length: 10.9 miles.

    Average run time: 3 to 6 hours.

Yuba River

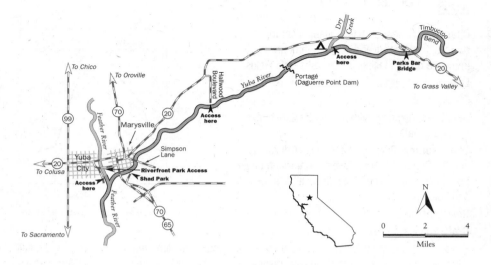

Optimal flow: 500 to 3,000 cfs (Yuba River below Englebright Dam gauge).

Class: II.

Skill level: Beginner.

Average gradient: 12 feet per mile.

For decades, the Sierra Club River Touring Section has conducted trips on this reach. The rocks along the right side create some fun waves, jets, and eddies for practice. You need to sustain a strong ferry to cross the fast, wide channel. For more variety, go upstream where the river charges between the rocky islands that once supported a bridge. Here the current is faster, the waves bouncier, and the eddies (particularly on river right) more placid than below. It takes some work to get there. Some paddlers like to explore the islands and riffles another mile upstream near Timbuctoo Bend.

With an average gradient of 12 feet per mile, the trip downstream is a fast float. You can kick back and relax or work out in the splashy wave trains and distinct eddies below the riffles.

Unlike many other dam-controlled rivers, the Yuba has remarkably little brush. Two miles below Parks Bar, the river splits around gravel bars. The right channel has eroded the bank and left two trees standing in fast water. You can avoid these obstacles by taking the other channel or executing a good eddy turn.

Dry Creek joins the Yuba in a beaver pond on the right, 3.5 miles below Parks Bar. Power lines cross the river above the confluence. On the south bank, opposite Dry Creek, are towering tailings piles. At lower river stages, the creek may flow swiftly near the river. This condition requires some lifting over one or two gravel riffles. Continuing upstream,

Dry Creek deepens and slows to provide 0.3 mile of paddling under a riparian forest canopy. Sycamore Campground occupies the west bank of Dry Creek.

The channel stays close to the north bank most of the 1.8 miles from Dry Creek to Daguerra Point Dam. Daguerra Point Dam funnels irrigation water into canals on the north side. Both ends of the dam support concrete fish ladders. From upstream, Daguerra Point Dam is difficult to see. Gravel has filled the 600-foot-wide river channel to the lip of the dam. Water pours directly over the top and down the rough dam face into a dangerous reversal below.

Portage on river left. One hundred yards above the dam, a quiet side channel offers easy paddling closer to the dam. From there, carry 0.25 mile up the dirt road to the hilltop oaks, then down to the base of the dam. A gravel bar parallels the dam to form a long pool for easy launching. In summer and autumn, you can watch large salmon jumping.

Steel towers support power lines across the river 1.5 miles and 2 miles below the dam. Here the dredger tailings diminish, then disappear. Wide, flat gravel bars line the river. Beyond the gravel bars, the banks rise 20 to 40 feet to well-tended orchards of walnuts, kiwi, and persimmons.

Small power lines spanning the river mark the take-out. Supported by wood poles, the wires are directly in line with Hallwood Boulevard on the right bank. The end of the road is 200 yards across the flat gravel bar.

Hallwood Boulevard to Marysville

Length: 7 miles.

Average run time: 2 to 5 hours.

Class: II.

Skill level: Beginner with fast-water experience.

Average gradient: 4 feet per mile.

Below Hallwood Boulevard the river displays increasing evidence of recent human activity. Pumps extract water for the orchards lining the riverbanks. About 2 miles below Hallwood, broken concrete riprap slows erosion on the right bank. Soon the river braids and fallen trees lie in the left channel. When you see the large Yuba-Sutter Recycling Center buildings above the right bank, the channel braids and turns abruptly to the left. A gravel bar, some brush, and a midstream snag are obstacles to avoid.

Soon the river channel narrows dramatically between clay banks lined with trees. Sand and silt replace gravel on the river bottom. A sandy beach beside slower water occurs about a mile upstream of Simpson Lane. Simpson Lane is the first bridge as you approach Marysville. The steep south bank provides an unattractive emergency take-out.

As the river arcs southwest, the water funnels through some faster chutes with a few waves. If you dump over here, you can go to the left shore on the gravel bars and beaches of Shad Park. Shad Park is the easiest take-out from a paddling perspective. On the down side, you will want a four-wheel-drive vehicle to negotiate the 200+ yards of loose sand and gravel near the river.

Continuing downstream under the first railroad bridge, Shad Park continues on the left. The river swirls around old broken bridge abutments that trap debris to form a low dam. The clearest low-water channel may be on the far left. At higher water, the river rushes around the pilings, producing some fast chutes requiring good boat alignment. Past the California Highway 65/70 bridge, more old pilings and another railroad bridge dominate the last river mile. Approaching the Feather River confluence, Riverfront Park occupies the right bank. Unfortunately the banks here are 40 feet high and steep, so taking out is not practical. However, two take-out options remain. Paddle to the confluence, then upstream on the Feather River. Look across the Feather for the concrete boat ramp on the Yuba City side. Look up and down the river for motor boats and jet skis, then paddle for the ramp. That is the shorter and easier take-out route. The other option is the Marysville Riverfront Park launch ramp, 0.75 mile up the Feather River against the current. Paddling this stretch is character-building work at the end of a long float trip. A small lagoon, dock, and ramp are 20 yards from vehicle access.

Access: Parks Bar bridge is 18 miles east of Marysville on CA 20. When the large concrete bridge comes into view, look for the Parks Bar side road on the right. Follow it about 0.5 mile, past some houses, and almost under the bridge. Carry along the gated road and path to the water under the bridge. Ample parking is available without blocking the gate or the haul road used by gravel trucks.

Dry Creek has a private campground currently named Sycamore Ranch. Located 14.4 miles east of Marysville, the campground is on the south side of CA 20.

Hallwood Boulevard is 7.4 miles east of Marysville on CA 20. Turn south 1.7 miles to the end of the road. Because this residential road has only three or four parking spaces, the neighbors advised you to find a shuttle driver to avoid leaving your vehicle here.

Shad Park is an informal expanse of sand and gravel on the south side of the Yuba just upstream of the CA 65/70 bridge. Take the first exit south of the river (North Beale and Feather River Boulevard). Go west on Feather River Boulevard to North Beale, then turn left. Go 0.5 mile north and turn right onto Shad Road just before the freeway entrance. Follow Shad Road to the park and paved parking. Local residents warn against driving over the soft, wide gravel and sand bars.

Riverfront Park is well developed with many sports fields, picnic areas, paved parking, rest rooms, and a paved launch ramp. In Marysville, turn west off CA 70, at the light onto Third Street or Fourth Street. Go 1 block, then turn south (left) onto "F" Street. Follow "F" Street and take the right fork up the levee on Biz Johnson Drive. (Do not go under the highway bridge.) Follow Biz Johnson Drive past the sports fields until you see signs for the launch ramp on your left.

Yuba City boat ramp is on the west side of the Feather River downstream of the Twin Cities Memorial Bridge. If you used CA 20 to cross the Feather River, turn south on Sutter Street. At the Memorial Bridge, Sutter Street becomes Second Street. If you used Marysville's Fifth Street to reach the Memorial Bridge, turn onto Second Street going south

Put in from the left bank after portaging Daguerra Point Dam.

in Yuba City. Continue south (bear left) on Second Street until you see the large sign for the launch ramp and paved parking area.

Shuttle: Parks Bar to Dry Creek: 4 miles (10 minutes). Dry Creek to Hallwood Boulevard: 9 miles (15 minutes). Hallwood Boulevard to Marysville or Yuba City: 10 miles (15 minutes).

For more information: (See Appendix B for phone numbers, websites, and street addresses.) Call Sycamore Campground for reservations.

Cache Creek—North Fork to Bear Creek

Character: These remote canyons provide a warm Class II stream with fine camping, big wildlife, and few people.

Length: 19 miles.

Average run time: About 8 hours, usually spread over 2 days.

Class: II.

Skill level: Intermediate.

Optimal flow: North Fork requires at least 100 cfs. Cache Creek requires at least 400 cfs at Rumsey Gauge.

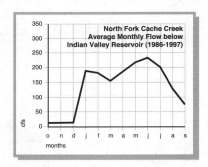

Water source: Clear Lake and Indian Valley Reservoir.

Average gradient: 18 feet per mile.

Best season: Spring, summer, and winter.

Craft: Canoes, kayaks, and inflatables including small rafts.

Hazards: Because of the remote backcountry wilderness location, help is far off and you must be self-sufficient. Cache Creek has the hazards of brush and rocks, plus some bears. Be extremely careful with fire as the wildfire hazard is often very high.

Maps: USGS 7.5 Lower lake, Wilson Valley, Glascock MT

Overview: The clear water of the North Fork Cache Creek comes from Indian Valley Reservoir some 11 miles upstream. Yolo County Flood Control and Water Conservation District operates Indian Valley Reservoir and Clear Lake to provide irrigation flows to Capay Valley farmers. The irrigation demand provides boating flows through the wilderness run, Rumsey Canyon, and Capay Valley. Without snowmelt, the water is relatively warm in the spring and almost tepid in summer.

Watch along the banks for impressive wildlife, like bear or elk. We saw bear scat and scratched trees near our camp, and another paddler saw the bear! The Department of Fish and Game protects Tule elk in the game preserves along the upper sections of Cache Creek. Overhead, we saw osprey and a bald eagle pair soaring the canyon in summer. Several bald eagle pairs are regularly visible in winter months when they feed on the carp in the creek. Note that the Wilson Valley area is closed from April 1 to June 30 for elk calving.

Recently the BLM purchased Kennedy Flats, Wilson Valley, and most of the other lands bordering Cache Creek down to and including the Bear Creek confluence at California Highway 16. The property adjacent to Mad Mike Rapid will stay private.

Streamside campsites are plentiful, particularly in Wilson Valley and Kennedy Flats. The long Redbud trail extends from the North Fork access, across the Peninsula, then along Wilson Valley. Bring lots of drinking water during the summer, as much as one gallon per person per day. Without local towns, highway traffic, or lights, the nighttime star

Cache Creek—North Fork to Bear Creek

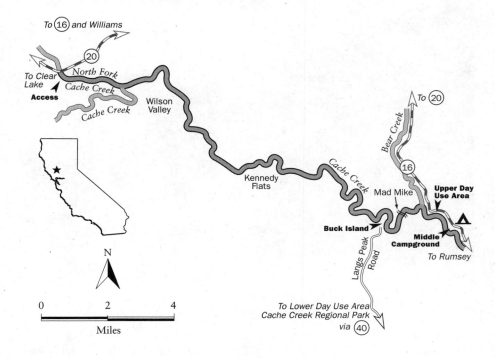

watching is great. Be really cautious with fire. The intensely hot summers dry everything to tinder and the dry brush has the explosive energy of gasoline. Open fires are illegal during declared fire season, usually starting in May or June. Then only stoves may be used outside designated campgrounds.

The paddling: From the CA 20 bridge to the confluence with Cache Creek, the North Fork is 2.5 miles of narrow channel (2 to 3 boat-lengths wide) mixed with brush, sharp blind turns, and trees. These obstacles reflect the dramatic changes to many stream channels caused by the great floods of 1997 and 1998. The North Fork obstacles are all negotiable with a little time and care. Along the way the shade opens up to reveal some walls of dark sedimentary rocks and sandy beaches.

The main stem of Cache Creek is much wider, with fast-moving, smooth water between the many short Class II riffles. Some riffles have bouncy wave trains, while others provide trees, strainers, or boulders for obstacles. Absent is the sharp river-bottom bedrock that dominates Rumsey Canyon.

Downstream 12.3 miles from the North Fork confluence, Buck Island is a put-in for the commercial raft trips into Rumsey Canyon. They follow a long, rough dirt road that starts at the low-water bridge over Cache Creek in Rumsey Canyon. A lonely picnic table and campsite decorate Buck Island. The rest of Buck Island and Buck Flats is private prop-

Cache Creek above Mad Mike rapid.

erty. Two miles below Buck Island, the creek makes a sinuous channel. When it heads northeast, look for the 2,800-foot Cortina Ridge above the nearby 1,800-foot Cache Creek Ridge. When you can see the high ridge, you are nearing Mad Mike Rapid.

A black shale cliff abruptly turns the channel to the north. Opposite the cliff, a private hunting camp sits on a riverside flat. Immediately downstream is Mad Mike, by far the most difficult rapid on the run. Mad Mike drops about 20 feet in 200 narrow yards. At summer flows of 400 cfs to 1,000 cfs, the run is straight forward. Select an approach through the guard rocks at the beginning, then avoid the one major submerged boulder under the picturesque tree. At high winter flows, lots of water hurrying downhill causes strong hydraulics. Beware! A portage is on the right bank. At the bottom a long, quiet pool leads to the Bear Creek confluence, 0.3 miles below.

Relax on the smooth water to Bear Creek, because that is where the Rumsey Canyon rapids begin. Here CA 16 joins the creek. Take out at any of the Yolo County parks along the river. See the next chapter for the Rumsey Canyon description.

Access: Access to the put-in and take-out are easy. At the CA 20 bridge over the North Fork Cache Creek, the BLM has established a put-in with parking lot, information kiosk, and toilet. It is on the west side of the river, 200 yards below the bridge.

The roads to Buck Island are steep, rough, and recommended only for four-wheel-drive vehicles. From CA 16, cross the low-water bridge at the Lower Cache Creek Park and follow Yolo County Road 40 for 5 miles. Climb the steep switchbacks to the junction with Fiske and Langs Peak Roads (4 corners). Follow Langs Peak Road 5 miles northwest along

Brush lines the North Fork Cache Creek.

the ridge tops that eventually descend to Buck Island. CR 40 and the low-water bridge are closed from mid-autumn to mid-spring, depending on weather conditions.

For the take-out, use the Yolo County Cache Creek Parks along CA 16 in Rumsey Canyon. In mid-August, the park charged $10 per car to park for two days in the middle campground group parking lot.

Shuttle: 20 miles (35 minutes).

For more information: (See Appendix B for phone numbers, websites, and street addresses.) For campground reservations and other information about the Cache Creek Regional Park, contact Yolo County Parks Department via telephone. Contact the BLM Ukiah Field Office for information about federal lands bordering Cache Creek.

34 Cache Creek—Rumsey Canyon

Character: A summer favorite, the warm shallow rapids and easy access of this stretch provide a great whitewater practice run.
Length: 8.4 miles.
Average run time: 3 to 4 hours.
Class: II, with one III.
Skill level: Beginner with fast water experience to intermediate.
Optimal flow: 500 to 1,000 cfs (Rumsey gauge).
Water source: Clear Lake and Indian Valley Reservoir.
Average gradient: 27 feet per mile.
Best season: Spring, summer, and winter.
Craft: Whitewater canoes, kayaks, and small rafts.
Hazards: A special hazard is the low-water bridge at the Lower County park. The culverts under the bridge often contain debris that will trap a boat, raft, or swimmer. The preferred portage is on river left in summer. When high water flows over the bridge, a dangerous reversal forms here. Land well above the bridge on river right. Also note that Rumsey Canyon bedrock is notoriously sharp. Definitely wear a helmet. Rowboat Rapid (aka The Mother), near the California Highway 16 bridge is much more difficult than the rest of the stream.
Maps: USGS 7.5 Rumsey, Glascock MT.

Overview: Cache Creek has cut through 2,000 feet of inclined and bent sedimentary rock to form Rumsey Canyon. Unlike most rivers where the ledges lie across the channel, in Rumsey Canyon the sharp edges of ledges parallel the streambed. The resulting bedrock rapids are well suited to boaters seeking a busy technical challenge to improve their skills. In the days of fiberglass boats, a time was usually set aside for repairs after a Rumsey Canyon run. Shallow with frequent pools, the river is so forgiving that commercial outfitters send thousands of people down the river in two-person rafts. Other folks try inner tubes at the risk of injuring their fannies. You can see enough of the creek from the road to give you a good idea of the paddling.

Winter rains can quickly raise the flow to thousands of cfs that quickly subside. Irrigation releases from Clear Lake and Indian Valley Reservoir prolong summer flows. Without snowmelt, the water is almost tepid in summer. Visitors can see wildflower displays and green canyons during the late winter and early spring months.

Cache Creek access is good with CA 16 closely paralleling the stream along the entire run. Much of the land is publicly owned. Yolo County Parks Department operates a large campground and two large picnic areas. Be aware that summer temperatures are often extremely hot and there is little shade.

The paddling: Loosen up your body and mind on the river bank because the rapids start at the put-in. Cloudy water hides many submerged rocks. On river right, just below Bear

Cache Creek—Rumsey Canyon and Capay Valley

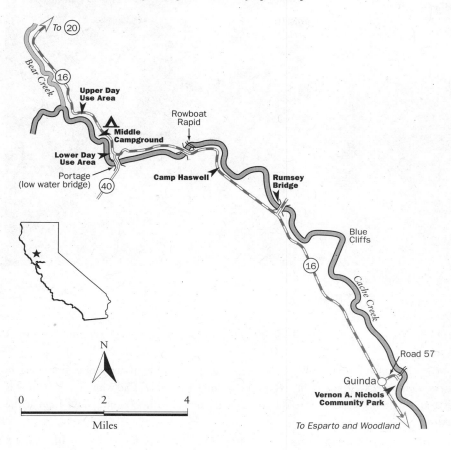

Creek, the current pushes into a wall that has upset many a neophyte paddler. The shallow, rocky Class II rapids require continuous river reading.

Several rapids are obscured from the road. These include a robust pair upstream from the campground and a long drop that follows a left turn above the low-water bridge. Fortunately a long, smooth run separates the rapid from the hazardous bridge, which should be portaged.

The CA 16 bridge marks the start of Rowboat Rapid. A Class III drop at the foot of a landslide, it is a steep rock garden at low flows. About 700 cfs, the route is a dog-leg turn to the right. At high water there are strong hydraulics. The action continues for another hundred yards before it slows. Since the left side erodes the landslide, the more reliable scouting route and portage are on river right. After Rowboat, the gradient slackens a little as it rounds a bend to the south. The big flat area on the right is Camp Haswell, a favored

Cache Creek below Camp Haswell at 700 cfs.

take-out. Camp Haswell is heavily used as a parking and staging area by commercial rafters in summer.

Continuing to Rumsey Bridge, you encounter more widely spaced rapids. Immediately below Camp Haswell, the right channel is no longer runable. The wide main channel is rock strewn at low water, but readily runable at 700 cfs with a bouncy wave train at the bottom.

The landscape changes as the canyon begins to open into Capay Valley. Instead of a steep-walled canyon, deeply cut banks, gravel bars, and occasional islands define the channel. Channels around the islands end in rapids with wave trains bouncy enough to be fun or to flip the careless.

Rumsey Bridge is a large, double-span, concrete structure. The take-out is on the left side gravel bar.

Access: Access is plentiful. The Bear Creek confluence has road-shoulder parking along CA 16 at the county line, 8.4 miles above Rumsey.

Cache Creek Regional Park Upper Unit adjacent to CA 16 has day-use parking 7.9 miles above Rumsey. Fee area.

Cache Creek Regional Park Middle Campground offers day-use and overnight parking. Check with the attendant to bring vehicles to the top of the road near the beach. The campground is a fee area 6.7 miles above Rumsey.

Cache Creek Regional Park Lower Unit, located 5.9 miles above Rumsey, gives access to the low-water bridge when it is open during the summer. When the gate is closed, it is a 0.5 mile hike down the road to the bridge.

CA 16 bridge, 3.7 miles above Rumsey, has limited road shoulder parking upstream of the bridge. You can walk to a good view of Rowboat rapid from here. If you are not confident about running Rowboat, you might park a vehicle nearby.

Camp Haswell is a former Boy Scout camp on a large flat 3 miles above Rumsey. During the summer, commercial rafts take out here and the gate is often open for the many shuttle busses. When the gate is closed, paddlers often park in the wide turnout adjacent to CA 16 and carry across the flat to the creek.

Rumsey Bridge is visible from CA 16 in the hamlet of Rumsey. Roadside parking exists east of the bridge. A well-worn path leads 75 yards down the riverbank to the gravel bar under the bridge. Rumsey is about 21 miles northwest of Esparto.

For more information: (See Appendix B for phone numbers, websites, and street addresses.) For campground reservations and other information about the Cache Creek Regional Park, contact Yolo County Parks Department via phone.

35 Cache Creek—Capay Valley

(see map on page 139)

Character: Seldom paddled, the stream meanders among bushy gravel bars and orchards.
Length: 7 miles.
Average run time: 2 to 3 hours.
Class: I+.
Skill level: Beginner with experience.
Optimal flow: 500 to 1,000 cfs (Rumsey gauge).
Water source: Clear Lake and Indian Valley Reservoir.
Average gradient: 13 feet per mile.
Best season: Spring, summer, and winter.
Craft: Canoes, kayaks, and rafts.
Hazards: Trees, like the one downstream of Blue Cliffs, have fallen into the river and may block the channel. Strong currents try to carry the boater into overhanging brush and trees. The most difficult whitewater rapid is plainly visible from the take-out at Nichols Park.
Maps: USGS 7.5 Rumsey, Guinda.

Overview: Released from the confines of Rumsey Canyon, Cache Creek meanders along the steep hills bordering the east side of Capay Valley. Rich in almond and walnut orchards, their blossoms make the valley beautiful in the late winter and early spring.

The stream banks support a variety of orchards, tamarisk islands, pampas grass, bamboo, and the usual cottonwoods, willows, and oaks. Great blue heron, egrets, osprey, and other large birds are commonly visible near the water, while turkey vultures soar overhead. The gravel bars are wider here but the land is private, so no camping is allowed.

The stream intersperses a mixture of Class I riffles, bushy islands, and cut banks between the quiet pools and runs. You can easily see the most difficult whitewater rapid immediately upstream of the take-out at Guinda.

The paddling: From Rumsey Bridge, Cache Creek turns east to run at the base of high bluffs. Opposite the bluffs, tamarisk and willows fringe the gravel bars. Several Class I riffles are scattered along the way.

Returning to a more southerly course, the creek heads toward some Rumsey homes. The 1997 and 1998 floods severely eroded the Capay Valley orchards and changed the creek's course. To protect their property from more erosion, Rumsey landowners placed large rocks (riprap) on the right bank.

Upstream are great views of the Rumsey Canyon. Downstream, the creek swings east toward the Blue Cliffs. Rising 500 feet above the creek, these mud and soft rock cliffs dominate the river. Swallow nests are common. Great blue heron play hide and seek from shallows and snags on the opposite bank. A ravine through the cliffs is a landmark of a brisk riffle among rocks at the cliff base.

A quarter mile beyond the cliffs, a large metal barn marks a real hazard. A giant valley oak blocks 75 percent of the channel. Passing next to the gravel bar on river left, you can see an immense stump mid-river.

About 1.5 miles upstream from Guinda on river left is a large slope with many landslides. Even in summer, the practiced eye can distinguish the potential landslides, suspended on the slope until the next wet season, when they will contribute rocks and gravel to the creek. Near the downstream end of the slope, the water abandons the right bank and swings toward the slope. In the middle of the fast riffles are several snags, which should be avoided. Their exact location will change each flood season, but others will take their place.

The last rapid above the Guinda bridge is the most technically challenging on this stretch. Scouting is easy. A short riffle leads to a longer drop on river right with several large rocks. Several options exist to run the drop and a large eddy allows paddlers time to line up for the slots. Since the rapid is within sight of the take-out, it is a good place for novices to practice eddy turns and ferries.

Access: The put-in at Rumsey Bridge is visible from California Highway 16 in the tiny hamlet of Rumsey. Roadside parking exists east of the bridge. A well-worn path leads 75 yards down the riverbank to the gravel bar under the bridge.

The take-out at Vernon A. Nichols Community Park is 0.2 miles south of the Guinda Grocery store and Post Office, east of CA 16 at the picnic sign. Go east on County Road 57 for 0.4 miles to the bridge. The easiest take-out is under the bridge on river right. Carry boats up the gentle path 75 yards to the gated day-use area. Park on the opposite side of the road.

Shuttle: 5.5 miles (10 minutes).

For more information: (See Appendix B for phone numbers, websites, and street addresses.) For campground reservations and other information about the Cache Creek Regional Park, contact Yolo County Parks Department via phone.

Folsom Lake—North Fork Arm

Character: The hills and narrowing canyon of this arm lure the paddler to explore quiet places, fish, and swim.

Length: Depending on lake level up to 4.4 miles long, 0.2 mile wide, 10.3 miles of shoreline.

Elevation: 466 feet.

Class: Flatwater lake.

Skill level: Beginner.

Best season: Year-round.

Craft: Canoes, kayaks, and power boats.

Hazards: Summer water skiers and jet skis play in the first mile. Winter storm torrents may fill the canyon.

Maps: USGS 7.5 Pilot Hill.

Overview: When the Army Corps of Engineers completed Folsom Dam in 1954, it created Folsom Lake. The U.S. Bureau of Reclamation owns the lake and surrounding lands and contracts with the California Department of Parks and Recreation for recreation management. With more than 1.5 million visitors annually, Folsom is one of Northern California's most popular state park areas.

The entire shore of the lake and the land for some distance beyond is within the Folsom Lake State Recreation Area and is open to the public. Summer daytime temperatures range from warm to hot, making water temperatures comfortable for swimming. Then grasses, brush, and trees become tinder dry, so fires and camping are only allowed in designated picnicking and camping areas. The Peninsula Campground is accessible by boat and car. Beals Point Campground is closer to Folsom, accessible from Auburn-Folsom Road. Folsom Lake State Recreation Area is a fee area.

Along the North Fork Arm, the landscape varies. Willow groves emerge from the water to tangle fishing lines. Away from the lake, the warmer slopes host oak and grass savannas mingled with digger pine and chaparral. Be cautious where you walk, because rattlesnakes are relatively common and poison oak is widespread. Where the slope's aspects provide cooler conditions, the vegetation changes to ponderosa pine, Douglas fir, and madrone. You may see black-tailed deer, ground squirrels, raccoons, skunks, opossums, gray foxes, rabbits, or coyotes. In recent years mountain lions have returned.

Like other large California reservoirs, flood managers partially drain Folsom Lake in the winter to increase flood protection for downstream communities. The North Fork Arm narrows and behaves more like a river with obvious current. During and after major storms, the current becomes powerful and loaded with debris.

Folsom Lake—North Fork Arm

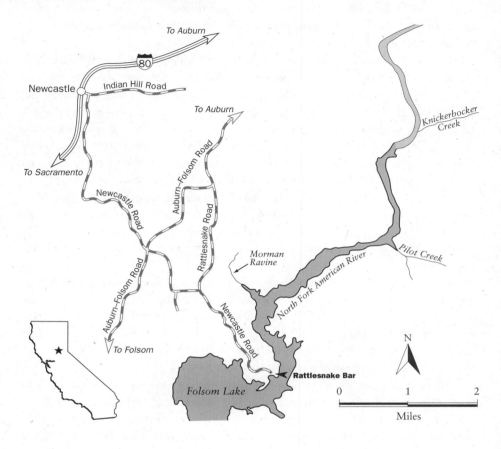

The paddling: Early mornings, evenings, and weekdays are the best times to enjoy the lake. Fish for bass, trout, kokanee, and catfish. Watch Canada geese fly from their nightly refuge on the lake to their daily feeding grounds. Bald eagles roost along the east shore during the winter and early spring. The water is usually smooth and motor boats are often absent.

Rattlesnake Bar access avoids the central portion of the lake frequented by many power boats that launch at Granite Bay, Beals Point, or Peninsula Campground. When Rattlesnake Bar boat ramp reaches the water, avoid using it on warm weekends because the ramp is often busy with motor boats and jet skis. In late summer and fall, the lake level drops below the boat ramp, but you can still launch hand-carried boats here.

Don't misjudge the delta breeze. It will feel much stronger on the return trip and if really strong will turn your paddling experience into a heavy workout.

Paddle along the shore of the lake to the north and west. Above the rocky cliffs on the west side, the remarkably level artifact that separates the trees from the high-water line is the North Fork Ditch. Constructed in the 1800s, the remains of the channel, abutments, and steel gates are intermittently visible the full length of the lake.

An easy mile from the ramp, you will reach the "5 mile per hour" zone. Water skiers and jet skis stay behind. Fisher folk, paddle craft, and a few explorers continue.

At another 0.3 miles, Mormon Ravine joins the east side of the lake amid some low willows. Even during the late summer, upstream irrigation canals sustain Mormon Ravine's flow. At high lake levels you can paddle past the powerhouse to see the water cascading down the shaded ravine. At low lake levels, the streambed is a shallow, rocky watercourse. The powerhouse sometimes discharges water without warning. The powerhouse road does not provide lake access, as it is private, gated, and closed to the public.

Paddling beyond Mormon Ravine, the 600-foot-wide lake bends to the northeast. The lower hillside is gentle and affords ample space to picnic. A wide grassy area extends high above the lake's north side. Near the top and plainly visibly, the Pioneer Express Trail, a popular hiking and horseback-riding route, parallels the water and connects Rattlesnake Bar to Auburn.

Approximately 2.6 miles from Rattlesnake Bar, the lake narrows. On the south side, low water levels expose rugged ledges. Some are good for sunbathing. Pilot Creek joins the south shore of the lake at 3.2 miles. Its narrow channel rises after a few yards to a steep, rocky creek bed. It is beautiful in the early spring, inviting exploration. Where the canyon turns north again, sand on the west bank makes an attractive beach. Above this point, the river flows become apparent and paddling becomes more difficult.

Feel for changes in the water temperature. During the summer, it changes abruptly from warm to cool to mountain-river cold. The water clarity improves dramatically to reveal the rocky river bottom. This phenomenon occurs where the clear, cold water from the North Fork of the American River slides under warmer lake water. The exact location of the phenomena changes throughout the summer, depending upon the water level.

Low water levels present a shallow, rocky Class I river. Higher lake levels flood over the river channels and make easy upstream paddling. Near the high-water mark, two huge gravel bars limit upstream progress to extensive walking, lining, or portaging. At this point you are about 4.5 miles from Rattlesnake Bar and 1.5 miles downstream of the proposed Auburn Dam site.

These giant gravel bars were once the contents of the Auburn coffer dam. The 1986 flood destroyed the coffer dam, sending 200,000 acre-feet of water rushing into Folsom Reservoir. This flood entirely filled the reservoir and forced flood managers to release 115,000 cfs down the Lower American River. Tested to their limits, the levees protected the city of Sacramento.

The Bureau of Reclamation has announced plans to plug the Auburn Dam diversion tunnel. When done, the North Fork would be a Class I–III whitewater stream from CA 49 to Folsom Reservoir. Since it is a political action, voice your encouragement to the Secretary of the Interior.

Access: Exit Interstate 80 at Newcastle and turn immediately south onto Newcastle Road. Follow Newcastle Road, cross Auburn-Folsom Road, bear right at Rattlesnake Road, following Newcastle Road to the Folsom Lake State Park Rattlesnake Bar entrance. Distance from the I–80 exit to the park gate is 5 miles. After the entrance kiosk, turn left along the paved road and follow it to the boat ramp and parking area. The park allows off-road access along the lakeshore.

Shuttle: None.

For more information: (See Appendix B for phone numbers, websites, and street addresses.) To learn current access hours and current fees, telephone the Folsom Lake State Recreation Area or view their website. To reserve a campsite, contact Reserve America.

37 Lake Natoma

Character: This narrow lake is a great place to fish, learn to paddle and sail, watch the wildlife, and relax in the metropolitan Sacramento Area.
Length: 4.5 miles long, 0.15 mile wide, 11.0 miles of shoreline. Surface area: 500 acres.
Elevation: 126 feet.
Best season: All year.
Class: Flatwater lake.
Skill level: Beginner.
Craft: Canoes, kayaks, sail craft, fishing boats, and rowing shells.
Hazards: Nimbus Dam is well marked with buoys.
Maps: USGS 7.5 Folsom. AAA Sacramento.

Overview: Only 20 minutes from downtown Sacramento, Lake Natoma is popular for canoeing, crew races, sailing, kayaking, and other aquatic sports. The area is steeped in California history.

According to *A History of the Lower American River*, by William C. Dillinger, "several hundred Negroes mined the bar adjacent the Folsom business district during 1849–50." Now named Negro Bar, this boat access, and picnic site, are part of Folsom Lake State Recreation Area.

Near Rainbow Bridge, Folsom Powerhouse was the source of the world's first long distance (22 miles) transmission of electrical power in 1895. A September 1895 celebration dubbed a "Grand Electric Carnival" was a night parade of illuminated floats mounted on electric streetcars rolling down Sacramento streets ablaze with electric lights. Lights visible for 50 miles outlined the Capitol building.

Another historical feature, Folsom Prison, was the topic of a Johnny Cash song. In 1880, inmates built Folsom Prison from granite quarried on the spot. Since the prison still tries to separate the public from the inmates, authorities prohibit paddling upstream of Rainbow Bridge.

Lake Natoma is part of the Folsom gold dredge fields, an area 10 miles long and up to 7 miles wide. The last dredge ceased operation in 1962. Even today, the huge piles of dredge tailings are plainly visible.

Created in 1954 as part of the Central Valley Project, Lake Natoma links Folsom Lake with the American River, and diverts water into the Folsom South Canal. Since water comes from the depths of Folsom Lake, Natoma's water temperature stays chilly all summer. At the west end of the lake, California State University at Sacramento Aquatic Center rents equipment and offers classes in sailing, canoeing, and kayaking. The center is also a hub for rowing and outrigger canoeing clubs. Open to the public, the center operates seven days a week, year-round.

Lake Natoma

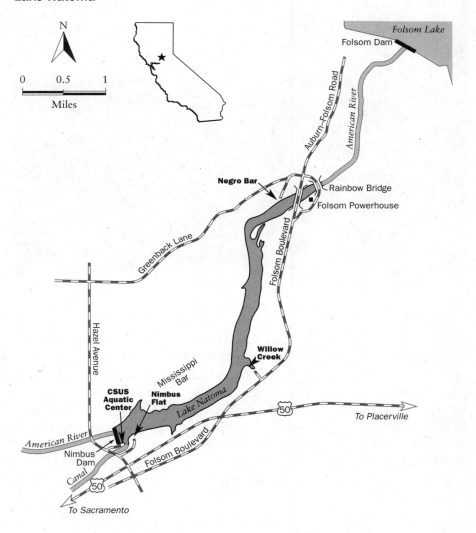

N

0   0.5   1
Miles

Folsom Lake

Folsom Dam

Auburn-Folsom Road

American River

Negro Bar

Rainbow Bridge

Folsom Powerhouse

Folsom Boulevard

Greenback Lane

Hazel Avenue

Willow Creek

Mississippi Bar

Lake Natoma

CSUS Aquatic Center

Nimbus Flat

50

To Placerville

American River

Nimbus Dam

Canal

50

Folsom Boulevard

To Sacramento

The bicycle trail along the north shore of Lake Natoma links Beals Point on Folsom Lake to the American River Bike Trail and downtown Sacramento. A new multi-purpose trail parallels Natoma's south shore to complete an off-highway circuit around the lake.

The paddling: One of the widest parts of the lake is directly across the water from the Aquatic Center. Here is cobble-studded Mississippi Bar, which extends almost a mile to the north and east. Before the gold rush, a fur trader set up business with the Indians on a large

The east end of Lake Natoma near Folsom.

sandbar. Later, many men exploited the rich gold deposits here. As late as 1900, two gold dredges operated here. Now the bicycle trail skirts the resultant piles of tailings.

The Nimbus Dam end is the focal point of much aquatic activity, including crew races and sailing. If the delta breeze blows, expect to see many windsurfers and laser sailboats. At the opposite end of the lake, Negro Bar launch ramp sits almost under the new Folsom Boulevard bridge. From here you can explore the islands along the Folsom shore or try your moving water skills near Rainbow Bridge. With a fair current from Folsom Dam and some large rocks, you can learn eddy turns and cross channel ferries in easy water.

Willow Creek access is on the south side between Folsom Powerhouse and Nimbus Dam. Egrets and herons have established rookeries adjacent to Willow Creek access and on the north lakeshore.

Access: CSUS Aquatic Center: From U.S. Highway 50, exit north onto Hazel Avenue. At the stop light before the bridge, turn east into the Aquatic Center (opposite Nimbus Fish Hatchery).

Nimbus Flat: From U.S. 50, exit north on Hazel Avenue. Turn east just before the Aquatic Center entrance. This fee area provides picnic sites, rest rooms, beach, and a launch ramp.

Willow Creek: About 0.3 miles northeast of the U.S. 50, Folsom exit onto Folsom Boulevard. Since Folsom Boulevard is a divided highway at this point, go north to Blue Ravine Road and come back about halfway toward U.S. 50. This lightly used fee area has a gravel launch ramp and parking area.

Negro Bar: Turn south from Greenback Lane some 0.3 mile west of Auburn Folsom Road. Like other Folsom Lake State Recreation Area components, this is a fee area.

Shuttle: Optional. From the Aquatic Center to Negro Bar is 6.0 miles (15 minutes). From the Aquatic Center to Willow Slough is 2.6 miles (10 minutes).

For more information: (See Appendix B for phone numbers, websites, and street addresses.) To reserve rental equipment, make appointments for lessons, or check operating hours call the CSUS Aquatic Center or visit their website. Reserve campsites at Folsom Lake by contacting ReserveAmerica. For status of other features of Folsom Lake State Recreation Area, call or visit their website.

American River Parkway

Character: Easy access, dependable flows, and natural surroundings attract thousands to float the American River.

Length: 23 miles.

Class: I to II.

Skill level: Beginner.

Optimal flow: 1,500 to 5,000 cfs (Nimbus Dam gauge).

Water source: Folsom and Natoma Lakes.

Average gradient: 3 feet per mile.

Best season: Year-round.

Craft: Canoes, kayaks, rafts, dories, and small power boats.

Hazards: Snags lie under the surface of this cold, strong river to catch the careless.

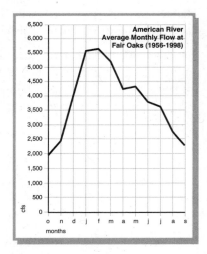

Maps: AAA Sacramento North, River Running the American River Parkway, USGS 7.5 Sacramento West, Sacramento East, Carmichael, Citrus Heights, Folsom.

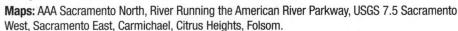

Overview: Since the California Gold Rush, the American River has been a focal point for navigation, commercial, and recreation activity. Now a recreational river in the National Wild and Scenic River System, the American River Parkway winds through the urban heart of Sacramento. With the urging of the Save the American River Association, Sacramento has acquired a wide riparian corridor protected from development. The corridor provides the multiple functions of flood control, wildlife habitat preservation, and play area for the region's one million residents.

Parks with good facilities line the river. Like Goethe Park, most are named after local personalities. Started in 1896, a paved bicycle trail now extends the full length of the parkway. The many access points are for day use, not overnight camping or parking. The Parkway charges use fees for parking and boat launching. Boats have a 5-mph speed limit, so the American River is a great place to paddle.

Winter stream flows average above 5,000 cfs and are frequently above 15,000 cfs. Summer flows are usually greater than 1,750 cfs. Future flow patterns may change depending on negotiated agreements for future water supply and preservation of the recreation, fishery, wildlife and aesthetic values of the river.

The paddling:

Sailor Bar to Goethe Park

    Length: 8 miles.

    Average run time: 2 to 4 hours.

American River Parkway

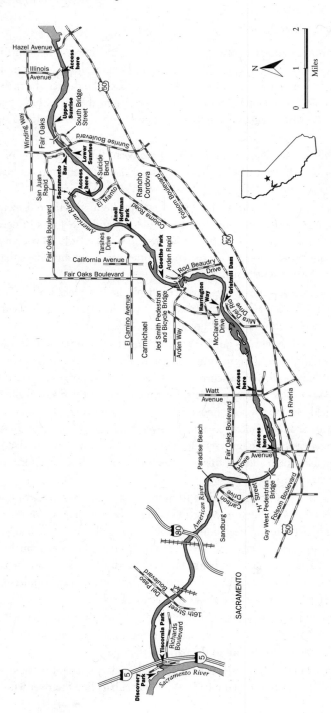

Class: I with one Class II.

Skill level: Beginner with experience.

Average gradient: 5 feet per mile.

This section is the most exciting and heavily used portion of the Lower American River. A short distance below Sailor Bar is a long diagonal gravel bar where salmon gather in the late summer and autumn. Enjoy the sight of them emerging from the deeper channels, skittering over the shallows, and bouncing against your canoe. On the gravel bars, flocks of seagulls wait for lunch, which will be the next salmon to spawn and expire. It is a sight to remember.

In contrast, think of how high the flows must have been during the spring of 1882. During that flood season the steamer Daisy made trips to Folsom to transport cobblestones and firewood to Sacramento.

From Sailor Bar and Upper Sunrise, the river flows quickly under the old metal Fair Oaks pedestrian bridge toward the large Sunrise Boulevard and Jim Jones bridges. On warm summer days, thousands of rafters float from here to Goethe Park. As you approach the bridges, keep your boats aligned with the current and watch for any snags that may have hung up on the bridge abutments.

Lower Sunrise access and Sacramento Bar access flank the Jim Jones Bridge. Pedestrians and bicyclists use this old gravel hauling structure. Every July the bridge is the transfer point from bicycles to boats in the annual Eppies Great Race.

Below Sunrise the wide river runs quickly between gravel bars. At 0.4 mile below Sunrise, the riffle slants right, skirting some brush on the bank. Suicide Bend is encountered 0.6 mile later. At the bend, much of the current starts left before a sharp right turn. On the left, a large strong eddy upsets unwary paddlers. Recent changes in the riverbed allow paddlers to avoid the eddy when flows are above 3,000 cfs by following the center channel between the gravel bars. From Suicide Bend, the river heads northward past El Manto Access. The parking area is visible on riverside cobbles. For folks wishing to play in San Juan Rapid without hassling a shuttle, this is a useful put-in. With some effort you can paddle back upstream from San Juan.

San Juan consists of a clay ledge extending from the right across two-thirds of the river. The ledge has runable slots through it. Most folks prefer the fast channel on the far left with the long, bouncy wave train directed into the 40-foot-high bank. Immediately left of the wave train is a sharp, fast eddy that exits to river left. On the right side, a much deeper and wider eddy circulates to the far right bank. The best scouting site is the large gravel bar on river left. San Juan Rapid is a favorite play spot for Sacramento area paddlers on hot summer evenings. The wave train and slots are good surfing spots.

After San Juan Rapid, the paddling is anticlimactic. The wide river slows and riffles disappear. Downstream 2 miles, picnickers, waders, and folks fishing enjoy Ansil Hoffman Park. The access is at the upstream end of the park on the right bank.

After a long turn to the south, riverside homes with wide yards and grouted stream banks announce the approach to Goethe Park. Wide gravel bars line the river left. When you can see the long Jed Smith bridge, take out over the left side gravel bar and up the sandy slope to the parking area and shuttle bus.

Goethe Park to Howe Avenue
Length: 6.1 miles.
Average run time: 2 to 4 hours.
Class: I with one Class II.
Skill level: Beginner with experience.
Average gradient: 3 feet per mile.

At Goethe Park the clear, fast river flows south under the Jed Smith bicycle bridge. The bridge provides a good view of the Arden Rapid, 150 yards downstream. The river here is 200 yards wide, and shallow. Each year, winter flood flows shift the gravel bars. Snags ground on the shallow bottom and islands. Often the central channel is deeper, with waves big enough to swamp open canoes. Some rocks produce holes for the open canoeist to avoid. Avoid the channels to the extreme right, since they flow into thick brush bordering William Pond Recreation Area, a restored gravel quarry that has stocked ponds for fishing, good bird-watching opportunities, and lengthy hiking trails to the river.

A quick mile below the bridge, the river narrows to a fast riffle and bends right. Expensive houses sit above the steep left bank. A surfing wave sometimes forms on the right. Another 0.5 mile downstream, Gristmill access is on the left bank and Harrington Way access provides easy access on the right. Be careful of where you walk on the Harrington side so you do not disrupt bird-nesting habitats.

From Harrington access you can see several brushy islands and a few snags in the broad river. Downstream 0.7 mile, the river separates into two channels. The left channel is slow, open, and wide. The right channel alternates between ponds and short riffles. Both are good fishing places.

As you approach Watt Avenue bridge, the current accelerates. At flows less than 3,000 cfs, the river exposes a gravel bar, clay bank, and riffle. The main flow tends to the center and right, but the Watt Avenue take-out is on the left. Upstream of the bridge is a simple gravel bar take-out. Just downstream from the bridge, gravel bars partly enclose a quiet lagoon. Outside the lagoon the current hastens. Beware of the large, circular fish trap on river right below the bridge.

The 1.5 miles between Watt Avenue and Howe Avenue contain a chain of secluded ponds favored by wildlife. Low levees with sandy banks separate the ponds from the main channel. To enter the ponds, look for breaks in the south bank 75 yards upstream and 50 yards downstream of the power line crossing. Another access to the ponds is 0.25 mile downstream, nearer the Howe Avenue bridge. The water between the ponds is shallow and may require walking at flows less than 3,000 cfs. Howe Avenue access is upstream of the bridge on river left.

Howe Avenue to Sacramento River Confluence

Length: 8 miles.

Average run time: 3 to 5 hours.

Class: I.

Skill level: Beginner.

Average gradient: 2 feet per mile.

Ten bridges mark your progress down the American between Howe Avenue and the Sacramento River confluence. Most of the adjacent lands were historically subject to flooding. The large structure below Howe Avenue is Sacramento's Fairbairn water intake and treatment plant. Extending from the intake works to H Street is the California State University at Sacramento campus. Guy West pedestrian bridge connects CSUS to the Campus Commons residential district on the right bank.

As the water quickens over shallow riffles below H Street, imagine what this area was like in 1930 when this was the site of a popular beach and a giant water slide. Now levees protect houses on the left and the Campus Commons Golf Course occupies the east bank.

Turning west, the river flows between Cal Expo with the Bushy Lake Nature Preserve to the north, and to the south Paradise Beach. Both are overflow areas at high water. The beaches' expansive gravel and sand bars make a popular neighborhood play area but lack easy boat access.

The I–80 bridges are near the site of Norris Ferry, a ford and later a cable ferry, which was a popular route to the northern mines of the early gold rush era. Slightly downstream was Sutter's Landing. A now filled-in river channel formerly swept southward and contributed to old Sacramento flooding.

Downstream, the river slows considerably. In the next 2 miles, two railroad bridges, a former railroad bridge—now bicycle bridge—and the twin concrete bridges of Twelfth and Sixteenth Streets cross the river. Homeless people camp nearby. Below the four bridges, the river is slow and deep. Some summer weekends, dozens of large pleasure boats anchor to worship the sun, fish, or party. The I–5 bridges indicate your approach to Discovery Park to the north and Tiscornia Parks to the south. Steel Jibboom Street bridge links Discovery and Tiscornia Parks.

The preferred take-out is Tiscornia Park on the left bank. Almost under the Jibboom Street bridge is an unpaved ramp for small boats. On weekends the paved Discovery Park ramps to the Sacramento River are very busy with power boats. Looking down the Sacramento River, you can see Sacramento skyscrapers over a mile away.

Access: Sailor Bar (north side of the river in Fair Oaks): From Sunrise Boulevard, go east 2.0 miles on Winding Way to Illinois Avenue, then south on Illinois to the park entrance.

Upper Sunrise and Lower Sunrise (south side of the river in Rancho Cordova): From U.S. Highway 50, go north 1.5 miles on Sunrise Boulevard. Turn east onto South Bridge Street past the commercial raft rentals and shuttle buses. Where the road intersects in a

Egret frequently visit the American River.

"T," turn east toward Upper Sunrise or turn west to go under Sunrise Boulevard to Lower Sunrise.

Sacramento Bar (north side of the river in Fair Oaks): From Sunrise Boulevard go west 0.1 mile on Fair Oaks Boulevard, then south at Pennsylvania. Go slowly through the residential neighborhood and down the hill to the river.

El Manto Drive (south side of the river in Rancho Cordova): From Sunrise Boulevard, go west on Coloma Road 0.9 mile to El Manto Drive. Follow El Manto north to the marked river access.

Ancil Hoffman Park (north side of the river in Carmichael): From Fair Oaks Boulevard intersection with El Camino Avenue, go east 0.4 mile on Van Alstine Avenue. Turn north on California 0.1 mile, then east on Tarshes Drive into the park. Park in the lot at the upstream end of the giant picnic area and carry 200 yards to the river.

Goethe Park (south side of the river in Rancho Cordova): From Folsom Boulevard (1.2 miles west of Coloma), go north on Rod Beaudry Road 0.7 mile into the park. Bear left at the intersections for the closest parking to the river. Look at the river to orient yourself to the bridge and the take-out. When available, use the shuttle buses to the Sunrise put-in.

Harrington Way (north side of the river in Carmichael): From Fair Oaks Boulevard, go east on Arden Way, then turn south onto Kingsford Drive that becomes Harrington Way and leads to riverside parking.

Gristmill Dam (south side of the river in Sacramento): From Folsom Boulevard, turn north onto Mira Del Rio Drive and follow it to the river.

Watt Avenue (south side of the river in Sacramento): Exit Watt Avenue onto La Riveria Drive. The access road is 50 yards east of Watt Avenue bridge.

Howe Avenue, La Riveria (south side of the river in Sacramento): Exit Howe Avenue onto La Riveria Drive. The access road is 100 yards east of Howe Avenue bridge.

Discovery Park (north side of the river in Sacramento): Exit I–5 onto Richards Boulevard. Turn west on Richards, then almost immediately turn north on Jibboom Street. Pay at the park kiosk, cross the steel bridge, then turn west toward the launch ramps.

Tiscornia Park (south side of the river in Sacramento): Exit I–5 onto Richards Boulevard. Turn west on Richards, then almost immediately turn north on Jibboom Street. Pay at park kiosk, and turn right into parking area. Do not go over the bridge.

Shuttle: Sunrise to Goethe Park: 6.5 miles (20 minutes). Goethe Park to Howe Avenue: 7.5 miles (15 minutes). Howe Avenue to Tiscornia Park: 9.0 miles (20 minutes).

For more information: (See Appendix B for phone numbers, websites, and street addresses.) Contact the Sacramento County American River Parkway via phone.

⬛ Cosumnes River Preserve

Character: This rare, free-flowing, canoeable water-way supports rich wildlife and riparian oak forests.

Class: I.

Skill level: Beginner.

Optimal flow: Low flow, real time tide levels gauge: Mokelumne River near Thorton (Benson Ferry). Tide differences for New Hope Bridge (4 miles downstream from Benson Ferry) are from Port Chicago: high tides: +4 hours, 22 minutes; low tides: +4 hours, 56 minutes. Winter and spring real time gauge: Cosumnes River at Michigan Bar.

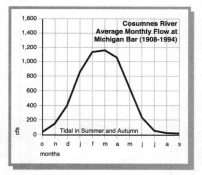

Best season: Year-round when the river is not flooding.

Craft: Open canoes, kayaks, and sea kayaks.

Hazards: Sharp branches submerged in opaque water can puncture inflatable craft. Spring and winter high flows drown the banks and you have to paddle through brush to reach dry ground.

Maps: USGS 7.5 Bruceville.

Overview: The last free-flowing river within the Central Valley, The Nature Conservancy has designated the Cosumnes one of the "Last Great Places" and created the Cosumnes River Preserve. With a consortium of partners, the 37,000-acre Cosumnes River Preserve works to preserve habitats from conversion to agricultural uses and urbanization, while promoting research, educating the public, and providing recreation.

The river's floods and dry periods foster dynamic processes, provide a variety of habitats, and promote abundant biological diversity. Today the Cosumnes River Preserve is one of the few remaining examples of pristine native habitat and wildlife that once characterized much of the Central Valley. Some notable features of the preserve are the Great Oaks Forest, the annual fall migration of sandhill cranes, and the winding waterways and wetlands. Scheduled activities usually include bird-watching tours, bird counts, and guided canoe trips. The preserve location on the Pacific Flyway attracts many resident and migratory wildlife species. To better enjoy the bird watching, obtain "A Field Checklist for Birds of the Cosumnes River Preserve" at the visitor center.

This is where the Cosumnes River meets the tidelands of the Sacramento–San Joaquin Delta. The water depth varies several feet every day, so consult tide tables to avoid being stranded on low water mud bars. As always, try to paddle with the tide rather than against it.

The paddling:

Cosumnes River to Tall Forest

Length: 5 to 6 miles round trip.

Average run time: 2 to 4 hours.

Cosumnes River Preserve

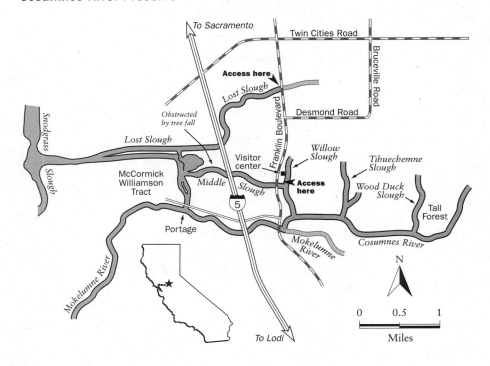

Class: I.

Skill level: Beginner.

Average gradient: Less than 1 foot per mile.

From the Cosumnes River Visitor Center, float along Willow Slough's intimate channel. The channel width is less than a canoe length. On the east side, dense thickets of button-bush emerge directly from the muddy water, looking like mangrove roots. You may hear the harsh squawk of a great blue heron taking flight around the bend. Roots and broken branches lay under water, sometimes bumping boats. Volunteers occasionally clear obstacles that fall into the slough. They would appreciate your help.

About 0.1 mile from the visitor center, a white sign supported above the water is a prominent landmark for finding your way back to Willow Slough. It reads, NO SHOOTING PAST THIS POINT. In a few more yards, Willow Slough joins with broad Middle Slough. Look west from the confluence and you will see the Franklin Boulevard bridge. The bridge is an important landmark when returning to the launch site.

The alternative put-in is 400 feet west, in a small slough next to the Franklin Boulevard bridge. A similar white sign marks this launch site. This waterway provides easier paddling and far fewer obstacles than Willow Slough.

Go south on Middle Slough. The tidal current may be noticeable. In 0.4 mile the slough joins the Cosumnes River. Fishermen often try their luck from the west bank. Look back and note the power lines in the distance and the tall communication towers to the west. If you miss the Middle Slough turnoff on your return, you will float downstream another 0.25 mile to the Mokelumne River. Benson's Ferry bridge at Thornton is unmistakable with the streamflow gauging station on the left abutment and the huge inverted staff gauge on the right side. The inverted gauge shows clearance from the water level to the underside of the bridge.

Paddling east up the Cosumnes, you will soon find two bridges, side by side. The larger is for the busy railroad, and the spindly structure appears to support a nonexistent pipeline. During the summer and autumn, the flow here ebbs and fills with the tides. Following winter storms and during spring snowmelt the river will be much higher with a strong current.

Explore Tihuechemne Slough 0.3 mile upstream of the bridges. The slough winds 0.7 miles to the north. Some side channels lead to marshes abundant with life. From the water you can see picturesque valley oaks. The Willow Slough Nature Trail wanders here through the oaks to the river edge. It is a wonderful place to see many birds, inspect riparian vegetation restoration results, and learn about floodplain flora and fauna. When the Michigan Bar streamflow gauge reads 1,100 cfs, the river overflows some banks in the slough, creating shallow streams through tunnels of willows and oaks. Return down Tihuechemne Slough to the Cosumnes River.

Continuing upstream, the river narrows dramatically and the current increases. Arching trees shade the entire channel. Fallen trees extend into the channel from both banks. At summer flows, maneuvering in either direction is easy. At flows above 500 cfs, take special care when paddling downstream to avoid being washed into these strainers. This narrow section is short and the channel soon widens.

The next 0.7 mile is amazingly straight. Tall cottonwoods and oaks line the south levee. Native grapes hang almost to river level. Just west of Wood Duck Slough is a grassy bank made to order for stretching your legs. The bank provides an inviting view of the "Tall Forest." The sight invites you to re-board your boat and explore Wood Duck Slough, which transports the paddler into the heart of the majestic Tall Forest with tall valley oaks overhanging the water to provide deep shade. The scene is reminiscent of Bogart and Hepburn on the *African Queen*. Branches reach out from the banks, making this a sinuous passage. Most of the banks are muddy and slippery. Look for the little critters that live in the banks. High water reaches the tops of the banks and moves back and forth from the river to the slough. At summer water levels a pump structure obstructs the upstream end of Wood Duck Slough. High water submerges parts of the structure, and a careful paddler can continue some distance.

Upstream from Wood Duck Slough, the Cosumnes River turns abruptly north and parallels the slough. This affords another view of the Tall Forest from a channel only a little less mystical and obstructed than Wood Duck Slough. When returning to your launch site, remember the landmarks. Downstream of the railroad bridge, turn right into Middle

Slough, watch for the Franklin Boulevard bridge, then look for the white sign marking your put-in.

Middle Slough and Lost Slough

Length: 5 to 7.5 miles round-trip.
Average run time: 2 to 4 hours.
Class: I.
Skill level: Beginner.
Average gradient: Less than 1 foot per mile.

Middle Slough and Lost Slough border the Lost Slough Managed Wetlands and the Willow Scrub Meadow and provide water-level views of the wildlife in this nature study preserve.

As described in the Tall Forest section, Middle Slough runs west under the Franklin Boulevard bridge. Sometimes it is possible to paddle around the fallen trees just west of Franklin Boulevard. To the north, 0.5 mile beyond the Willow Slough parking area, Lost Slough flows under Franklin Boulevard. On the west side of that narrow bridge, only a thin fishing track leads to a hummock above Lost Slough. Broken pilings and debris discourage landing under the bridge.

A reasonable option is to paddle down the Mokelumne River 1.4 miles. You will pass under Franklin Boulevard and I–5. The levee-lined Mokelumne channel swings first southwest, then northwest, then west into a long straight section. At 100 yards, look for slippery concrete riprap on the right bank. Portage across the gravel road to a dirt clearing into a slough heading north.

The west bank is a high levee bordering the McCormick Williamson tract. A much lower levee borders the slough's east side. Two long, thin islands split the broadening slough—paddle on the east side of the second island. Several breaks in the low levee allow canoes and kayaks to reach Middle Slough to the east. Middle Slough connects with Lost Slough to the north. If you elect to continue north instead of entering Middle Slough, then you will lengthen your tour by at least 3.5 miles. A long, thin continuous island splits Lost Slough for 1.7 miles between Snodgrass Slough and Middle Slough. You have to paddle west to Snodgrass, then go around the end of the island, and paddle east to reach the confluence of Lost and Middle Sloughs.

Along Middle Slough, calm ponds, shallow and deeper channels, and tule marshes give delightful variety to paddlers and bird watchers. The only disruption is traffic noise near I–5. As evidenced by the small docks and tree swings, local landowners enjoy summer days here. The slough continues 0.5 mile east of I–5 until the channel thins and fallen trees block return to Franklin Boulevard.

Following Middle Slough north and west leads to open ponds and the much larger Lost Slough. Signs at the confluence advise, "Nature Study Preserve boats not to exceed idle speed and 55 dba." Lost Slough is arrow-straight east and west. Paddle past large floating docks tied to the north bank near I–5. East of I–5, Lost Slough broadens, turns north-

Tall Forest of the Cosumnes River Preserve provides an inviting backdrop for a canoe ride.

ward, and borders the Lost Slough managed wetlands. Turning again, the channel looks more natural and shrinks as it approaches Franklin Boulevard. Expect to see egrets and great blue herons.

To get back to your vehicle, retrace your path to the Mokelumne or risk the narrow Franklin Boulevard bridge over Lost Slough and hike back to your parking place.

Access: From I–5, travel east 1 mile on Twin Cities Road. At Franklin Boulevard, turn south for 2 miles to the Cosumnes River Preserve Visitor Center. Here is the public put-in/take-out. After unloading your gear at the parking lot, you should park outside the gate on the wide Franklin Boulevard shoulder.

Two put-ins/take-outs are near the visitor center. One is a few yards south of the Visitor Center down an old levee into the narrow, sometimes shallow Willow Slough. The second is at a much wider and easier-to-navigate arm of Middle Slough. From the parking lot, follow the mowed footpath 200 yards across the field to a bare spot just east of the Franklin Boulevard bridge. When winter floods or snowmelt flood the field, put in cautiously on Willow Slough.

Shuttle: None.

For more information: (See Appendix B for phone numbers, websites, and street addresses.) Contact the Cosumnes River Preserve via phone or Internet for scheduled trips and volunteer activities.

Mokelumne River—Electra Run

Character: This small, scenic canyon is a favorite run for training up-and-coming whitewater boaters.

Length: 3 miles.

Average run time: 1 to 2 hours.

Class: II.

Skill level: Beginner with whitewater experience to intermediate.

Optimal flow: 500 to 1,200 cfs inflow to Pardee Reservoir.

Water source: Electra powerhouse releases.

Average gradient: 22 feet per mile.

Best season: Spring through autumn.

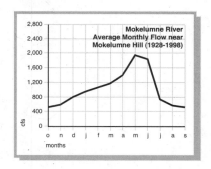

Craft: Whitewater canoes, kayaks, inflatable kayaks, and small rafts.

Hazards: Spring snowmelt can sustain flows that run through trees and brush, making take-out and rescue extremely difficult. The afterbay dam, between the powerhouse and put-in, has narrow slots that should not be run.

Maps: USGS 7.5 Mokelumne Hill.

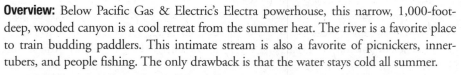

Overview: Below Pacific Gas & Electric's Electra powerhouse, this narrow, 1,000-foot-deep, wooded canyon is a cool retreat from the summer heat. The river is a favorite place to train budding paddlers. This intimate stream is also a favorite of picnickers, inner-tubers, and people fishing. The only drawback is that the water stays cold all summer.

With a paved road closely paralleling the river, you can run the short reach several times a day, with time for lunch on the beach. The narrow road is close enough to see many, but not the biggest, rapids.

Parking is limited to a small area near the put-in, a few spots along the road, and a wide, flat area near the afterbay dam. Bring a good shuttle vehicle and someone willing to drive it. Since the Amador County Sheriff enforces camping prohibitions, try the Indian Grinding Rock State Historic Park for camping or the towns of Jackson or Mokelumne Hill for other accommodations.

Access near California Highway 49 has deteriorated over the years and is currently limited by private landowners who exclude boaters from a historic take-out, upstream from the bridge on river left. Due to the CA 49 curve and narrow shoulders by the bridge, you might consider parking elsewhere.

East Bay Municipal Utility District has a history of jealously claiming the river, lands and access downstream of CA 49.

The paddling: A sandy beach put-in provides a choice of sun or shade, and a beautiful large pool. It is a great spot for novice paddlers to get used to their boats and try a roll or two. Upstream 75 yards, the modest Maytag hole can sharpen your bracing skills.

Mokelumne River—Electra Run

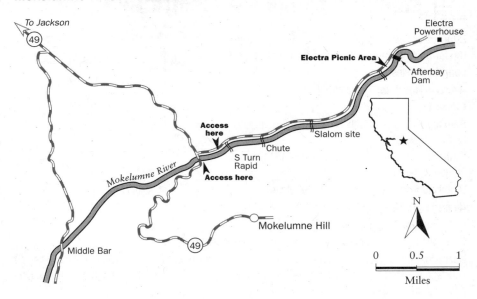

The run starts with broad, easy rapids. It is good practice for reading water, catching eddies, and fine-tuning communications with your paddling partner. A mile downstream the river narrows and increases in velocity as it approaches large boulders with well-defined eddies. The combination of rapids and excellent roadside viewing make this a fun slalom site. Farther downstream, the channel constricts into a chute filled with steep, exciting haystacks. Some neophyte open-canoeists may want to look it over. A recovery pool waits at the bottom.

The final challenge above CA 49 is the "S" turn. Out of sight from the road, the rocky channel turns left, then increases speed as it careens off ledges and turns right. Your friends can watch from the big eddy on the bottom right. Eddies on both sides of the rapid give you a chance to paddle upstream and try surfing.

Some boaters choose to take out at the "S" turn and shuttle back to the put-in for another run. Otherwise, continue downstream past the old concrete abutments and take out upstream of the CA 49 bridge.

Access: CA 49 bridge: Go south from Jackson 4.0 miles on CA 49 to the highway bridge.

Electra Picnic Area: 100 yards north of the bridge, Electra Road turns uphill, then follows the river 3 miles to the small parking area and beach.

Shuttle: 3 miles (10 minutes).

For more information: (See Appendix B for phone numbers, websites, and street addresses.) Contact the Bureau of Land Management or whitewater information. For camping, check with Indian Grinding Rock State Historic Park via phone or Internet.

41 Mokelumne River below Camanche

Character: The Mokelumne is a great place on a hot summer day with delightful shade trees, cold water, and fine fishing.

Length: 4 miles.

Average run time: 2 to 3 hours.

Class: I.

Skill level: Beginners with experience.

Optimal flow: 250 to 1,500 cfs.

Water Source: Camanche Reservoir.

Average gradient: 5 feet per mile.

Best season: Spring, summer, and autumn.

Craft: Canoes, kayaks, and inflatables.

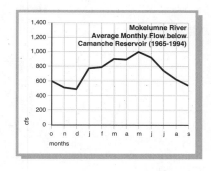

Hazards: Fast flows in the first mile of paddling, an abundance of snags, and low hanging branches throughout the reach require paddlers to maneuver adroitly to avoid a dunking into the cold water.

Maps: USGS 7.5 Clements.

Overview: Downstream of Camanche Reservoir, the Mokelumne starts cold and fast. Readily visible numbered blocks mark the many salmon redds. Avoid damaging the redds by not wading near them.

Bring your fishing rod! In summer, trout bite in the main stream, and black bass lurk in the backwater dredge ponds. Salmon fishing is limited to early September through mid-October when the adult salmon return. Steelhead season lasts from January 1 into mid-February. Check the California regulations for special fishing rules here.

Tall cottonwoods and oaks line most of the riverbanks and contribute to the cool air. Buckeye blossoms scent the air in spring and early summer. Upstream of the California Highway 88 bridge, cattle ranches occupy the adjacent lands. Downstream, expensive homes dot the riparian landscape. Trees and brush hide the gold-dredging tailing mounds, but several dredge ponds, providing bass habitat, still connect with the river. The take-out is the site of the Lone Star Mill, first built in 1855.

The paddling: The large pool near the lower parking area is a good place to practice if the people fishing along the banks are not too close together. The river current is fast, 4 to 5 miles per hour. Beware of trees in the water and hanging over the river at the first real bend in the channel. After 0.5 mile the flow slows to a more normal pace.

For landmarks note that the right bank is low and slopes gently. Several fallen trees are not too difficult to get around. The trees standing on the bank show high-water marks 3 to 5 feet above the summer flow level. Abruptly, the right bank climbs into a low bluff with a deep pool. Nearby is a huge oak. Stay alert where the river turns, then carefully paddle

Mokelumne River below Camanche

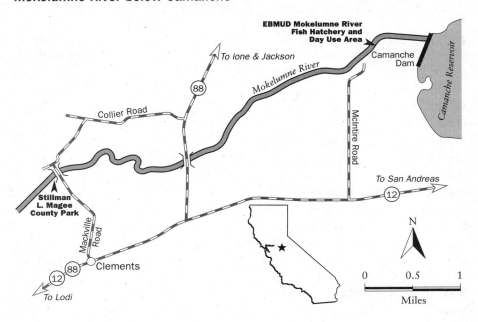

through. Downstream 0.5 mile, a skillful paddler might squeeze under a big oak that leans from the left bank. Alternatively, the rest of the channel has ample space to paddle. Behind the oak are the piles of gold-dredge tailings.

The first bridge is CA 88. On the right is a lagoon where we noted a swan. Large houses dot the left bank. An island divides the flow and the current accelerates. We paddled the left side, although both sides were negotiable. Continue your vigilance for snags in the river.

Three miles from the put-in, the river turns abruptly right and then left. Irrigation pumps draw from the deep eddies separated by shallower fast-moving water. Soon a few more houses come into view, some with expansive lawns down to the river's edge. Half a mile upstream from the Mackville Road bridge, trees on the left screen dredge tailings. A high bank appears on the right, a warning sign for more snags in the river.

The second bridge (Mackville Road) is the take-out. Land on the left bank and carry the boats 150 yards along the foot path adjacent to the bridge to the parking area.

Access: From CA 99 in Lodi, follow CA 12 east 11.5 miles to Clements. The take-out is 1 mile north of Clements on Mackville Road. The county prohibits parking along the road near the bridge, so pay the day-use fees to park in Stillman L. Magee County Park.

To get to the put-in, return to Clements, then turn east on CA 12. Stay on CA 12 for another 1.6 miles past the CA 88 junction (total of 3 miles from Clements). Turn north onto McIntire Road at the sign reading "Mokelumne River Fish Installation." Follow McIntire Road past the ostrich farm to the East Bay Municipal Utility District recreation area below the fish hatchery.

Shuttle: 6 miles (10 minutes).

For more information: (See Appendix B for phone numbers, websites, and street addresses.) Call East Bay Municipal Utility District for put-in information or visit their Internet site.

42 Stanislaus River—Knights Ferry to McHenry Recreation Area

Character: A quick-flowing stream in a tree-shaded intimate channel that is inviting most of the year.

Length: 27 miles.

Class: I with one Class II.

Skill level: Beginner.

Optimal flow: 300 to 1,000 cfs (Orange Blossom gauge).

Water source: New Melones Reservoir.

Average gradient: 5 feet per mile.

Best season: Spring and summer.

Craft: Canoes, kayaks, and inflatables, including small rafts.

Hazards: Russian Rapid near Knights Ferry has a well-marked portage trail. Otherwise, be alert for occasional fallen trees in the channel.

Maps: USGS 7.5 Knights Ferry, Oakdale, Escalon, Riverbank.

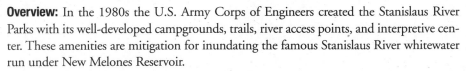

Overview: In the 1980s the U.S. Army Corps of Engineers created the Stanislaus River Parks with its well-developed campgrounds, trails, river access points, and interpretive center. These amenities are mitigation for inundating the famous Stanislaus River whitewater run under New Melones Reservoir.

Once the Stanislaus county seat, the historic community of Knights Ferry is worth exploring. The 140-year-old, 360-foot-long covered bridge, restored mill, and office are within easy walking distance of the put-in.

Boating regulations allow only electric motors between Horseshoe Road and Orange Blossom Bridge. Ten-horsepower gas motors may operate at 5 m.p.h. maximum speed between Orange Blossom Bridge and CA 120 in Oakdale.

Remember to bring drinking water, pay for your camping permit, and perhaps reserve a campsite in advance. Ask at the interpretive center about overnight parking.

The paddling:

Knights Ferry to Valley Oak Recreation Area

> **Length:** 10 miles.
>
> **Average run time:** 4 to 6 hours.
>
> **Gradient:** 5 feet per mile.
>
> **Class:** I with one Class II.
>
> **Skill level:** Beginner.

At the put-in, the clear, cold Stanislaus is only three canoe lengths wide. Paddle upstream 200 yards to enjoy water level views of the old covered bridge. To sharpen skills at fast-

Stanislaus River—Knights Ferry to McHenry Recreation Area

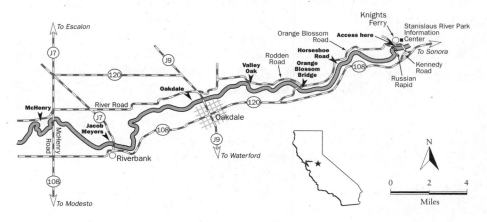

water ferries and turns, continue upstream to the chutes and eddies. This swift water practice may soon pay off at Russian Rapid.

Returning downstream, the few houses of Knights Ferry are soon left behind. The bank on river left is a brush-covered gravel bar, while the right bank climbs upward as the river begins a long, gradual turn to the left. A large sign on the left bank announces the start of the portage trail around Russian Rapid. Use the portage trail if you are new to canoeing or uncomfortable with Class II whitewater. Russian Rapid is by far the most difficult rapid below Knights Ferry.

In 150 yards, Russian Rapid contains one hole, a midstream tree, and bouncy surfing waves at the bottom. A continuous ledge forms the right side from top to bottom at 450 cfs. At higher discharges, the water flows over the wide, downstream part of the ledge. The slippery, narrow path on the right bank affords great views for photographing and scouting the rapid, but stay close to the river to respect private property rights. The bottom of the rapid offers good rescue pools, surf waves, and an early lunch site.

Below Russian Rapid, the river is much easier. Wide and narrow sections alternate slow and fast. In the fall, salmon spawn in the riffles. A deep pool forms below Lovers Leap on river left. The mile-long straight section provides distant vistas of the surrounding hills. Look for hawks, vultures, great blue herons, and other wildlife as you enjoy the river. The colder waters of the deeper pools provide trout habitat through the warm summer months.

A mile past Lovers Leap, where the river turns southwest, is the Horseshoe Road Recreation Area. A large Corps sign announces this take-out option on river right. Horseshoe also offers boat-in camping. Obtain permits at the campground honor system kiosk or at the USCE Knights Ferry Information Center.

Horseshoe Road Recreation Area exhibits some of the few gold-dredge tailings still clearly visible along the Stanislaus. Quiet ponds invite exploration for wildlife. The Corps' "Birds of the Lower Stanislaus River" lists more than 180 species.

An abrupt turn to the right brings the Orange Blossom Bridge into view, 7 miles from the put-in. Take out under the bridge on river right. Available here are permanent rest rooms, drinking water, picnic tables, and paved daytime parking which is gated at night.

An option is to continue past Orange Blossom Bridge to Valley Oak Recreation Area. The current is quick. The channel is free of brush, and the tall shade trees lining both banks make this a delightful stretch of river. Several riffles with wave trains provide splash relief from summer heat. Be alert for snags where some tall shade trees have fallen into the river. Some trees show signs of saw cuts where limbs have been cleared from the river.

About 1.4 miles below the Orange Blossom, look for a house on top of a high bluff on the left side. Below the bluff, the Stanislaus turns sharply right, with a large snag blocking the right two-thirds of the river.

Valley Oak Recreation Area is about 2.5 miles below Orange Blossom Bridge. Look carefully for the wooden railroad-tie steps in the right bank for the take-out. If you miss it, a second set of steps is 100 yards downstream at the boat-in campsite. The picnic tables are visible from the river. Sometimes the recreation area is marked by a sign. When you do the shuttle, check for distinctive landmarks at the take-out, or create one that is environmentally acceptable.

Valley Oak to McHenry Recreation Area

Length: 17 miles.
Average run time: 6 to 9 hours.
Class: I.
Skill level: Beginner.
Average gradient: 4 feet per mile.

From the campground the river begins to swing northward and the streamside bluffs begin to drop away, providing a wider horizon. Snags warrant your attention as the channel bends west. At the top of a bluff, a palatial house dominates the scene 0.5 mile above a small beach on river right.

More snags lie in easy current at the distinct right bend a mile from Oakdale. Closer to town, a waterfall intermittently plunges 90 feet from a water tank. Fortunately the falling water cascades onto the left bank and is not usually a hazard to boaters. Houses again line the blufftops approaching Oakdale. Under the CA 120 and railroad bridges, a low rock pile blocks the right two-thirds of the channel. Downstream of Oakdale the river bluffs retreat and the stream character changes. Low banks with wide gravel bars topped with brush form the channel. The current flows intermittently fast and slow.

Where the river zigzags left then right, a sign hangs from a pipeline high above the river. It advises that a research area exists downstream and recommends that boaters stay to river

Russian Rapid is the most difficult rapid on the Stanislaus River below Knights Ferry.

left. Soon wide gravel bars and ponds appear. The access to Oakdale Recreation Area is on river right. The first access point, with its railroad-tie stairs, is at the far side of a pond. The river flows through more ponds—often populated by ducks, egrets, and herons—to a second take-out. Easier to see than the first, this part of the Oakdale Recreation Area provides a riverside gravel road that ends at a gate, a signpost, and a rest room. If you plan to take out here, look at it carefully so you will recognize it when you approach from the river.

The alternate route to these ponds is on the far left, in an obscure channel with many snags. Continuing west across the ponds is easier. Paddle around the gravel bars and through the lazy eddies. The ponds end at a runable breach in the low levees that form the pond. At low flow, you may scrape some rocks.

Soon the river channel narrows again and the current accelerates. An orchard occupies a low terrace on the right. Then a high bluff slopes steeply to the river. The bluff falls away and a mile-long straight section leads into San Joaquin County. Orchards line both sides of the river. The banks are occasionally covered with broken concrete riprap. Approximately 3 miles from Riverbank the river makes a long "S" turn, first west, then south, then east, and finally south again. The current is strong and the landowners have lined the banks with broken concrete to reduce erosion. Tall trees provide shade, and a few fallen trees are in the river.

From Riverbank 1.5 miles, the river runs due south toward a tall bluff with CA 108 on top. Directly below lie snags that are relatively easy to negotiate. As the channel turns west, the current alternates between gentle riffles and slow pools. Directly under the Sante Fe Avenue bridge, the Jacob Meyers Park concrete ramp on river right is impossible to miss.

Beginning about a mile below Riverbank, the bluffs retreat from the water for the next two miles. When the river narrows again, you are approaching the McHenry Avenue bridge. This reach is less scenic, with broken concrete riprap, industrial land uses, and the outfall pipe by the bridge. Much of the 1.4 miles along the north bank from McHenry Avenue to the take-out is now managed as part of the McHenry Recreation Area. The water still flows quickly in the narrow channel lined with fallen trees.

Past the golf course, the river turns abruptly northward. The right bank is covered with new erosion-control riprap and a boat ramp. Around the bend is a wide beach next to the day-use area. Take your choice of take-out: the ramp is steep but the beach is a longer carry.

Access: Knights Ferry Recreation Area: From Oakdale follow CA 108/120 east for 12 miles. Turn north on Kennedy Road, then turn left onto Sonora Road. Cross the river and turn right to the paved parking area, put-in, and Stanislaus River Park Information Center.

Horseshoe Road Recreation Area is off Orange Blossom Road 3.5 miles east of Orange Blossom bridge toward Knights Ferry. From Knights Ferry take Sonora Road west, through the town. Turn left and follow Orange Blossom Road for about 2.2 miles. Horseshoe Road Recreation Area access is on the right.

Orange Blossom Road bridge: From Oakdale follow CA 108 east 3.6 miles, then turn north onto Orange Blossom Road. Orange Blossom Road crosses the bridge at 1.5 miles.

The paved parking area, with permanent rest rooms and picnic tables, is immediately downstream of the bridge on the north bank. From Valley Oak Recreation Area follow Rodden Road east to Orange Blossom Road and bridge.

Valley Oak Recreation Area: 4 miles east of the stoplight on Stanislaus County Road J9 (Valley Home, Oakdale-Waterford Road), turn south off Rodden Road at the sign that reads "Valley Oak Recreation Area." The paved road is 50 feet east of the much more visible sign "Arbini Road" and leads to the paved parking area. Follow the unpaved service road 200 level yards to the river. Steps lead down to the water. Large oaks shade most of the area. The environmental campground is several hundred yards downstream with its own landing place. The Corps requires campers to obtain camping permits from the visitor center in Knights Ferry or at the campground honor vault. Be sure to look at the take-out since the landing is obscure and the sign is sometimes absent.

Oakdale Recreation Area and Fishing Access, Oakdale: West 0.4 miles from the intersection with Stanislaus County Road J9 (Valley Home–Oakdale–Waterford Road), turn from River Road south onto Liberini Road North. Liberini Road is paved and extends 0.7 miles to the parking area, rest rooms, and the river. A gravel road extends along several ponds and the river channel to give a choice of easy put-ins. The area is scenic and quiet. Be sure to look carefully for take-out landmarks since the landing is obscure and the sign is sometimes absent.

Jacob Meyers Park in Riverbank is at the north end of the Sante Fe Road bridge, between Sante Fe Road and the railroad bridge. Downstream 50 feet of the highway bridge, a narrow concrete boat ramp extends to the river. The Corps removed the line of old broken pilings in 2000. Although there is ample parking, the park is not a good place to leave a vehicle overnight.

McHenry Avenue Recreation Area joins the River Road, 0.8 mile west of the McHenry Avenue intersection, east of the railroad tracks and wastewater treatment plant. Follow the paved entrance road past the kiosk to the day-use areas and steep, unpaved launch ramp beside the riprap banks. The less steep take-out is downstream at the day-use area, across the sand bar and up the wooden stairs.

Shuttle: Knights Ferry to Valley Oak: 9.5 miles (25 minutes). Valley Oak to Oakdale: 5.4 miles (15 minutes). Valley Oak to Jacob Meyers: 9.5 miles (25 minutes). Valley Oak to McHenry: 17 miles (40 minutes).

For more information: (See Appendix B for phone numbers, websites, and street addresses.) Contact the U.S. Army Corps of Engineers Stanislaus River Parks for camping permits and river information via telephone, or check their website.

43 Tuolumne River—La Grange to Roberts Ferry

Character: The object of epic river conservation struggles, the remnant flows of the Tuolumne River twist through the gold-dredge tailings near historic La Grange.

Length: 10.3 miles.

Average run time: 1.5 hours to Basso Bridge, 2.5 hours more to Turlock Lake State Recreation Area campground, and another hour to Roberts Ferry.

Class: I with some brush.

Skill level: Beginner with experience.

Optimal flow: 400 to 600 cfs (La Grange gauge).

Water source: New Don Pedro Reservoir minus diversions.

Average gradient: 6 feet per mile.

Best season: Autumn through spring except during flood flows.

Craft: Canoes, kayaks, and small rafts.

Hazards: When winter and spring flows rise to many thousands of cfs, the river is powerful, cold, very fast, and treacherous.

Maps: USGS 7.5 La Grange, Cooperstown.

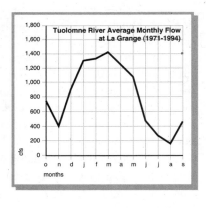

Overview: The 148-mile Tuolumne River originates at the 12,000-foot Sierra Crest in Yosemite National Park. From granite peaks and the Mount Lyell glacier, the Tuolumne cascades down narrow canyons and slides through lush meadows before O'Shaughnessy Dam captures the river in Hetch Hetchy Canyon. John Muir fought valiantly to save Hetch Hetchy's splendor as equal to Yosemite Canyon. Muir and the fledgling Sierra Club lost that battle and Congress enacted the Raker Act in 1914. The act authorized the City of San Francisco to dam Hetch Hetchy and divert much of its flow through tunnels, power plants, and aqueducts to San Francisco. The remaining water flows through the Grand Canyon of the Tuolumne to huge New Don Pedro Reservoir. Modesto Irrigation District and Turlock Irrigation District divert water from New Don Pedro Reservoir at La Grange Dam. Only 2 miles by road upstream from the community of La Grange, the dam is worth seeing. Built in 1894 of huge granite blocks wedged into the narrow canyon, the dam diverts the river into canals carved into the canyon walls. Except during flood periods when La Grange Dam overflows, the little powerhouse beside the dam sends the limp remainder of the Tuolumne to the lower river.

Threatened with extinction, salmon spawn again in the Tuolumne these days due in part to restored spawning gravels, increased seasonal San Joaquin River flows, and a seasonal ban on all sport fishing.

Tuolumne River—La Grange to Roberts Ferry and Fox Grove Park

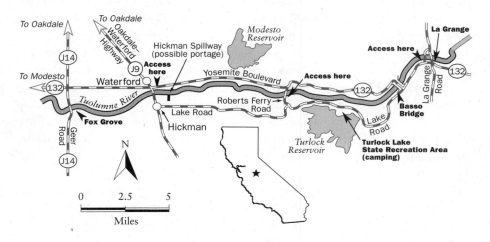

The paddling: At La Grange, the Tuolumne emerges from its narrow canyon to sparkle over a wide cobbled bed. The cobblestone bottom provides easy Class I riffles. At 400 cfs, adept paddlers can avoid scraping and walking the boats. At lower summer flows, walking in the cool water is a welcome relief from the valley heat.

The wide stream channel is a remnant of the gold dredging that denuded many of California's river bottoms in the earlier 1900s. The huge floating dredges gouged the rivers, separated out the gold, then dumped the remaining rock in vast piles of cobbles extending hundreds of yards from the river.

Nearing the mouth of Lower Dominici Creek, about 0.5 mile above Basso Bridge, many swallows nest in the low sedimentary cliffs that line the river right. Overhead look for larger birds such as hawks, turkey vultures, lots of ducks, great blue heron, and an occasional osprey. You can take out on river left at the new Basso Bridge or continue to Turlock Lake State Recreation Area Campground, 5 miles downstream. Be advised to visit the take-out at Turlock Lake State Recreation Area before you put in so you can recognize the unmarked take-out.

For 2 miles below Basso Bridge, the river alternates between long ponds and faster riffles. Gravel bars and willow thickets form the shores. In the fall, salmon use the riffles and skitter between the canoes. In one clear section, steel sheeting and concrete emerge from the riverbed. Since the chutes and riffles between the brush change each year, each trip is a new adventure.

Around one sharp bend, a tiny island divides the river. Most of the flow goes left, then hooks 90 degrees to slide under a fallen tree. At 400 cfs, the right channel is fast, steep, and so shallow that we needed to lift our boats over the cobbles.

After the roads leave the river near river mile 46, tall stately oaks line the left side. At Peaslee Creek, the left bank rises abruptly to 100-foot cliffs. Oaks dot these steep hills that continue downstream past the Turlock SRA campground. On the way, enjoy the occasional sandbars and deep pools by the cliffs. One of the stronger riffles gushes past mushroom boulders on river left, forming good eddies for talented boaters. Another sharp left turn leads to a high bank covered with lush ferns, a tantalizing spot on a hot summer day.

The unmarked take-out for the Turlock SRA campground is at a small slough downstream of several islands and a broad meander to the north. Look for two landmarks: 1) A tall chimney high on the left hillside (also visible from Lake Road) is 1 mile upstream from the campground. 2) On river right is a broad, flat privately owned area that looks good for camping and may have picnic tables. Turlock Lake SRA Campground is immediately downstream on the left.

If you are floating to Waterford or beyond, note the Hickman Spillway warning signs. The next chapter discusses the spillway that is downstream from Roberts Ferry.

Downstream of Turlock SRA the river is mostly flat water with a few riffles. The oak-studded bluffs and brush-shrouded tailings change sides. Land on river left, just upstream from the Roberts Ferry bridge.

Access: Roberts Ferry Road connects California Highway 132 and Lake Road with a new bridge. From Modesto, take CA 132 east 14 miles to Waterford. Continue on CA 132 paralleling the river for another 8 miles to Roberts Ferry Road. Turn south and cross the bridge. On the upstream side, a narrow road parallels the river and provides parking space.

Turlock Lake SRA campground can be reached from Roberts Ferry bridge by continuing south another 0.8 mile to Lake Road. Go east on Lake Road 2.1 miles to the campground entrance. Crowned by tall valley oaks, cottonwoods, walnuts, and sycamores, the 66 campsites are open all year. This fee campground is an easy put-in and take-out next to the river but is screened by vegetation. So visit the take-out before you put in so you can recognize the unmarked take-out from the river.

If the Roberts Ferry bridge is closed, get to Turlock Lake SRA Campground from Waterford. From CA 132 in Waterford turn right on Hickman Road (County Road J9) and drive 1 mile to Lake Road. Turn left on Lake Road and drive 10 miles to Turlock Lake SRA.

Basso Bridge is where CA 132 crosses the Tuolumne River almost 8 miles east of Roberts Ferry Road. A designated Wildlife Viewing Area, this access has a large paved parking area, permanent rest rooms, and concrete boat ramp. The access is on river left, immediately downstream from the bridge. Turlock SRA Campground is 7.5 miles along Lake Road on the south side of the river. The tall old chimney on the right signals that you are about 1 mile from the campground turnoff.

La Grange has two access points. The more developed access is next to the new bridge near La Grange. From Basso Bridge follow CA 132 east 2.1 miles to the next highway bridge. The access is immediately on the left, between CA 132 and the "new" La Grange bridge. Parking and river access is on river left, downstream from the bridge. Carry about 200 yards to the river.

High bluffs border the Tuolumne River near Turlock Lake State Recreation Area.

Old La Grange Bridge is 0.5 mile upstream. Follow CA 132 to the little town of La Grange. Look for the short road leading steeply downhill to the old bridge. Unload near the bridge and carry 200 yards over easy ground. Park in town along the main street.

Shuttle: La Grange to Basso Bridge: 2.2 miles (5 minutes). Basso Bridge to Turlock Lake SRA: 7.5 miles (15 minutes). Turlock Lake SRA to Roberts Ferry Road: 2.9 miles (10 minutes).

For more information: (See Appendix B for phone numbers, websites, and street addresses.) Call the Turlock Irrigation District for Hickman Spillway discharge schedules. To learn more about the park, call the Turlock Lake State Recreation Area or view their Internet site. For camping reservations, contact ReserveAmerica.

44 Tuolumne River—Roberts Ferry to Fox Grove Park

(see map on page 177)

Character: Bring your fishing pole for some slow paddling through long ponds, a few riffles, and some impressive gravel-mining operations.
Length: 13.4 miles.
Average run time: 4 to 6 hours.
Class: I.
Skill level: Beginner with experience.
Optimal flow: 400 to 1,000 cfs (Modesto gauge).
Average gradient: 3.5 feet per mile.
Best season: Autumn through spring, except during floods.
Craft: Canoes, kayaks, rafts, and dories.
Hazards: When Hickman Spillway discharges heavy flows to the river, it may cause severe turbulence.
Maps: USGS 7.5 Cooperstown, Denair, Paulsell, Waterford.

Overview: Below Roberts Ferry, the river changes to wide, slow reaches with a few riffles and streamside gravel quarries. The Department of Fish and Game enforces a seasonal ban on all sport fishing.

The paddling: Signs warn that the Hickman Spillway sometimes releases flows to the Tuolumne River. The spillway is 7 miles downstream of Roberts Ferry. Below Roberts Ferry the geologic flood channel widens as the bluffs retreat from the river. After a few gravel bar riffles, you come to the first of several haul road bridges for gravel-mining operations. Gravel miners no longer quarry directly from the river, nor are there any cables to impede your float trip.

About 2 miles below Roberts Ferry, the landscape varies. Low bluffs on the north side support oaks and grass. The other side is flat gravel bar covered with willows. Soon a huge quarry structure comes into view. It is actually a mile downstream on river right. Before you get there, you will pass under another haul road. An unusual bridge supports a conveyor high across the river.

Downstream from the conveyor, the channel narrows as the river swings north. It becomes more attractive as it parallels CA 132 on the bluff above. Another mile downstream, an obsolete bridge spans the river. Enjoy the blackberries, figs and grapevines that soon appear. Where the channel approaches the bluffs on the south side of the floodplain, the course turns sharply northeast. Look for a snag in the middle of a riffle. As the river arcs north, there is a good gravel bar for lunch.

Next a power line crosses the river, then some houses and a picturesque red barn appear on the right bank. These are landmarks that the Hickman Spillway is about 0.5 mile ahead. Warning signs may be visible on the banks. The Hickman Spillway is a concrete chute that drops 100 vertical feet from the Turlock Main Canal to the river. The river channel is wide and the north bank provides a level portage, should it be necessary. For most spillway discharges and river flows, paddlers can avoid the turbulence by staying close to the north bank, opposite the spillway.

If you plan to take out at Waterford, start looking. A brushy gravel bar hides Big Bear Park Campground. When you can see the Waterford bridge, you have past Big Bear and it is time to land on the right bank to find the take-out. The worst case is to land near the bridge and carry to Baker Street.

Just upstream from the Stanislaus J9 bridge, a large tree has fallen midstream. The route is obvious, so if you maintain control of your boat, you should enjoy the fast water that begins under the bridge. Beyond the bridge, a huge nursery occupies the long river terrace on the left. Broken concrete riprap lines the banks. Soon the channel snakes between gravel bars, brush, and snags. Look carefully to the right and you may see another spillway recessed from the river. Some 2 miles below the bridge are some broken concrete pilings, then the stream velocity increases. Enjoy the faster pace while it lasts.

The last 3 miles are wide, flat, and slow. Waterfowl and fishing boats enjoy the ponds. Some tall cottonwoods mark the north bank. When the large "WSP" silo appears, you are about a mile from the take-out. A white house sprawls on river right with sweeping lawns and a picturesque weeping willow. When the Geer Road bridge comes into view, paddle to the cove along the left bank with the Fox Grove boat ramp. That is the take-out.

Access: Fox Grove Park: From Modesto, take CA 132 east 8 miles to Geer Road. Turn south on Geer Road, then 0.2 mile past the Tuolumne River bridge turn east to the Fox Grove access road.

Waterford: From Fox Grove return to CA 132 and turn east for 4.8 miles. There are two access points on the north side of the river in Waterford. Big Bear Park is a private campground 0.2 mile east of Stanislaus County Road J9 on CA 132. Call 209–874–4000 in advance for river access.

Far less formal is Baker Street. From CA 132 turn toward the river one block east of J9. Baker Street has a small community park with foot access. Closer to the J9 bridge is a local fishing access near some commercial buildings. Landowners have posted and gated the old access on the south side of the river.

Roberts Ferry Road connects CA 132 and Lake Road with a new bridge. From Waterford, travel east 8 miles along CA 132 to Roberts Ferry Road. Turn south and cross the bridge. On the upstream side, a narrow road parallels the river and provides parking space. Alternatively, from Waterford go across the river on Hickman Road (Stanislaus County Road J9) and drive 1 mile to Lake Road. Turn left on Lake Road and drive 8 miles to

Roberts Ferry Road. On the way, you will pass Hall Road with its gated access to the Hickman Spillway.

Shuttle: Roberts Ferry to Waterford: 8 miles (10 minutes). Waterford to Fox Grove: 7 miles (10 minutes).

For more information: (See Appendix B for phone numbers, websites, and street addresses.) Call Big Bear Park for private campground reservations or to make group takeout arrangements. Call the Turlock Irrigation District for Hickman Spillway discharge schedules.

Ahjumawi Lava Springs State Park

Character: Within sight of Lassen Peak and Mount Shasta, these remote waters offer fine camping on some of the world's largest spring systems.

Size: 4 miles long, 0.1 to 1 mile wide, 13+ miles of shoreline.

Elevation: 3,300 feet.

Class: Flatwater lake.

Skill level: Beginner.

Water source: Natural springs feed the lake, so it remains at almost constant level.

Best season: Summer and autumn; open year-round.

Craft: Canoes, kayaks, inflatables, and row boats.

Hazards: Because of the remote wilderness location, help is far off and you must be self-sufficient. Hiking the sharp, rugged lava rocks demands sturdy footwear. Remember that rattlesnakes live in the area. Power boats use the adjacent lakes.

Maps: USGS 7.5 Fall River Mills, Timbered Crater.

Overview: Tucked into the far northeast corner of Shasta County, Ahjumawi sounds like paradise revisited. The state parks brochure calls Ahjumawi "a place of exceptional, even primeval beauty." Lava beds collect and store snowmelt for summer-long release to many crystalline springs feeding Big Lake, Horr Pond, Ja She Creek, and the Tule Rivers. Ahjumawi is a wonderful place to hike, view wildlife, fish, and explore by paddle and foot.

You can only reach the park by boat. No public roads exist and the park prohibits private motor vehicles. Outside the park, motorboats ply the lakes and rivers.

Ahjumawi State Park, 6,000 acres big, includes Horr Pond and the land north of the lakes. Most of the land to the south of Tule River, Little Tule River, and Big Lake are private property, as is the land to the east of Big Lake.

Three primitive campsites are found at each of three campgrounds with nearby vault toilets. Camp only at these campsites and keep fires in the fire rings. Water is available from the nearby springs, but you should purify it. Soft, silty lake bottoms discourage swimming. Pets should be left at home.

At 3,300 feet of elevation, the summer days are hot and the evenings cool. As in many other areas, the wind will be calm in the morning and strengthen in the afternoon. One advantage of the location is that these lakes are not subject to the Central Valley wind machine that blows up the Sierra canyons much of the summer. On the other hand, the breeze helps to keep the mosquitos away.

The paddling: Put in at the Rat Farm, a Pacific Gas & Electric site for boat launching. Then paddle 0.5 mile north along a slim finger of water to Big Lake. Big Lake opens to the east and north. The campgrounds are to the west. Horr Pond campsite is closest, a paddle of a little over a mile. Along the way are tiny, tree-studded islets with aquamarine bays. They enclose Horr Pond. This is a great place to try fishing for trout and bass. Crystal

Ahjumawi Lava Springs State Park

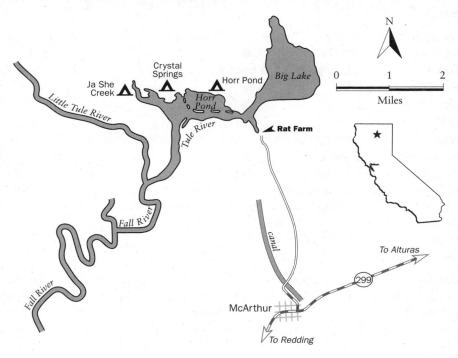

Springs is a 1.2-mile hike by land or a 1.5-mile paddle from Horr Pond camp. Crystal and Ja She Creek campsites are in the headwater springs of Ja She Creek.

These springs are famous for their rock fish-traps used by the Ahjumawi Indians. The rock formations are still there. Fish swim to the uprising water of the springs to spawn. Native Americans built small rock walls that would block the exits. Then they could easily spear or grab the fish.

With bald eagles and ospreys gliding overhead, marshy shores stalked by great blue heron, and Mount Shasta shining in the distance, this place "where the waters come together" will make you want to explore every part of it.

Access: From Redding, follow CA 299 east to the small town of McArthur. Turn north onto Main Street, past the fairgrounds, then cross over to the east side of the canal and follow the unpaved road to the site of the Rat Farm, some 3.7 miles from town. This is the only public launch site on Horr Pond and Big Lake.

Shuttle: None.

For more information: (See Appendix B for phone numbers, websites, and street addresses.) Call McArthur–Burney Falls Memorial State Park for operating information about Ahjumawi or visit their website.

46 Eagle Lake

Character: Wildlife and fish abound at this huge remote gem bounded by mountain forest and high desert.

Size: 13 miles long, up to 5 miles wide, 60 miles of shoreline, 25,000 acres.

Elevation: 5,100 feet.

Class: Flatwater lake. SCRS I to II.

Skill level: Beginner to intermediate.

Best season: May to October.

Craft: Canoes, kayaks, sail craft, and power boats.

Hazards: Eagle Lake is notorious for gentle morning breezes that blow into afternoon gales pushing 3-foot waves. Other hazards are springtime cold water, occasional summer thunderstorms, and large power boats.

Maps: Eagle Lake by Bob Reedy, Lassen National Forest, USGS 7.5 Pike's Point, Galletin Peak, Troxel Point, Spalding Tract.

Overview: Cascade mountain forests, Great Basin Desert, and Modoc Lava Plateau all come together at Eagle Lake. California's second-largest natural lake is a closed basin, meaning a few streams flow in, but no streams flow out. As a result, the lake has accumulated salts that make the water alkaline.

A product of this circumstance are the Eagle Lake rainbow trout. Fisheries biologists believe Eagle Lake trout to be a subspecies adapted to the lake's alkaline waters, where no other trout will survive. The popular trout quickly grow to 18 inches long and weigh 3 to 5 pounds. Two fish per day is the limit.

Diverse habitat supports a wonderful variety of wildlife. You can expect to see osprey, white pelicans, western grebes, ducks, and bald eagles in the summer. Mule deer are common, and pronghorn antelope visit the basin. Summer days are warm, but the nights are cool. Spring and autumn days have fewer motorboats and cooler weather. Early morning breezes often become blustery. Toward evening the winds may die down.

Lassen National Forest and the BLM provide many campgrounds around the lake. Forest Service campgrounds are on the south shore. BLM offers one developed campground at the north shore and allows shoreline camping for fully self-contained campers at Rocky Point and at designated points along the north shore and California Highway 139. Most campgrounds open by mid-May. Fees vary with location and season. Campers may use Forest Service lands if they are more than 1 mile from developed campgrounds. Camp at least 100 feet away from the water. Use existing fire rings, fire pans, or stoves. The state, Forest Service, and BLM require campfire permits for any open burning except in designated campgrounds. Other seasonal fire restrictions may apply.

The paddling: Early morning and evening are quiet times to view wildlife and enjoy smooth water. Eagle Lake is large and the winds do not allow paddling most afternoons except in protective areas, so plan your exploration accordingly.

Eagle Lake

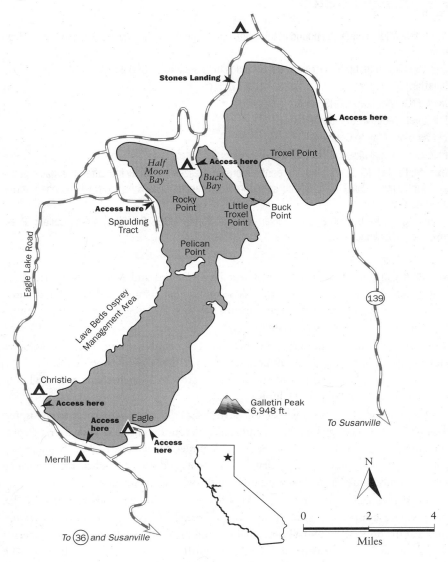

Several long peninsulas divide the lake into large lobes that are like several separate lakes. The largest and deepest is the southern lobe. Merrill and Christie campgrounds are the nicest developed locations around the lake. Merrill is popular with the fishing motor boat set since the shore is smooth and the campsites are close-by. Christie is more wooded and a better starting point to explore the southwestern shoreline. Remember that the waters south of Pelican Point are the largest and most exposed part of the lake.

Western grebes like this one congregate at Eagle Lake.

The 5.5 miles of rugged shoreline from Christie Beach to Pelican Point has many small inlets and points to explore. Along the southern third, Brockman Flat Lava Beds come down to the water's edge. An Osprey Management Area contains this shoreline, including Pelican Point. At higher lake levels, Pelican Point becomes an island. North of Pelican Point, the lake is less than 20 feet deep. Spalding Tract residential development occupies 2 miles of lakeshore in Half Moon Bay. The bay's west and north shorelines are marshy with aquatic grass growing 100 yards into the shallow lake. In sharp contrast, Rocky Point's east shore is steep lava rock down to the water. Not a place to be paddling during a westerly wind!

Near Rocky Point is Buck Bay. A dirt road to the BLM camping area and fishing access leads down the west side. The topography shelters the 0.8-mile-wide bay on three sides, but the mouth is exposed to the prevailing southwesterlies. From the north end to the tip of Buck Point is 2.4 miles. The channel between Buck Point and Troxel Point is 0.6 miles wide. It leads to the shallow, northernmost lobe of the lake. The shorelines are sandy, with grass growing from the shallows closest to shore. Little of the shoreline is appealing for camping.

The most interesting views are along the eastern sides of the southern lobe. Black Mountain rises 1,100 feet above the water and Galletin Peak summits at 6,948 feet. Here the lake reaches its deepest point, more than 70 feet. This shoreline is home to the CSU Chico Biological Station and the Lassen Youth Camp.

Eagle Lake Marina is protected by high sea walls.

Access: Eagle Lake Marina: From CA 36, turn north on Lassen County Road A-1 (Eagle Lake Road) about 3 miles west of the CA 139 junction in Susanville. Follow A-1 north for 12 miles to the south shore of the lake. Galletin, Merrill, Christie, and Marina campgrounds and day-use areas facilitate hand-launch boats. The Marina has a concrete launch behind a protective breakwater. All roads are paved.

Spalding Tract: From the south shore follow A-1 around the west side of the lake to the Spalding Tract turnoff. Go to the lakeshore, then turn north to the marina and launch ramp.

Rocky Point: From Spalding Tract, follow A-1 eastward, climbing the hill north of Rocky Point. Stop and enjoy the great view. Continue north back down to lake level and turn south onto the dirt road to the BLM Rocky Point Fishing Access.

Stone Landing: From A-1 at the northwest corner of the lake, take the side road to the docks at Stones Landing.

BLM access on CA 139: 4 miles south of the CA 139 junction with A-1. An easily accessible gravel ramp leads to shallow water.

Shuttle: Varies from none to 1 hour.

For more information: (See Appendix B for phone numbers, websites, and street addresses.) To verify that the campgrounds are open, contact the Lassen National Forest Eagle Lake Ranger Station. To check the status of BLM lands, call the Eagle Lake Field Office or view their website.

⛆ 47 Juniper Lake

Character: Sparkling mountain lake beside the Lassen Wilderness Area.
Size: 1.5 miles long, 0.8 mile wide, 5.0 miles of shoreline.
Elevation: 6,792 feet.
Class: Flatwater lake.
Skill level: Beginner.
Best season: July to September. Closed due to snow the rest of the year.
Craft: Canoes, kayaks, and other non-motorized craft.
Hazards: Cold mountain water offsets Juniper Lake's charms all summer long. Afternoon winds can make paddling difficult. Avoid being on the lake when summer thunderstorms threaten.
Maps: Lassen Volcanic National Park, Lassen National Forest, USGS 7.5 Mount Harkness.

Overview: Juniper Lake lies on a vast lava plateau more than 1 mile above sea level. The Tahoe clear water is fed by snowmelt from the surrounding peaks stretching above 7,500 feet. Lassen's 10,457-foot peak is easily visible 11 miles to the west. About one-third of the shoreline is designated wilderness area. Private cabins blend in with the northwest shore. The nearby trailheads offer attractive hiking trails to other lakes and mountains.

Lassen Volcanic National Park is a fee area. The park requires reservations for group camping at Juniper Lake Campground. Depending on snowmelt, cars may be left some distance from the designated campsites. Bring drinking water or be prepared to treat it. Lakeside camping is prohibited.

The paddling: Halfway between the earth and the sky, paddling on Juniper Lake is like floating above shimmering blue and violet crystals. Streamers of sunlight stab to the depths. Even in shallow areas, the clarity of the water makes the true depth hard to judge.

To the east, the heights of Eagle Cliffs overlook the lake. To the south, snow drapes the slopes of Mt. Harkness for much of the summer. Saddle Mountain guards the west. From the eastern half of the lake, Lassen Peak protrudes above the richly forested hills.

With a perimeter of only 5 miles, you can easily paddle around the lake in three hours. Early mornings often provide mirror-smooth water that clearly shows the bottom features. As the sky changes hue, the colors of the lake change, too. The afternoons offer warm sunshine, which is quickly offset by a dip in the lake. Beware of afternoon breezes that become strong winds. The park service requires that a personal floatation device be used by everyone floating on the lake.

Juniper Lake

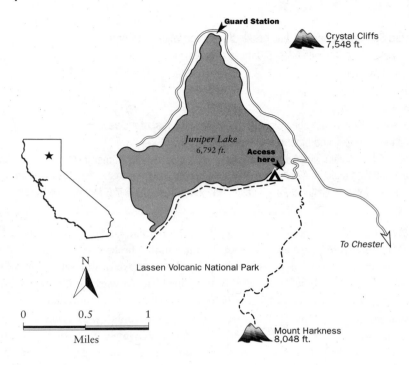

Access: In the southeast corner of Lassen Volcanic National Park, Juniper Lake is accessible after the snow melts in June. From California Highway 36 in Chester, turn north on Feather River Drive. Follow the signs 13 miles to Juniper Lake. The first 6 miles of the road are paved before it changes to a steep gravel road. LVNP advises that trailers not use the road.

Two launching sites exist: A 100-yard carry near the picnic site and campground at the east end of the lake; and 1.4 miles farther, the road is right beside the water. Good parking is available at the adjacent trailhead.

For more information: (See Appendix B for phone numbers, websites, and street addresses.) To verify that the road is open and that the campground is available for use, call Lassen Volcanic National Park or view their Internet site.

High mountain air and crystal clear water are two of the attractions of Juniper Lake in Lassen Volcanic National Park.

48 Round Valley Reservoir

Character: Small, quiet, picturesque high-country lake with good warm-water fishing.
Size: 1.2 miles long, 0.5 mile wide, oval shape.
Elevation: 4,470 feet.
Class: Flatwater lake.
Skill level: Beginner.
Best season: May to October. Access is difficult due to snow the rest of the year.
Craft: Canoes, kayaks, and other small craft.
Hazards: Snowmelt feeds Round Valley Reservoir so the water is cold early in the summer. Afternoon winds can make paddling difficult. Avoid being on the lake when summer thunderstorms threaten.
Maps: Plumas National Forest, USGS 7.5 Crescent Mills.

Overview: Round Valley Reservoir exudes relaxation. Lily pads dot much of the surface, and people fish for bass, bluegill, and catfish. The Indian Valley Chamber of Commerce claims that the California record for largemouth black bass was a 14-pounder taken from Round Valley in 1948. Even when we visited on the Fourth of July it was uncrowded.

The 4,500-foot elevation offers cool evenings. The pine- and fir-covered hillsides reach above 5,500 feet in the lovely Sierra-Cascade setting of the Plumas National Forest.

A Forest Service picnic area is found on the northeast shore about 0.5 mile from the dam. The only remaining campground at the lake is the privately operated Round Valley Lake Resort, 1 mile from the dam. No telephone or electricity exists at the lake. The resort offers running water, hot showers, and flush toilets for a fee. They allow no swimming since the lake is a public water supply for the town of Greenville.

The paddling: The lake's perimeter is less than 5 miles, an easy distance to paddle in two hours. One can explore the lily pads of the north and west shores where the bass may lie, or paddle the open water. Early mornings usually offer the quietest water. The afternoons offer warm sunshine. Beware of afternoon breezes that become winds.

Access: From California Highway 89 south of Greenville, turn west onto Hideaway Road at the Greenville town line. Look for the "Round Valley Lake" sign. Follow Hideaway Road parallel to the railroad tracks to Round Valley Road. Turn left and climb 2.1 miles along the paved, steep, crooked Round Valley Road to Round Valley Reservoir. Signs advise against trailers.

Alternatively, from the center of Greenville on CA 89, turn right (south) on Main Street. Main Street soon becomes Wolf Creek Road, then crosses the railroad tracks. Continue to the junction with Hideaway Road, and bear right onto Round Valley Road.

Two easy launching sites exist: 1) Where Round Valley Road meets the lake next to the small dam, the shore is gentle and you can drive a vehicle to the water's edge. Parking is nearby. 2) From the dam, turn left and follow the paved road 0.9 mile to the Round Val-

Round Valley Reservoir

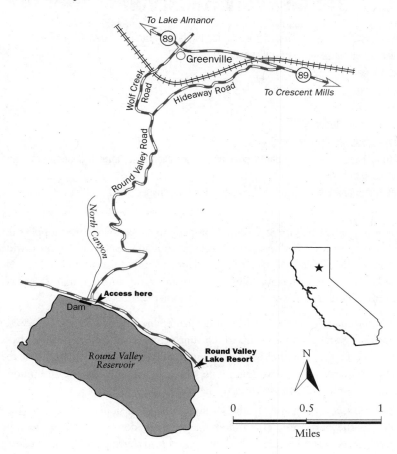

ley Lake Resort. The resort offers easy put-in, a small dock, and canoe and fishing boat rentals.

For more information: (See Appendix B for phone numbers, websites, and street addresses.) Contact the Round Valley Lake Resort by telephone or visit their website.

Mountain Meadow Reservoir

Character: A big sky and Lassen Peak dominate this big lake in remote mountains.

Size: 5,800 acres, 6.5 miles long, 1.5 miles wide.

Elevation: 5,046 feet.

Class: Flatwater lake.

Skill level: Beginner.

Best season: May to October.

Craft: Canoes, kayaks, and power boats.

Hazards: Natural hazards are springtime cold water, occasional summer thunderstorms, and winds on a large open lake.

Maps: Plumas National Forest, USGS 7.5 Westwood East, Westwood West.

Overview: Built by the Pacific Gas & Electric Company to supplement water supplies for the North Fork Feather River hydropower projects, Mountain Meadow Reservoir is wide and shallow. The only recreational facility is the launch ramp adjacent the Indian Ole Dam. Private lands surround the lake. Summer days are warm, but the nights are cool. Spring and autumn days have fewer motorboats and cooler weather.

The paddling: Paddling this big shallow lake under azure blue skies is a delight. The western end consists of several deeper bays up to 0.5 mile across. To the east, the lake opens dramatically. Much of the shoreline is shallow, inundated grasslands. Four miles of the northeast shore are marsh. With these conditions, expect to get your feet wet and muddy when you land along the eastern two-thirds of the lake.

In mid-lake the scenery is grand. To the south, pine-covered slopes rise to 7,490-foot Keddie Ridge. To the northwest, 10,457-foot Lassen Peak dominates the scene. The extreme western end of the lake is accessible from a gravel road skirting the water. The carry is 100 yards between the cow patties. Early morning and evening are quiet times to view wildlife and enjoy smooth water. Plan your actions in case strong winds pick up.

Access: From Chester travel 10 miles east on California Highway 36 to the junction with CA 147. Go south on CA 147 toward Clear Creek, then turn east on Lassen County Road A21 toward Westwood. Follow Lassen A21 about 0.8 miles to a well-used gravel road heading south. (If you pass the Lassen Power Plant, you have gone too far east.) Turn south and follow the forks southeastward to Indian Ole Dam and a dirt parking area.

The east shore is accessible from a dirt road connecting to Plumas National Forest Road 28N02 at Section 24, Township 28 North, Range 9 East. To get there, go west of Westwood on CA 36, turn south on Lassen A21 for 0.3 mile, then turn east onto Old Town Road. After several miles Old Town Road passes through a big wooden arch, skirts the marshes, and continues past a quarry reaching the unnamed road about 6.5 miles from Lassen A21. Turn west.

Mountain Meadow Reservoir

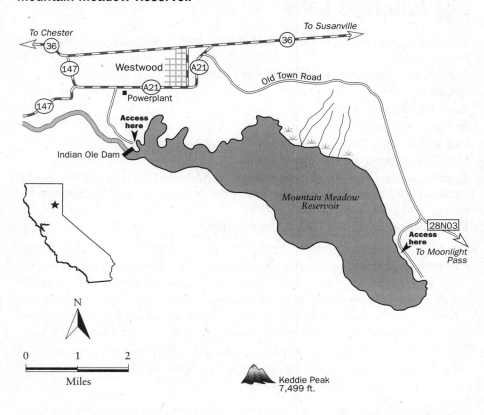

To Chester

To Susanville

36

36

147

Westwood

A21

Old Town Road

A21

147

Powerplant

Access here

Indian Ole Dam

Mountain Meadow Reservoir

28N03

Access here

To Moonlight Pass

N

0   1   2

Miles

Keddie Peak
7,499 ft.

For more information: (See Appendix B for phone numbers, websites, and street addresses.) To verify that nearby campgrounds are open, call the Plumas National Forest or the Lassen National Forest or view their websites. To reserve a campsite, contact the National Recreation Reservation System.

50 | Antelope Lake

Character: Antelope Recreation Area provides camping, boating, and fishing in a lovely forested mountain setting.

Size: 930 acres, irregular shaped, approximately 3 miles long.

Elevation: 5,025 feet.

Class: Flatwater lake.

Skill level: Beginner.

Best season: May to October.

Craft: Canoes, kayaks, and power boats.

Hazards: The popularity of power boats and jet skis on Antelope Lake is the primary hazard to paddlers. Other hazards include springtime cold water, occasional summer thunderstorms, and visits by bears in the campgrounds.

Maps: Plumas National Forest, USGS 7.5 Antelope Lake.

Overview: Located on Upper Indian Creek, Antelope Lake is the northernmost reservoir of the State Water Project. Its recreational features include three campgrounds, three day-use areas, and a three-lane boat ramp. The campgrounds have piped water, flush or vault toilets, stoves or fire circles, tables with benches, and parking spaces. The Forest Service permits camping only at the 194 campsites. Antelope Recreation Area is a fee area.

The California Department of Fish and Game stocks the lake with rainbow and brook trout. Summer days are warm, but the nights are cool. Spring and autumn days have fewer motor boats and cooler weather.

The paddling: Paddling is a delight along the many bays and peninsulas of Antelope Lake's 15 miles of shoreline. Early morning and evening are quiet times to view wildlife and enjoy smooth water. Later when the motorboaters emerge, there are many sandy places along the shoreline to fish, picnic, and swim. The pine-covered hillsides are a delight to explore. The irregular shape of the lake makes it easy to paddle from the middle of the water to shore.

Access: From California Highway 89, 6 miles north of the junction of CA 70 and CA 89, take Arlington Road (Road A22) east to Taylorsville, continue on to Genessee, then follow Indian Creek Road to Antelope Lake (27 miles from CA 89). Hand-launch boats can put in at Lone Rock and Long Point Campgrounds, the day-use areas, or the boat ramp on the north shore. All roads are paved.

For more information: (See Appendix B for phone numbers, websites, and street addresses.) To verify that the campgrounds are open, contact the Plumas National Forest. To reserve a campsite, contact the National Recreation Reservation System.

Antelope Lake

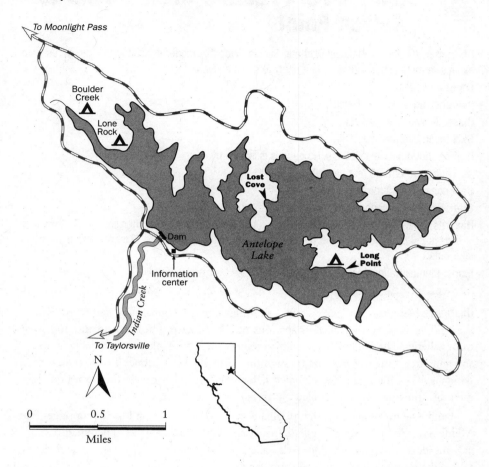

Middle Fork Feather River—Sloat to Nelson Point

Character: An original National Wild and Scenic River, this moderate whitewater run drops from expansive mountain meadows into a richly forested canyon.

Length: 8 miles.

Average run time: 3 to 5 hours.

Class: II+ with one Class III-.

Skill level: Intermediate.

Optimal flow: 500 to 1,500 cfs. No gauges exist nearby.

Average gradient: 30 feet per mile.

Best season: April through June.

Craft: Whitewater canoes, kayaks, and inflatables.

Hazards: Since the Middle Fork Feather is runable during and soon after snowmelt, the water is always cold. Do not miss the take-out, since it leads to a remote Class V canyon with few take-outs.

Maps: Plumas National Forest, USGS 7.5 Blue Nose Mtn. and Johnsville.

Overview: Designated in 1969 as one of the original nine National Wild and Scenic Rivers, the Middle Fork Feather exhibits spacious meadows, deep, forested canyons, and great trout fisheries. The Union Pacific railroad follows the right bank but is generally unobtrusive and after 3 miles disappears through the Spring Garden Tunnel. Before the canyon's national designation, engineers studied it for stair-stepped hydroelectric power development like the now concrete-girdled North Fork Feather River.

Unlike many Sierra rivers that originate as steep snowfields on high Sierra ridges, the Middle Fork of the Feather originates between 4,000 and 5,000 feet. The broad pastures and meadows of Sierra and Mohawk Valleys soak up copious winter snows and slowly release the moisture to the river all spring and early summer.

I've run this reach as early as April and as late as June. Recent rainfall and snowmelt add to the whitewater challenge. At low summer flows, you bump through the riffles, float the pools, and enjoy the scenery. The Merrimac gauge is so far downstream and collects water from so many tributaries that its readings are not suitable indicators of the Sloat run.

Note: Do not confuse this run with the very remote and extremely difficult canyon from Nelson Point to Milsap Bar.

The paddling: At Sloat, the river left provides a convenient gravel bar put-in. The opposite bank is steeply cut cobbles. Shake the kinks out quickly because the water converges at the first turn to form a chute with bouncy waves and a strong eddy on river right.

The run continues with Class II gravel bar rapids at every turn. It is busy enough so that you don't readily notice that the pine-covered terraces are dipping into a steeper canyon. After 1.5 miles, both banks climb into fir-draped slopes. About the place that the

Middle Fork Feather River—Sloat to Nelson Point

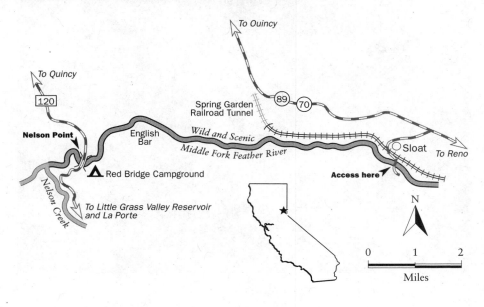

railroad seeks a flatter grade through a tunnel, the river steepens to provide some spicy bedrock rapids. With holes and boulders to negotiate, at 600 cfs or more, some of the rapids may rate Class III.

Three miles from the Red Bridge takeout, the river has cut a canyon 1,800 feet deep. Below English Bar the rapids ease a little and the pools lengthen, so enjoy the tranquility. Soon Red Bridge comes into view. **That is the take-out with no alternative downstream!**

Access: From Quincy go east 2.9 miles on California Highway 70 to the stoplight at the Safeway Store. Continue on CA 70 another 11 miles. Turn south toward the Sloat Mill and go 1.2 miles across the railroad tracks and the river. Almost immediately turn left onto a road into undeveloped real estate lots. Put in 50 to 100 yards upstream of the bridge. As an alternative, park on the north side of the river near the stock corral.

To get to the take-out, go back toward Quincy on CA 70. East of the Safeway stoplight, turn south onto Forest Service Road 120 toward LaPorte. The road leads 7.8 miles beside spacious meadows, climbs over the hills and through the woods to the river crossing at Red Bridge. On the north side of the bridge is a small day-use area with an easy take-out and parking next to the river. On the south side Red Bridge campground is perched above the river near the site of Nelson Point.

Shuttle: 20 miles (40 minutes).

Middle Fork Feather River between Sloat and Nelson Point.

For more information: (See Appendix B for phone numbers, websites, and street addresses.) Contact the Plumas National Forest by telephone or visit their website for campground information.

![52] Little Grass Valley Reservoir

Character: Rimmed with campgrounds, this isolated reservoir provides boating and fishing in a scenic, forested mountain location.

Size: 3 miles long, 0.5 mile wide at the narrowest point, 16 miles of shoreline. The reservoir's 1,930 acres are shaped like a goat.

Elevation: 5,046 feet.

Class: Flatwater lake.

Skill level: Beginner.

Best season: June through October.

Craft: Canoes, kayaks, and powerboats.

Hazards: Power boats and jet skis are the primary hazards. Natural hazards are springtime cold water, occasional summer thunderstorms, and isolation from communities with hospitals.

Maps: Plumas National Forest, USGS 7.5 American House, La Porte.

Overview: In the 1850s, the gold miners were snowbound at La Porte. Some Norwegians made traditional long skis steered with a pole. These led to some of the earliest ski races in the United States. Today the deep snows around La Porte still attract winter recreation, including Boy Scout Frostbite Camporees and snowmobiling.

Some private cabins adjoin the road and the lake from La Porte toward the dam. Except for this 2 miles of private property, the Plumas National Forest provides public access to the lake. Running Dear, Red Feather, Little Beaver, Wyandotte, Peninsula Tent, and Black Rock campgrounds have tables, stoves, water, and toilets. They permit camping only at the 290 designated campsites. Little Grass Valley Reservoir is a fee area.

Fishing is very popular for German brown and rainbow trout and catfish. Swimming is pleasant at the day-use beaches. Summer days are warm, but the nights are cool. Spring and autumn days have fewer motorboats and cooler weather. Campgrounds are open from June 1 through October 31, snow permitting.

The paddling: The long arms of this clear lake are a delight to paddle. The bare face of Grass Valley Bald Mountain looks down from the north. Osprey float overhead and maintain a nest in a snag on the high ground above Wyandotte Campground. The red fir growing along the rocky shoreline is a sign of the cold winters.

You can easily paddle the length of the lake and return in a few hours. Plan a full day to carefully explore all the shoreline. Early morning and evening are quiet times to view wildlife, enjoy the smooth surface water, and try your luck fishing.

Access: From Marysville follow California Highway 20 east 11.5 miles, then turn north on Marysville Road (E21) toward Browns Valley and La Porte. Continue 55 winding miles through Browns Valley, Challenge, and Strawberry Valley to La Porte. Follow the signs 2 more miles to Little Grass Valley Reservoir and a paved road around the lake.

Little Grass Valley Reservoir

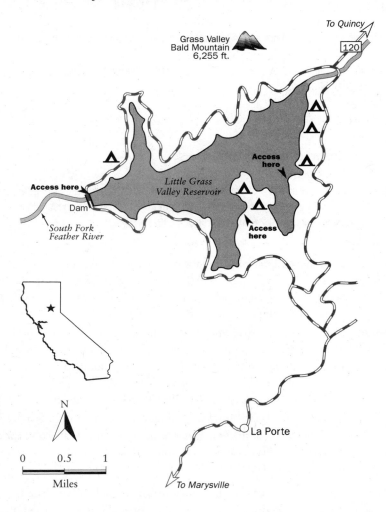

If your approach is from Reno or Quincy, take CA 70 to Forest Service Road 120, at the stoplight 2.9 miles east of Quincy. Take this mountain road 7.8 miles past picturesque meadows, over forested hills, and down into the Middle Fork Feather River Canyon. Cross this National Wild and Scenic River, then ascend steeply for 20 unpaved miles. Pass Pilot Peak (7,457 feet) and follow intermittently paved FR 22N60 to Little Grass Valley Reservoir.

Three boat ramps and two day-use areas give great lake access for hand-launch boats.

Shuttle: None.

For more information: (See Appendix B for phone numbers, websites, and street addresses.) During the spring and autumn, learn if the campgrounds and roads are open by calling the Plumas National Forest or checking their website. For campsite reservations contact the National Recreation Reservation System.

53 Bear River—Colfax to Dog Bar

Character: This intimate stream has fun riffles when releases are high enough.

Length: 4.6 miles.

Average run time: 2 to 4 hours.

Class: II.

Skill level: Intermediate.

Optimal flow: 450 to 1,000 cfs (inflow to Lake Combie).

Water source: Rollins Reservoir minus Bear Canal diversions.

Average gradient: 17 feet per mile.

Best season: Winter and spring.

Craft: Whitewater canoes, kayaks, inflatable kayaks, and rafts.

Hazards: Cold water flows from Rollins Reservoir. Brush grows on a few gravel bars. The last drop above Dog Bar is more demanding than the rest of the reach.

Maps: USGS 7.5 Colfax, Lake Combie.

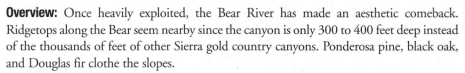

Overview: Once heavily exploited, the Bear River has made an aesthetic comeback. Ridgetops along the Bear seem nearby since the canyon is only 300 to 400 feet deep instead of the thousands of feet of other Sierra gold country canyons. Ponderosa pine, black oak, and Douglas fir clothe the slopes.

At Taylor Crossing, the mining equipment and mounds of black and white rock are relics from the gravel quarry days. Homes above the Nevada County riverbanks now enjoy canyon views. Nevada Irrigation District releases water from Rollins Reservoir to supply the Bear River Canal and Lake Combie. The portion going to Lake Combie flows in this river reach. Placer County operates the popular Bear River Park and Campground. Make camping reservations well in advance.

For many years, the River Touring Chapter of the Sierra Club paddled 4 more miles from Dog Bar to Lake Combie. The former take-out has been sold, the lands surrounding the lake are now private residences, and a gravel operation gates and posts its roads against trespass. So no public access from the Bear River is currently available near Lake Combie.

The paddling: The delightful Bear is not often run due to the rarity of adequate flows during warm weather. Enjoy the river when the chance occurs.

At the put-in, the Bear runs clear, fast, and shallow. Almost immediately, an easy rapid provides warm-up practice and displays the degree of difficulty for most of this stretch. It is a good place to practice eddy turns and ferries across the wide stream. Downstream 0.25 mile, the Bear turns abruptly south through a brushy gravel bar. Most of the water initially slides to the right and center, before it returns to the left. A clear channel starts near the

Bear River—Colfax to Dog Bar

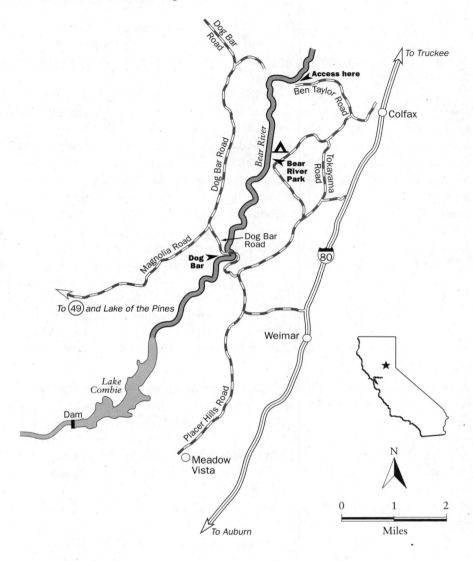

head of the riffle on river left. Such conditions can change with any winter storm. A little farther, the river braids through more brush. The good news is that very little brush exists below here.

For over a mile the canyon runs due south. The winding channel provides frequent Class II gravel bar rapids. At 600 cfs, you can easily find a channel. Occasional boulders provided fun sport and midstream eddies. Downstream, a hillside house and power lines

with orange balls become prominent. They mark another rapid, maybe a little more difficult than the earlier ones.

This is also the upstream end of Placer County's Bear River Park at Plumtree Crossing.
The popular campsites and day-use facilities stretch 1.5 miles along the left bank. Inner
tubing, sun bathing, and gold panning are common. The day-use area is the midpoint of
the boating run and an ideal intermediate put-in or take-out.

Past the Plumtree day-use area, the river curves into a long rapid. Downstream the
group campground sits on the left bank and some homes are set back on the right side. At
a bouncy rapid, the river abruptly narrows to one-third of its earlier width. Then the river
turns westward and enters a mini-gorge, and the rapids become a challenge to open canoes.

The *pièce de résistance* of the run is a drop between boulders into a hole only one and
one-half boat lengths from a vertical wall at right angles to the channel. A small eddy on
the left provides a place to land and inspect the drop. Ledges clutter the river right. The
center offers a clear channel over a submerged boulder into a hole ready to swamp the
unwary. A route tight against the left bank misses the hole. Generous eddies at the bottom
provided good picture-taking locations. Faint-hearted paddlers can portage on the left. (A
0.25 mile hike upstream from the Dog Bar Bridge provides a good view of this drop.)

Below the drop, smooth water flows through a rock-walled mini-gorge. The locals like
it for swimming, fishing, and its proximity to Dog Bar Bridge. The take-out is below the
bridge on the right. For those with excess energy, a line of widely spaced boulders offers
more play at the bottom of Dog Bar. Take out here unless you have personal acquaintances
that own waterfront property on Lake Combie! There is no public access for the next 5
miles of river.

Access: Ben Taylor Road near Colfax: Exit Interstate 80 at Colfax and follow signs to Old
Colfax. After crossing the railroad tracks go straight onto Grass Valley Road to first stop
sign. Turn left onto Rising Sun, which curves around the hill to another intersection with
stop signs. Turn right onto Ben Taylor Road, which heads down the hill past Colfax High
School, bears left, and narrows. It ends at a broad circle above the river. The upstream footpath winds down through blackberries to the river. (Although tempting, the gated and
posted downstream road is a longer carry to the river.)

Bear River Park: From Colfax go west on Tokayama Road that becomes Placer Hills
Road. Turn north (downhill) to the park.

Dog Bar Road bridge: For the shuttle, follow Ben Taylor Road back to the stop signs.
Go west on Tokayama Road which becomes Placer Hills Road. Follow Placer Hills Road
to Dog Bar Road. Go down the winding, sometimes one-lane Dog Bar Road to the bridge.
Although the easiest take-out is downstream on river right, the Nevada County enforces
its no-parking signs, so park on the Placer County (south) side.

Shuttle: 8.7 miles (20 minutes).

For more information: (See Appendix B for phone numbers, websites, and street
addresses.) Call Placer County for campground reservations. For streamflows, call Nevada
Irrigation District Operations Center.

54 Lake Spaulding

Character: A gigantic granite bowl that captures Sierra sunlight, exhilarating air, and liquid snow.
Size: 2.0 miles long, 0.5 miles wide, and 9.0 miles of shoreline.
Elevation: 5,011 feet.
Class: Flatwater lake.
Skill level: Beginner.
Best season: Summer and autumn.
Craft: Canoes, kayaks, and power boats.
Hazards: The potential hazards of Lake Spaulding are easily avoidable. Buoys mark the discharge from the Rim Powerhouse. Motor craft prefer the middle of the lake, so stay close to the shore. When snowmelt fills the South Fork of the Yuba River in May and June, the torrent roars down the cataract through the narrow gorge and into the lake. Stay out of the gorge if the current is strong, since the turbulence can easily upset a boat.
Maps: Tahoe National Forest, USGS 7.5 Blue Canyon, Cisco Grove.

Overview: Lake Spaulding practically shouts for paddlers to visit. The skies are normally deep blue and the water sparkling clear. Mountain ridges soar 2,000 feet above lake level. Easily accessible in a spectacular setting, Lake Spaulding is a major storage reservoir for Pacific Gas & Electric Company's Drum Spaulding Hydroelectric Project. Pines and open granite surround the lake.

The coves and inlets on the east side of the lake provide some seclusion, particularly on weekdays. Smooth granite slabs make comfortable spots to soak up the Sierra's brilliant sunshine. By midsummer, Castle Peak's crystalline snowmelt warms enough for enjoyable swimming. The high elevation, reflection from the granite and water, and bright sun can quickly cause sunburn.

The west side of the lake offers great views, particularly the point immediately south of Rim Powerhouse. Grouse Ridge parallels the north side of the lake. Six miles to the east, Old Man Mountain is a steep granite crag that seems to be sheered on the north side. Four miles to the southeast, several antennas identify Cisco Butte. You can find the transcontinental railroad and Interstate 80, but they are not intrusive by sight or sound.

Pacific Gas & Electric operates this fee area with drive-in and walk-in camping areas near the boat-launching area.

The paddling: The boat ramp provides an easy put-in. By paddling along the west side you can easily look into the coves on the east side of the lake. It is a quick way of locating the neighbors.

Alternatively, following the eastern shoreline is enticing, since new surprises appear around each point and inlet. Some coves are small. Zebra-like stripes coat the granite. The cove near Gonelson Canyon has permanent islands and good campsites among the pines

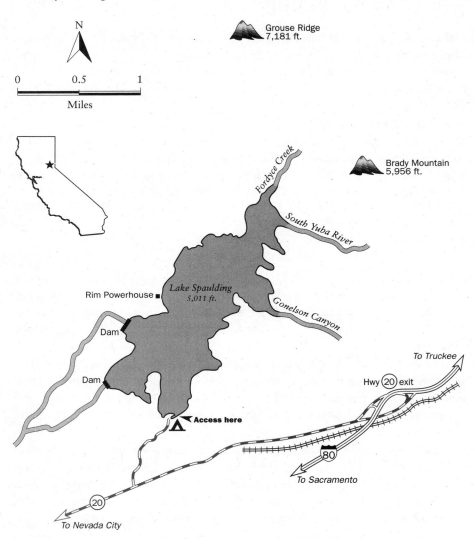

at the far end. Continuing northeast toward the head of the lake, Grouse Ridge dominates the northern skyline. A second, long cove invites inspection.

Beyond, ice and water have chiseled a long, narrow cleft in the granite. This is the South Yuba River. Beware during high runoff, as the current in the gorge is powerful with potentially hazardous turbulence in the recently thawed water. Late in the summer, the river dwindles and the lake level drops, so paddling far up this mini-gorge to the cataract is easy. The rock walls magnify the sound of water flowing under great boulders. Further

Bound by granite, Lake Spaulding offers a delightful paddlers' retreat that is easily accessible.

exploration would require a rock scramble up the steep, algae-covered slabs of granite. The pool above is pretty, but the abundant algae hint at pollutants from upstream communities. The most enticing view is looking down the gorge to the lake.

The remaining tributary to explore is Fordyce Creek at the north end of the lake. In marked contrast to the South Yuba, Fordyce is broad and boulder-strewn. Even in late summer, Fordyce, Sterling, and Meadow Lakes provide ample flows down Fordyce Creek into Lake Spaulding.

If you follow the west shore back toward the launch ramp, turn around and enjoy the view of the mountains to the east.

Access: From I–80, exit at California Highway 20. Go east on CA 20 for 2 miles, then turn right at the sign marked Lake Spaulding Recreation Area. For 0.7 miles, follow the narrow, paved road past the Pacific Gas & Electric employee houses and the camping area to the large, paved parking area above the boat ramp.

Shuttle: None.

For more information: (See Appendix B for phone numbers, websites, and street addresses.) Contact the Pacific Gas & Electric Company to learn current fees and campground availability. Contact the Tahoe National Forest, Big Bend Visitor Center about the surrounding area. They are located near I–80 at the Rainbow–Big Bend Exit.

55 Lake Valley Reservoir

Character: Forested mountain lake that is great for the family.
Elevation: 5,786 feet.
Size: 1.8 miles long, 0.25 miles wide, and 4.5 miles of shoreline.
Class: Flatwater lake.
Skill level: Beginner.
Best season: Summer and autumn.
Craft: Canoes, kayaks, and power boats.
Hazards: The hazards of Lake Valley Reservoir are few. Although motorboats are allowed, signs prohibit water skiing and jet skis. In the spring and early summer, the water is liquid snow, very cold.
Maps: Tahoe National Forest, USGS 7.5 Cisco Grove.

Overview: Peaceful Lake Valley Reservoir invites family outings. The lakeshore varies from rocky to grassy banks. Dense forests surround the lake below ridge tops rising 500 to 1,000 feet above the water. Lake Valley Reservoir is a component of Pacific Gas & Electric's Drum Spaulding Hydropower Project.

Glacier-polished granite adorns two islands that are great for sunbathing, fishing, and midsummer swimming. Sometimes yellowjackets welcome shoreline visitors. The high elevation, reflection from the granite and water, and bright sun can quickly cause sunburn.

A major feature on the west shore of the lake is Sky Mountain Camp. Their summer program offers canoeing and other aquatic activities.

Except at the campground, the shoreline is uncomfortably steep for camping. Pacific Gas & Electric operates Lodgepole Campground (fee area) near the end of Lake Valley Road west of the dam.

A major wildfire in 2001 spared the views from the lake, but destroyed nearby Eagle Mountain Nordic Center and Mountain Bike Park. Snowflower Thousand Trails Camp and hostel are nearby.

The paddling: The boat ramp at Silvertip Picnic Area provides an easy put-in and take-out. The adjacent parking usually has space for another vehicle. Since the shoreline is thickly forested, the best views are from the water. In the distance to the south, cliffs rise 600 feet above the lake. The shoreline at that end of the lake becomes grassy at lower water levels. Closer are two islands inviting exploration.

To the immediate west of the put-in is the low dam created in 1911 by Pacific Gas & Electric. The 940-foot-long structure captures water that would otherwise flow into the Wild and Scenic North Fork of the American River. Instead, Pacific Gas & Electric diverts the water to the Drum-Spaulding hydroelectric project on the Bear and South Yuba Rivers. The dam offers the most direct lake access from the Lodgepole Campground.

Lake Valley Reservoir

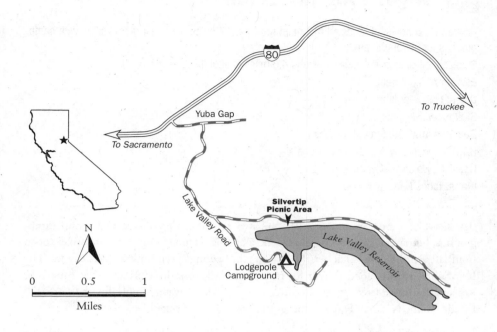

Sky Mountain campers swarm around the northernmost island and the nearby cove. The camp's permanent buildings are prominent on the west shore. Farther to the south is another island of similar size. Both have lots of bare, polished rock. Close to the second island are a few rocky islets that emerge as fishing and swimming platforms at lower water levels.

Like other mountain lakes, the breeze increases in the late afternoon. Even if it becomes too strong, this lake is small and roads encompass the reservoir.

As you return to the launch ramp, look around and enjoy the view of the mountains.

Access: From Interstate 80, exit at Yuba Gap. Go south on Lake Valley Road, bearing right at the "Y" by the big tree. Stay on Lake Valley Road past Eagle Mountain Nordic Center and Mountain Bike Park to the junction at 1.4 miles. Go left on the unpaved Mears Meadow Road (Forest Service Road 19) to Silvertip Picnic area and a concrete boat ramp. The total distance from I–80 is 1.8 miles.

Shuttle: None.

For more information: (See Appendix B for phone numbers, websites, and street addresses.) To learn current fees and campground availability, contact Pacific Gas & Electric or Eagle Mountain Nordic Center and Mountain Bike Park. Inquire about hostel availability at Snowflower Thousand Trails. Call them or check their Internet sites.

56 Sugar Pine Reservoir

Character: A beautiful, forested mountain reservoir 17 miles northeast of Foresthill, with campgrounds for the entire family.
Size: 1.1 miles long, 0.4 mile wide, and 4.0 miles of shoreline.
Elevation: 3,602 feet.
Class: Flatwater lake.
Skill level: Beginner.
Best season: April through October.
Craft: Canoes, kayaks, and power boats.
Hazards: No special hazards.
Maps: Tahoe National Forest.

Overview: Scattered around this lake are two family campgrounds, two group campgrounds, hiking trails, sandy shorelines, and a boat-launching ramp. They are usually open from late April to mid October. The 10-m.p.h. boating speed limit attracts canoes. The Fish Sniffer reports good fishing for trout and black bass. In 1981 the U.S. Bureau of Reclamation completed Sugar Pine Reservoir as a local water supply for the Foresthill Divide. Tahoe National Forest manages this concession-operated fee area.

The paddling: The launch ramp and nearby ample parking makes an attractive put-in. The forested hills are gentle right down to the sandy shores. Comfortable summer weather and excellent camping facilities make this a favorite place for family visits.

With a perimeter of only 4 miles, you can easily paddle around the lake in two or three hours. Since the lake is only a mile long, you are never very far from either camp or the launch ramp. It is really beautiful under a full moon.

Access: Exit Interstate 80 for the Foresthill Road near Auburn. Follow Foresthill Road across the North Fork American River. Continue past the Foresthill Ranger Station for 10 miles. At the Sugar Pine Reservoir sign turn north on Forest Service Road 10. Go 5.5 miles, past the OHV staging area to the boat ramp, paved parking, and rest rooms. Follow the road across the dam to reach the campgrounds.

Shuttle: None.

For more information: (See Appendix B for phone numbers, websites, and street addresses.) During the spring and autumn contact the Foresthill Ranger District by phone to learn if the campgrounds and roads are open. For campsite reservations contact the National Recreation Reservation System.

Sugar Pine Reservoir

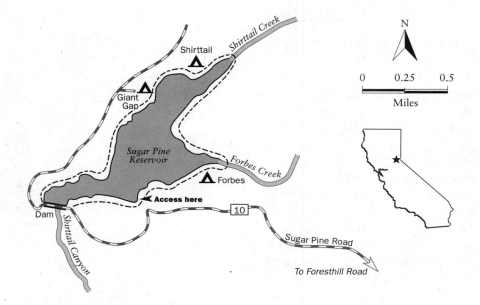

57 North Fork American River—Colfax to Lake Clementine

Character: Wild in every sense, this is a crown jewel of Sierra whitewater.

Length: 14 miles.

Class: II to IV.

Skill level: Intermediate to expert.

Optimal flow: 500 to 1,500 cfs (North Fork Dam gauge). Rafts up to 3,000 cfs.

Water source: Sierra snowmelt.

Average gradient: 31 feet per mile.

Best season: Spring through early summer.

Craft: Whitewater canoes, kayaks, and rafts.

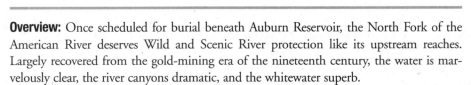

Hazards: At high flows the upper run is for experts only. Severe rapids warrant scouting and, at some flows, portaging. Be prepared for turbulent high water and very cold snowmelt in spring.

Maps: USGS 7.5 Greenwood, Colfax.

Overview: Once scheduled for burial beneath Auburn Reservoir, the North Fork of the American River deserves Wild and Scenic River protection like its upstream reaches. Largely recovered from the gold-mining era of the nineteenth century, the water is marvelously clear, the river canyons dramatic, and the whitewater superb.

Only three roads cross the river and none follow its shores. Be self-sufficient and prepared to handle your own emergencies. The way out is along the river, not up the 1,400 vertical feet of steep slopes, poison oak, and rattlesnakes.

Mother's Day weekend is often a prime time to be on the North Fork. Fed entirely by Sierra snowmelt, early May flows have yet to reach their peak, and the days are warm. If it is a big snowmelt year, flows will stay above 2,000 cfs for several weeks before and after Memorial Day. When that occurs, desirable flows sometimes last into mid-July.

Mineral Bar is a primitive campground at the Colfax–Iowa Hill bridge. Auburn State Recreation Area manages the river from here to Lake Clementine.

The paddling:

Colfax–Iowa Hill Bridge to Yankee Jim Bridge (Shirttail Canyon)

Length: 4.8 miles.

Average run time: 3 to 5 hours.

Class: IV.

Skill level: Expert.

Average gradient: 44 feet per mile.

North Fork American River—Colfax to Lake Clementine

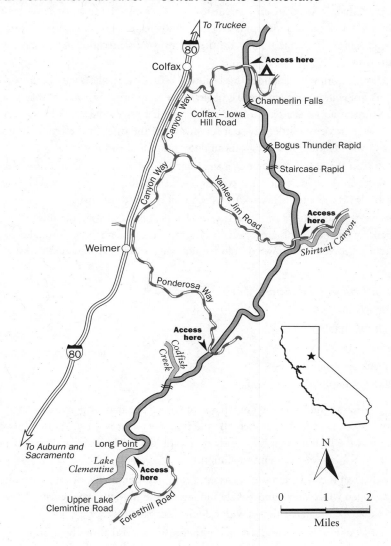

Mild riffles at the put-in present no hint of the demanding whitewater 0.25 mile down-stream. The bedrock walls converge, the channel steepens, and boaters need to catch eddies behind every rock. It is definitely a technical big-water challenge of paddle a drop, catch an eddy, and look over your shoulder for the next slot. Then do it all again.

Rafters like higher water than kayakers and whitewater canoeists. The California Department of Boating and Waterways suggests a flow range of 1,500 to 3,000 cfs for rafts. Many kayakers prefer the less powerful range of 500 to 1,500 cfs.

Chamberlin Falls drops into a two-way reversal. Not only can the hole hold a boat, but the eddy immediately downstream recirculates you back into the hole. At flows between 1,000 and 1,500 cfs, the channel splits around a midstream rock, allowing an alternative route on the right. The slippery rocks on the left provide a precarious place to scout or portage the drop.

The action continues throughout this beautiful bedrock canyon. Bogus Thunder, once named Fen's Folly after early kayaker Fen Salter, is a steep drop over ledges that deserves scouting. Staircase Rapid is a series of three ledges with a huge hole at the bottom. Scout it. Just below Staircase is a little play spot for kayaks on the right. If the water conditions are right and you're feeling up to it, you can do pop-ups and endos there.

Downstream the rapids continue at a less frantic, Class III pace. As you near Shirttail Canyon on warm days, look for some well-exposed sunbathers on the rocks. The Yankee Jim Road bridge is the middle take-out. A steep trail climbs to the bridge.

Between 350 and 500 cfs the river is very technical but lacks the big push of higher flows. Then the emerald pools are especially alluring. Still, it is not a place to take novices or inner tubes. People have drowned in low water when caught by undercut rocks.

Yankee Jim Bridge to Ponderosa Way

Length: 4.5 miles.
Average run time: 3 to 5 hours.
Class: II+.
Skill level: Intermediate.
Average gradient: 24 feet per mile.

The bridge yields a tantalizing view of what is to come. The narrow gorge stair-steps into a huge pool favored by local swimmers. By the time the water is warm enough for pleasant swimming, the boating season is nearly over. Still, the pools are luxurious attractions. Check out the fishing for trout and smallmouth bass.

While this run is easier than the upstream action, it is definitely not for new whitewater boaters. Open whitewater canoeists should have some tune-up experience. The whitewater is suitable for inflatable kayaks with experienced paddlers.

The first set of rapids is relatively easy, but they soon descend abruptly to Bunch Creek. At low water (less than 600 cfs) they require good route-finding skills to avoid the many rocks. At higher flows (above 1,000 cfs) you will want to eddy hop, watch for the holes, and play the waves. Below Bunch Creek, the mile-long straight section eases up to frequent Class II rapids. Around Sore Finger Point they become more demanding and continue almost to the Ponderosa Way bridge.

Recreational gold mining is popular in this area. They use small dredges and sluice pans to work the gravels. This activity is permitted here but prohibited in the designated Wild and Scenic River portion upstream of Iowa Hill Bridge.

Bogus Thunder Rapid on the North Fork American River.

Ponderosa Way to Lake Clementine

Length: 4.4 miles.

Average run time: 2 to 4 hours.

Class: II.

Skill level: Intermediate.

Average gradient: 19 feet per mile.

The Ponderosa bridge put-in is a popular summer swimming hole. A half mile downstream is a challenging rapid. At the end, a ledge extends from the right to produce a sizable hole in higher water. Soon the channel becomes wider. Cobbles and gravel replace boulder and bedrock rapids. Ample gravel bars offer lunch stops. Below 600 cfs, the wide gravel bar rapids reduce the water depth and massage the bottom of your boat. The long diagonal gravel bar at the mouth to Codfish Creek deserves some attention. The top left is shallow and the flow invites the paddler to go right. This is a trap, as the lower part of the bar runs down the middle of the river and supports a nasty growth of willows straining the flows.

Approaching Long Point, the river turns abruptly eastward. On the right side a shallow cave lies at water level. About 0.25 mile downstream, before the river turns right, snags await the unwary floater.

On busy summer days, the dust from vehicles on the Upper Lake Clementine Road blows upstream around Long Point to advise you that Lake Clementine is near.

The gated, steep, unpaved road is closed during winter months and may not be open until the boating season is nearly over. Early season paddlers must then hike their gear 1.4 miles up the hill to Foresthill Road or paddle 3.5 more miles to the boat ramp at the dam. See the next chapter about Lake Clementine.

Access: Colfax–Iowa Hill bridge: Exit Interstate 80 in Colfax. Go west 0.3 mile on Canyon Way to Colfax–Iowa Hill Road. Turn north, past the fire station, 3.0 miles to the river.

Yankee Jim Road bridge: Go west 1.8 miles from Iowa Hill Road including 0.7 mile past the next I–80 exit to Yankee Jim Road. Turn north and descend 4.5 miles to the river.

Ponderosa Way bridge: Continue west 2.8 miles on Canyon Way to Weimar or go west on I–80 one exit. Canyon Way and Ponderosa Way intersect about 0.2 mile east of the Weimar exit. Go north on Ponderosa Way, cross the railroad tracks, then descend 5.1 sinuous miles to the river.

Lake Clementine: Please see next chapter.

Shuttle: Colfax–Iowa Hill to Yankee Jim: 9.3 miles (25 minutes). Yankee Jim to Ponderosa Way: 12.5 miles (35 minutes). Ponderosa Way to Upper Lake Clementine: 22 miles (45 minutes).

For more information: (See Appendix B for phone numbers, websites, and street addresses.) Call the Auburn State Recreation Area for whitewater or camping information, or visit their website.

58 Lake Clementine

Character: Easy access makes this canyon lake a great place to relax and enjoy Sierra Foothills wildlife.
Size: 3.8 miles long, 0.1 mile wide, 8.8 miles of shoreline. Surface area: 280 acres.
Elevation: 715 feet.
Class: Flatwater lake.
Craft: Canoes, kayaks, fishing boats, and power boats.
Hazards: Summer water skiers share the lake at speeds up to 40 m.p.h. Beware of water spilling over the top of North Fork Dam.
Maps: USGS 7.5 Auburn, Greenwood.

Overview: In 1939 the Army Corps of Engineers created Lake Clementine when they built North Fork Dam. They built the dam to stop gold-mining debris from clogging the Lower American River. Later slated for inundation by the unbuilt Auburn Dam, popular Lake Clementine is now a part of the Auburn State Recreation Area.

A boat-launch ramp and small marina are near the dam. Several miles upstream, 20 boat-in campsites occupy sandbars. During the summer, campsites that are not reserved in advance may be available on a first come, first served basis.

The park rules stipulate that water skiing and boating be done only in a counterclockwise direction. The maximum speed within buoyed areas is 5 m.p.h. No wake is allowed at the ramp, marina, and camping areas. No swimming or water skiing is allowed in the marina area. No power boats are allowed upstream from the last boat-in camp to Upper Lake Clementine, and no dogs in boat-in camp and day-use areas. Lastly, users must pay boat-launch and camping fees.

To avoid the water skiers, visit Lake Clementine during summer weekdays or in the spring or autumn. On summer weekends, launch from the upper end where power boats are prohibited.

The paddling: Only a few minutes from I–80, the deep canyon setting quickly removes you from the hassle and hustle of the workaday world. Limestone cliffs, such as Robbers Roost, look over the narrow, winding waterway. A concrete ramp provides easy launching near the dam. Ten minutes of paddling leaves the launch area and marina behind.

Whether you are enjoying a leisurely day-long float or a brisk evening workout, Lake Clementine is a delight. During the quiet times, you can expect to see deer, waterfowl, and maybe a mountain lion. By mid-summer the clear water warms up enough for you to enjoy swimming. Only in the last mile does the water show any current. Here the water displays its finest emerald green. It may also feel a bit cooler, having just arrived from the distant Sierra snows.

The boat-in campsites are scattered along the upper third of the lake. Most are situated on enticing sandbars with partial shade from the strong Sierra sun. All have nearby floating toilets.

Lake Clementine

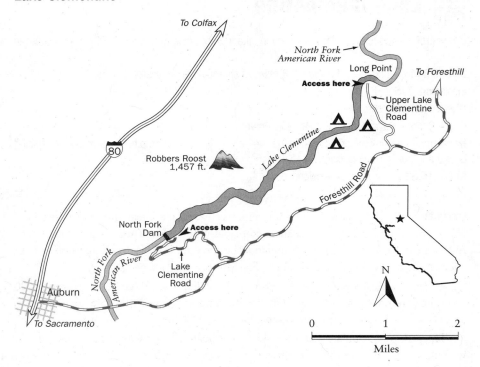

The pools and beaches near the Upper Lake Clementine parking area are popular for swimming and picnicking. This is the take-out for the North Fork American River Ponderosa Road run described in the previous chapter. At low water, you can wade the river to hike the trails along the spine of Long Point. The shady trail offers some views looking upstream. At higher water you can try your skills paddling upstream around Long Point.

Access: Exit Interstate 80 for the Foresthill Road near Auburn. Go 3.2 miles along Foresthill Road across the North Fork American River to the Lake Clementine Road. Turn left. First go up a hill, then descend 2.5 miles on a steep, paved, lane-and a-half road to the lake. Unload at the launch ramp and park in a designated spot up the hill.

At 5.7 miles from the Foresthill exit, unpaved Upper Clementine Road bounces steeply 1.4 miles down to the lake's east end. This popular day-use area has a large cobble parking area that is closer to the boat-in campsites. This road is closed to vehicles in wet weather. During the summer it is open from 7:00 A.M. to 9:00 P.M.

Shuttle: Optional in summer. Distance is 6.6 miles (25 minutes).

For more information: (See Appendix B for phone numbers, websites, and street addresses.) Call the Auburn State Recreation Area for campground and road information or visit their website.

59 **French Meadows Reservoir**

Character: A high, forested mountain reservoir with campgrounds only 9 miles from the Sierra Crest.
Size: 2.9 miles long, 0.6 mile wide, and 7.3 miles of shoreline.
Elevation: 5,263 feet.
Class: Flatwater lake.
Skill level: Beginner.
Craft: Canoes, kayaks, and power boats.
Hazards: No special hazards.
Maps: Tahoe National Forest, USGS 7.5 Bunker Hill.

Overview: Scattered around the lake are four family campgrounds, two group campgrounds, hiking trails, sandy shorelines, and two boat-launching ramps. Depending on snow conditions, they are usually open from June to October. Since a state game refuge surrounds the entire reservoir, no firearms are permitted. Placer County Water Agency completed French Meadows Reservoir for water supply and power generation. Tahoe National Forest manages this concession-operated fee area.

The paddling: Both the north and south sides of the lake have launch ramps and adjacent parking. Bring your fishing rod: maybe the trout will bite. Look east to enjoy a fine view of Granite Chief and Squaw Peaks, both more than 8,500 feet. In the early summer they will still shimmer with snow that feeds the lake.

With a perimeter of only 7.3 miles, this lake can be paddled around in a morning or an afternoon. Since the lake is only 0.6 mile wide, you are never very far from either side, should the afternoon winds pick up.

The forested hills are gentle right down to the stony shores. Sun-bleached old stumps dot the shores and provide ready-made seats. Summer days are comfortable and the nights are cool, thanks to the altitude.

Access: Exit Interstate 80 for the Foresthill Road near Auburn. Follow the Foresthill Road to Foresthill, then turn right onto paved Mosquito Ridge Road. This road provides a grand tour to the headwaters of the Middle Fork American River. Cross the North Fork of the Middle Fork bridge. Pass the turnoff to Ralston Afterbay with a great view of Horseshoe Bar, where gold miners diverted the river through a tunnel. Maybe stop at the inspiring Placer Big Trees Grove, then continue along the ridgetop road to the dam. After crossing the dam, the launch ramp and parking area are 2.5 miles around the lake's south side.

Shuttle: None.

French Meadows Reservoir

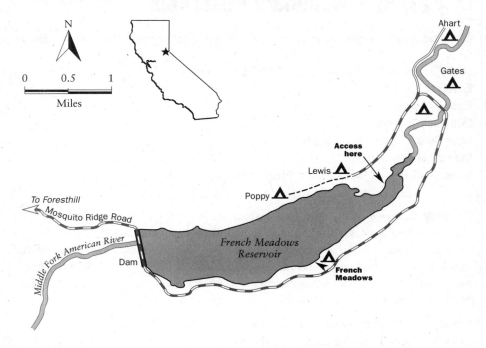

For more information: (See Appendix B for phone numbers, websites, and street addresses.) During the spring and autumn call the Tahoe National Forest Foresthill Ranger District to learn if the campgrounds and roads are open. For campsite reservations contact the National Recreation Reservation System.

Middle Fork American River— Greenwood Bridge to Mammoth Bar

Character: Reliable flows, a short shuttle, and fun fishing in a rugged gold mining canyon add to this whitewater run.

Length: 6.6 miles.

Average run time: 3 to 4 hours.

Class: II.

Skill level: Intermediate.

Optimal flow: 600 to 2,000 cfs at Middle Fork American (Oxbow Powerhouse gauge).

Water source: Frenchman and Hell Hole Reservoirs.

Best season: Spring, summer, and autumn.

Average gradient: 18 feet per mile.

Craft: Whitewater canoes, kayaks, inflatable kayaks, and rafts.

Hazards: Summer-long cold water is always a whitewater concern. Pick your poison: Both rattlesnakes and poison oak are present.

Maps: USGS 7.5 Auburn, Greenwood.

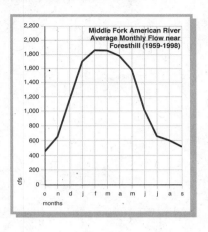

Overview: Imagine being a visitor to the Middle Fork's gold mines of the 1850s. More than 10,000 men lived and worked at Maine Bar, Kenebec Bar, and Poverty Bar. Machines and men dug deep into the riverbed gravels, obliterating the original streambed. Wood and canvas flumes carried water for mining operations. The miners stripped pines and firs from the canyon slopes. Since then, 150 years have healed the Middle Fork Canyon, but this will all be inundated if Auburn Dam is built.

French Meadows and Hell Hole Reservoirs capture river flows that Placer County Water Agency releases through Oxbow Powerhouse. The result is one of the longest boating seasons in the Sierra. Some years you can plan on Halloween trips here.

Drivers Flat Road offers good views of the biggest rapids. You can see them close up with a short hike from the put-in. Infrequently, the first rapid below the campground may be too shallow, and then the river is too low. By late summer, flows vary with hydropower fluctuations. Check the recent flow patterns. Remember that releases originate 15 miles upstream and may not reach Greenwood crossing until midday. With time to wait, walk the jeep road a mile upstream to see the falls at Ruck-A-Chucky Rapids.

Expect to see mountain bikers, horses, and hikers. Each July the Western States 100-Mile Endurance Run and the Tevis Cup 100-mile horseback ride use trails that cross and parallel this river.

The Auburn State Recreation Area limits camping to the unimproved areas near the put-in and 1 mile downstream at Cherokee Bar.

Middle Fork American River—Greenwood Bridge to Mammoth Bar

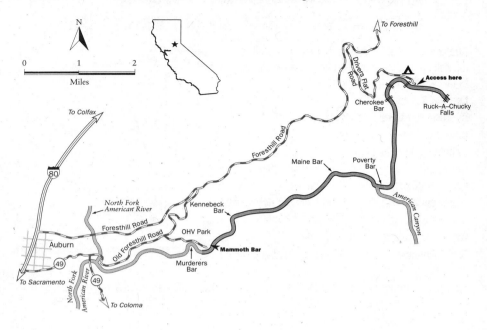

The paddling: The rapids near the put-in are the trickiest of the run. Ledges stretch across the river with narrow slots and standing waves. These chutes and short pools offer good whitewater practice. If you want to start more gradually, put in downstream at the campground where there are a long pool and sandy banks.

All the river bends have gravel bar rapids with standing waves that are just large enough to challenge open canoes with possible swamping. The first waves above Cherokee Bar are the biggest. The 1.5-mile straight stretch ends at Poverty Bar with a sand beach on the right. Slightly downstream on river left is the brush-obscured mouth of American Canyon. The canyon has attractive falls and pools accessible by trail from the next gravel bar downstream. Follow the trail upstream, past the creek crossing, and up the hill where the pools become visible.

Occasional boulders and ledges require enthusiastic maneuvering. The approaches to some rapids can be wide and shallow enough to line a canoe to get to the deeper channel. Watch for brush hanging from the banks. Large sand and gravel bars line most of the river. Broken trees and renewed sand deposits are evidence of the 1997 and 1998 floods.

Even at this low elevation, the north- and east-facing slopes have stands of Douglas fir and black oak. Ponderosa pine is common. Oak woodlands and open grass cover the upper slopes.

Dust from motorcycles may signal the Mammoth Bar take-out at a left bend. The upstream end of the bar (river right) has a fine eddy for a take-out, but this may require a long carry over cobbles unless you have a four-wheel-drive vehicle. Look it over. Another choice is to float another 100 yards downstream for much shorter access to vehicles. A seasonal sign announces the take-out. Do not float downstream to Murders Bar, as that rapid is as lethal as its name.

Access: Greenwood Bridge (site): Exit Interstate 80 for the Foresthill Road near Auburn. Go 7.5 miles along Foresthill Road across the North Fork American River high bridge. Turn right at Drivers Flat Road (sign reads "American River 3 miles"). Initially paved, Drivers Flat Road becomes gravel, then forks left at a parking lot (sign reads "Ruck-A-Chucky"), then steeply descends the canyon as a bumpy, narrow dirt road. At the bottom, cross a concrete low-water bridge to a primitive campground with day-use parking. A short distance upstream is the designated raft access and another parking area. Since parking near the put-in is limited, and serves both this stretch of river and the upstream whitewater run popular with outfitters, large groups should arrange to leave their vehicles at the upper parking lot near the Foresthill Road.

Mammoth Bar OHV Park: Turn off the Foresthill Road opposite the Lake Clementine Road and descend the Old Foresthill Road to the OHV Park turnoff. Turn onto the gravel road and drive as far as you dare toward the upstream end of the cobble bar. **Note the lockup time for the OHV Park and finish your take-out before they lock the gate.** The Old Foresthill Road connects with California Highway 49 by the old North Fork bridge at the canyon bottom.

Shuttle: 9.5 miles (25 minutes).

For more information: (See Appendix B for phone numbers, websites, and street addresses.) Call the Auburn State Recreation Area for whitewater or camping information, or visit their website.

61 South Fork American River—Chili Bar to Folsom Lake

Character: Summer-long flows, exciting pool and drop rapids, and California's gold discovery site attract crowds of rafters.

Length: 20.7 miles.

Class: II to IV.

Skill level: Intermediate to expert.

Optimal flow: 500 cfs (1000 cfs for rafts) to 2,000 cfs (Chili Bar Powerhouse).

Water source: Chili Bar Reservoir.

Average Gradient: 22 feet per mile.

Best season: Spring through autumn. Weekdays are best to avoid crowds.

Craft: Whitewater canoes, kayaks, and rafts.

Hazards: In spring expert paddlers should be prepared for turbulent high water, very cold snowmelt, and brush hazards. Hydroelectric operations may quickly change streamflows.

Maps: USGS 7.5 Garden Valley, Coloma, Pilot Hill.

South Fork American River Average Monthly Flow near Placerville (1965-1998)

Overview: *Paddling Northern California* includes this run because it is attractive, fun, rich in California history, and has a good section for open whitewater canoeists. Unfortunately, the river is too crowded during spring and summer weekends, so try to plan your trip for a weekday.

The South Fork American has three runs with different character. Chili Bar is the most difficult, combining greater steepness, strong hydraulics, and demanding technical paddling. Coloma to Lotus is the easiest, but is still powerful above 1,000 cfs and suitable for open whitewater canoeists wanting to improve their skills. Folsom Gorge is a big step up from Coloma. The Gorge is a fast roller-coaster ride, best attempted by rafters, paddlers in decked boats, or whitewater canoeists with advanced skills.

Its popularity has resulted in large crowds. Paddling out of an eddy during summer weekends is like entering a Los Angeles freeway at rush hour. The best South Fork experience is on weekdays or in the autumn. Even then you will have company.

"How much water and when?" is an often-repeated question. Like other Sierra rivers, the spring snowmelt provides torrents of cold, clear water. The amount and duration vary from year to year. A big-water year can provide flows more than 3,000 cfs for many weeks into June. During drought years, hydropower releases of 500 cfs to 1,500 cfs may dominate early summer. These releases come from Pacific Gas & Electric's Chili Bar Powerhouse. An informal agreement between Pacific Gas & Electric and rafting outfitters provides for flow releases at the Chili Bar put-in from mid-morning to early afternoon. The same releases may not arrive in Coloma until early afternoon. Check recent release patterns on the Internet. At 500 cfs, kayaks can run the river, but that flow is undesirably low for rafts.

South Fork American River—Chili Bar to Folsom Lake

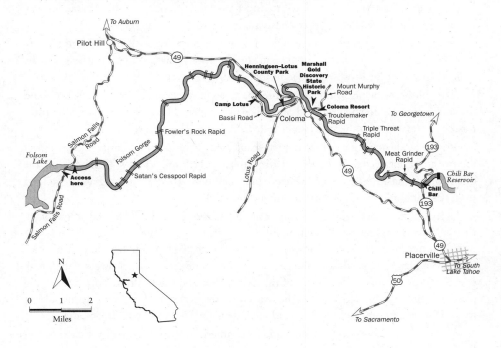

Commercial campgrounds, historic attractions, and eating places are plentiful in Coloma and Lotus.

This river is lined with many privately owned homes. Please respect and heed private property rights and rules for quiet zones. El Dorado County details the rules on annual waterproof permits that you should obtain at the put-ins. Free waterproof maps show public lands for lunch stops, toilets, and access points.

The paddling:
Chili Bar to Coloma
Length: 5.5 miles
Average run time: 2 to 4 hours.
Class: III to IV.
Skill level: Advanced.
Average gradient: 33 feet per mile.

Put in at the Chili Bar gravel flat below the California Highway 193 bridge. In the center channel is a hole that has been the site of the Chili Bar Whitewater Rodeo. If it is a summer weekend, many rafts may be around you, some with crews learning how to paddle. If it is spring, then the snowmelt will be flowing high and fast down this rollicking, powerful river.

Downstream 0.2 mile, several points of a ledge protrude across the surface. Beyond is Meatgrinder (Quartermile) Rapid. Meatgrinder is long, fast, rocky, has big hydraulics, and requires your full attention. This is a nasty place to swim.

Racehorse Rapid drives into the right rock wall as the river turns left. After that there is a good eddy, the gradient flattens, and during lower flows you get a little rest. The braided area with the brush and grass in the middle is African Queen.

The third mile begins with Triple Threat, a series of three rapids that all have holes and big waves. It is the downstream end of public land managed by BLM, so it is a good place for lunch and to watch the whitewater rodeos sometimes held here.

Private lands occupy much of the riverbank from here to below Lotus. Please respect the private property rights. Starting at river mile 4.5 (1.5 miles below Triple Threat) the quiet zone begins. Respect homeowners' rural tranquility by not shouting and refraining from water fights. The quiet zone continues to mile 11.5.

S-Turn, a.k.a. Troublemaker, is the finale to this run. Large boulders and ledges block the right two-thirds of the channel. Scout on the left where all the onlookers decorate the rocks. From a rocky entrance, the water funnels left, through a hole next to a giant mid-stream boulder, then swirls into the left side ledges. The current then surges right to fall over the second drop. In the middle of the second drop, Gunsight Rock forms a wrapping place for rafters undecided between the two slots. Upsets abound, so it is a favorite subject for professional photographers. You can purchase their pictures of you in Coloma.

From here to the take-outs (Coloma Resort, American River Resort, CA 49, Ponderosa Park, or El Dorado County's Henningsen–Lotus County Park) the river is easy compared with the Chili Bar run. A few rapids need some attention.

Coloma to Lotus

Length: 3.5 miles.
Average run time: 1 to 2 hours.
Class: II.
Skill level: Intermediate.
Average gradient: 17 feet per mile.

While this run is much easier than Chili Bar, it is definitely not for the first-time canoeist. The North Beach area of Marshall Gold Discovery State Historic Park allows a start on slow-moving Coloma Lake, where you can get a feel for the river. Downstream 0.4 mile is an easy rapid with a hole. Where the river turns south, a rapid called Old Scary awaits. It used to be a turning (over) point for many neophytes. Now the river splits. Be alert for the strong eddies.

After the CA 49 bridge, the Henningsen–Lotus County Park is 0.5 mile downstream on the left. Some ledges and practice spots persist to the pool at Camp Lotus. Take out on river left at Camp Lotus unless you plan to run The Gorge!

Folsom Gorge—Lotus to Folsom Lake

Length: 11.5 miles.

Average run time: 4 to 6 hours.

Class: III.

Skill level: Intermediate to expert.

Average gradient: 19 feet per mile.

Put in at Henningsen–Lotus County Park or Camp Lotus. This run starts easily and increases in difficulty. The rapids are many and rafters have given most of them names. Barking Dog comes just below Camp Lotus, then comes a rock island called Current Diver. Two miles below Camp Lotus, wide rocky Highway Rapid may demand some careful water reading. Afterwards, you come closer to CA 49 behind the rafting camps on the right.

A foot access on the right follows Greenwood Creek across BLM lands. It is also the end of the Coloma-Lotus quiet zone.

The river narrows into a long bouncy wave train with good eddies. It is a favorite play spot for whitewater canoes and kayaks. Soon look for a beach and BLM toilet on river right. As the rapids get spicier, watch the distant hilltops for the Lollypop Tree. A round-shaped tree with a bite missing, the tree marks the entrance to the rock walls and rapids of Folsom Gorge. As the channel doglegs right approaching Norton's Ravine (about 0.5 mile above Fowler's Rock), there is a small beach on the right. The toilet there is the last one until the take-out.

The entrance to The Gorge is marked by Fowler's Rock, a house-sized boulder with a hole to the left. Much of the current flows between the rock and the left wall. It is a favorite spot for rafts to wrap.

As the rocky gorge constricts, the water accelerates into big, churning waves. If you swim, you may be in the water a long while if your friends do not help.

Satan's Cesspool is the focal point of the run. Fast water from a smaller drop and a long wave train drive into Satan's. The bedrock rises from the left side, funneling the river into a narrow, nonsymmetrical drop next to a bedrock island. At higher flows, a wide eddy branches to the island's right, leading to a technical chicken chute. You have to be alert to catch it. Most kayakers catch the eddy on the left 25 yards above Satan's, pick their line, then power into the current to run the curling wave in the drop. Smile as you run this rapid, because it is a favorite photographer's site.

The gorge and whitewater action continue for 2 more miles. Squirrely water squirms under you below Satan's. Try not to swim. The ledges are hard. At Bouncing Rock Rapid the river bends left but the current drives over a ledge on the right, creating a diagonal wave with a hole on the right. Hospital Bar has a sharp drop with a steep, long wave train. Those waves are a "face wash" to surf. Depending on reservoir level you may find Surprise Rapid uncovered.

If Folsom Reservoir is high, then the last 1.5 miles will be flat water. Do not be too surprised to see motorboats towing rafts. Salmon Falls bridge marks the take-out. Paddle to the right bank upstream of the bridge. Many people use the loading zone, so try to load your stuff quickly. Commercial outfitters and their shuttle vehicles use the take-out 0.5 mile downstream on river left.

Access: All of the access points are fee areas. Chili Bar, Henningsen-Lotus, Marshall State Park, and Salmon Falls are day-use.

Chili Bar: From U.S. Highway 50 at Placerville, exit north onto CA 49. Follow CA 49 about 0.7 mile to CA 193. Take CA 193 into the steep canyon, cross the bridge, and turn left into Chili Bar (about 2.4 miles from CA 49).

Coloma, the private campground, will allow boaters who are staying overnight to take out. American River Resort borders S-Turn upstream of Coloma, off CA 49. On the opposite side of the river, Coloma Resort can be reached by crossing the one-lane bridge on Mount Murphy Road and turning upstream. North Beach of the Marshall State Park serves as a put-in for noncommercial craft. Ponderosa Park is a private campground on the right bank between Old Scary and CA 49.

Henningsen–Lotus County Park (take-out for Chili Bar trips): From the CA 49 bridge over the South Fork of the American River, go south on Lotus Road about 0.5 mile to the parking area and river access. Gated at night, the park provides toilets, outside shower, paved parking, and an easy launch. Alternatively, from U.S. 50, exit at Shingle Springs, and just north of the freeway bridge turn east onto North Shingle Road. Follow it 4 miles to Rescue. Bear right on Green Valley–Lotus Road for 0.6 mile, then go left (north) at the "Y" on Lotus Road to the park.

Camp Lotus: From Lotus Road (1 mile south of the CA 49 bridge), turn west onto Bassi Road. Follow it about 0.8 mile to private Camp Lotus on the right.

Salmon Falls Road bridge at Folsom Lake: From the CA 49 bridge over the South Fork of the American River, go west and north on CA 49 to Pilot Hill, about 6 miles. Turn south onto Salmon Falls Road, descending the curvy, narrow, paved road with scenic views about 6 miles to the river. Paved parking can be found on the north side of the bridge, road-shoulder parking on the south side. South of the bridge 0.5 mile is the large parking area for commercial and private boaters.

Alternatively from U.S. 50, exit at El Dorado Hills and go north on El Dorado Hills Boulevard. Continue north across Green Valley Road where El Dorado Boulevard becomes Salmon Falls Road. Follow Salmon Falls Road north to the bridge.

Shuttle: Chili Bar to Henningsen–Lotus County Park: 11.5 miles (40 minutes). Coloma to Camp Lotus: 2.6 miles (15 minutes). Henningsen–Lotus County Park to Salmon Falls bridge: 12 miles (30 minutes).

For more information: (See Appendix B for phone numbers, websites, and street addresses.) Contact the BLM Folsom Field Office about whitewater by phone or visit their website. Alternatively, contact El Dorado County Parks by phone or see their website. Contact information for stores, equipment rentals, campgrounds, and current conditions can be found at: www.coloma.com.

62 Truckee River—Tahoe City to River Ranch

Character: Crystal clear water, a sandy bottom, and spectacular Tahoe scenery combine to make this one of the most popular beginner float runs in Northern California.

Length: 4 miles.

Average run time: 2 to 3 hours.

Class: I with one II.

Skill level: Beginner.

Optimal flow: 200 to 800 cfs (Tahoe City gauge station per Federal Watermaster).

Water source: Lake Tahoe.

Average gradient: 12 feet per mile.

Best season: Late spring through autumn.

Craft: Canoes, kayaks, inner tubes, and small rafts.

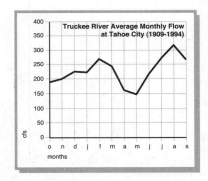

Hazards: Placer County ordinance forbids the floating or entering river when flows exceed 1,205 cfs between Tahoe City and River Ranch due to extremely low clearance between the river surface and several bridges.

Maps: Tahoe National Forest, USGS 7.5 Tahoe City.

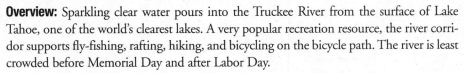

Overview: Sparkling clear water pours into the Truckee River from the surface of Lake Tahoe, one of the world's clearest lakes. A very popular recreation resource, the river corridor supports fly-fishing, rafting, hiking, and bicycling on the bicycle path. The river is least crowded before Memorial Day and after Labor Day.

From Tahoe City to Alpine Meadows Road, California Highway 89 runs along the right shore. The road provides an almost continuous view of the adjacent river. You can easily see flow conditions and rafts on the river. A half dozen small bridges cross the river to private land and private cabins.

Several Tahoe City outfitters rent rafts, provide parking, and shuttle buses from May through September. Shuttle buses pick up boaters at Bell's Landing or River Ranch, then return to the Tahoe City parking lots.

Paddlers begin their journey at the improved put-in facilities 100 yards below Fanny Bridge in Tahoe City. Folks with their own boats frequently use the 64 Acres public parking lot near the footbridge. Inner-tubers should be aware that the water stays very cold until midsummer.

Truckee River summer flows are often shallow. A federal watermaster schedules annual water releases from the top 6 feet of Lake Tahoe. The watermaster balances Tahoe flows with releases from Boca and Prosser Reservoirs. Together they provide water to Reno, irrigated lands near Fernley, Lahonton Reservoir near Fallon, and the Piute Indians at the river's natural destination, Pyramid Lake.

Truckee River—Tahoe City to River Ranch and Floriston

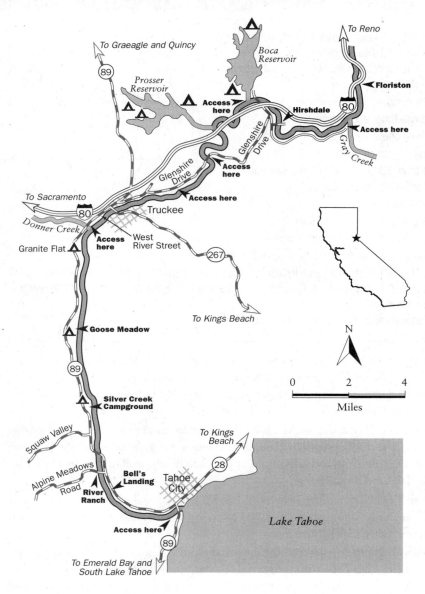

To Graeagle and Quincy

89

To Reno

Boca Reservoir

Prosser Reservoir

Floriston

Access here

Hirshdale

80

Access here

Glenshire Drive

Access here

Gray Creek

Glenshire Drive

Access here

To Sacramento

80

Donner Creek

Truckee

Access here

West River Street

267

Granite Flat

To Kings Beach

Goose Meadow

N

89

0   2   4

Miles

Silver Creek Campground

Squaw Valley

To Kings Beach

28

Alpine Meadows Road

Bell's Landing

Tahoe City

River Ranch

Lake Tahoe

Access here

89

To Emerald Bay and South Lake Tahoe

Land managers have posted rules to make the river enjoyable for everyone. They are as follows: Wear life jackets. Do not use glass bottles or containers. Use the trash cans and portable rest rooms strategically located on islands and the riverbanks. Respect private property by not trespassing and keeping noise levels down. Pull out only in designated areas to avoid fragile riverbanks. Do not go beyond River Ranch.

The paddling: Below the put-in 200 yards, a large pipe crosses the river. This is the lowest of the bridge crossings, clearing the water by two or three feet at normal flows. At any flow you should duck to get under it.

As soon as you leave Tahoe City, the first fast-water riffle occurs. Like many others to follow, enjoying the bounce and splash is easy and fun. Interspersed with the riffles are runs of smooth, fast water and slower pools suitable for wading or swimming—if you enjoy cool water.

Several islands make you choose which side to float around. You cannot go wrong. A couple of these have pleasant, sandy beaches. Grasses and alder adorn the banks and ducks frequently greet floaters, looking for handouts.

Much of this river stretch has a sandy bottom. The fir forest on river left grows down to the riverbank. Look right to the canyon cliffs to see the rocky crags of lava flows that once blocked Lake Tahoe. Today these crags bear such names as Ramparts, Thunder Cliffs, Fir Crags, and Twin Crags.

Some of the prettiest scenery is near the end. A bridge with a red beam announces this section. Two channels meander through a long, wide, flooded meadow. This wide, slow section is important because it is the end of the Class I water. On the right, the bicycle path dips almost to river level for an easy take-out at Bell's Landing, immediately up the bank.

Downstream, several fast riffles carry you toward a picturesque house on the sharp "U" bend in the river channel. Beyond that house are 100 yards of Class II rapids to River Ranch Lodge. The rapids are shallow and rocky. Rafts often bounce from rock to rock. A long tree lying on the left side of the river is a concern during high water. The rapid pauses at River Ranch pool where the rafting companies have take-out and shuttle facilities. River Ranch has a great sun deck beside the river, a fun place to eat and drink.

Before condominiums were built opposite River Ranch, the River Touring Section held annual summer whitewater slaloms on the rapids below the pool. We had great fun running the race course, being with friends in the mountains, and partying on the broad deck.

Access: Tahoe City has three parking areas. The first is called 64 Acres and is located 0.1 mile south of Fanny Bridge off California Highway 89. Second is Fanny Bridge Rafts, immediately south of Fanny Bridge off CA 89. Third is Truckee River Rafting on CA 89 just west of the "Y." The commercial rafters include parking and shuttle bus service when renting their equipment.

Bell's Landing is 0.1 mile upstream of River Ranch along CA 89. A highway turnout and limited free public parking is beside the bicycle trail. Rafting outfitters operate a larger parking lot on the other side of CA 89.

Shuttle: 4 miles (15 minutes). Buses are available to parking lots.

For more information: (See Appendix B for phone numbers, websites, and street addresses.) To ask about rafting rental operations and bus shuttle service, telephone the Truckee River Raft Company. To learn the opening dates of Silver Creek, Goose Meadows, and Granite Flat Campgrounds, call the Tahoe National Forest, Truckee Ranger District. Truckee and Tahoe City have a plentitude of overnight accommodations, restaurants, and support services. For restaurants and lodging call the Truckee Donner Chamber of Commerce or visit their website.

Truckee River—River Ranch to Floriston

(see map on page 232)

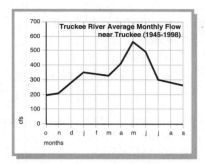

Truckee River Average Monthly Flow near Truckee (1945-1998)

Character: This modest-size whitewater stream drops from the fir forests near Tahoe to deep canyons entering Nevada.

Length: 27 miles.

Elevation: 6,160 feet at the put-in.

Class: II to IV.

Skill level: Intermediate to advanced.

Water source: Lake Tahoe, Boca Reservoir, and several tributaries during snowmelt.

Best season: Late spring through autumn, depending on reservoir releases.

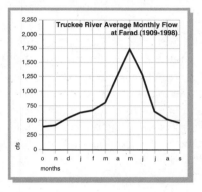

Truckee River Average Monthly Flow at Farad (1909-1998)

Craft: Whitewater canoes, kayaks, and inflatable kayaks.

Hazards: This is a rocky, high-elevation mountain stream. Trees fall and sometimes block the channel. Abutments of small bridges add to the obstacles. Between Gray Creek and Floriston, the channel steepens dramatically to a Class IV rock stairway.

Maps: Tahoe National Forest, USGS 7.5 Tahoe City, Truckee, Martis Peak, Boca.

Overview: Easy access, steady whitewater, streamside camping, and beautiful surroundings attract paddlers to the Truckee River. From River Ranch to the town of Truckee, California Highway 89 parallels the river. Forest Service campgrounds alternate with private cabins beside Class II whitewater. Below Donner Creek, the Truckee River turns east through the town of Truckee in a Class III boulder slalom. Then the river cuts through a canyon with easier, well-spaced rocks. The scenery improves as the canyon deepens on the way to Gray Creek. Below Gray Creek the channel drops steeply into a Class IV boulder-hopping challenge.

Snowmelt and water deliveries to Nevada affect stream flows in the different reaches. The tributaries between Bear Creek (from Alpine Meadows) and Donner Lake deliver snowmelt that combines with Lake Tahoe releases to dominate the flow as far as Boca. Scheduled releases from Boca Reservoir may dominate downstream flows when Tahoe releases and snowmelt are low.

The paddling:

River Ranch to Silver Creek

Length: 3 miles.

Average run time: 2 hours.

Class: III.

Skill level: Intermediate.

Average gradient: 50 feet per mile.

Optimal flow: 300 to 600 cfs (Truckee River near Truckee gauge).

This short run is a rock slalom requiring precise turns on short notice. From River Ranch pool the river drops through the rocky slalom site leading to the Alpine Meadows Road bridge. Although the gradient moderates for 0.5 mile by the old Deer Park picnic area, fallen trees have historically obstructed part of the channel.

After the CA 89 bridge, the river drops faster. Steep slopes confine the narrow, rock-strewn riverbed. Be ready to catch an eddy if a tree looms in your path. You can easily inspect a mile of this run from the new bicycle path.

CA 89 turns away from the river near Squaw Valley. The wooded right bank rises 1,700 feet to the ridge top. Abutments from the several bridges add obstacles and eddies to the river. Downstream of Squaw Creek (river left) the gradient eases and the highway returns to the river. The two separate again 0.3 mile above the take-out. Take out immediately below the next bridge. On river left is Silver Creek campground. This is the put-in for the next reach.

Silver Creek to Donner Creek

Length: 7 miles.

Average run time: 3 to 4 hours.

Class: II.

Skill level: Intermediate.

Average gradient: 30 feet per mile.

Optimal flow: 300 to 600 cfs (Truckee River near Truckee gauge).

Put-in at Silver Creek Campground for a fun whitewater run that is a major step easier than the previous stretch. Since the river is shallow and CA 89 is never far away, this is a good place to train folks wishing to improve their whitewater skills. The mountain air, many campsites, and brilliant sunshine add to the delights.

During snowmelt season, the tributary streams from Alpine Meadows, Squaw Valley, and the neighboring mountains will add more water than that released from Lake Tahoe; thus the reference gauge is near Granite Flat Campground.

We have successfully run the river at lower flows than appear appropriate from CA 89. At 250 cfs, you can reduce scraping by using some careful route finding. At any level, the paddling includes many eddy turns, midstream rocks, shallow riffles, and occasional snags. A few chutes add some bouncy excitement. One challenge involves strong currents trying to erode a house-size boulder found midstream. Another occurs where the river zigs right from the highway and a streamside cabin. The rocky rapid then zags left close to fallen trees.

Children playing, folks fishing, and occasional air-mattress riders are typical of summer days. They are most frequently encountered near Goose Meadows and Granite Flat Campgrounds, both possible take-out spots. During the early summer the meadows are lush green, painted with wildflowers.

West River Street replaces CA 89 at the Donner Creek confluence. Large, flat concrete slabs still stand in the river. Land on river left. A gravel bar and picnic area provide an easy take-out.

Donner Creek to Glenshire Drive Bridge

Length: 5.8 miles.
Average run time: 2 to 4 hours.
Class: III.
Skill level: Intermediate.
Average gradient: 41 feet per mile.
Optimal flow: 400 to 700 cfs (Truckee River near Truckee gauge).

Put in at the Donner Creek confluence. The river heads east into the center of Truckee. Buildings replace trees, and the banks run up to houses and businesses. Upstream of CA 267 large rocks create a long, busy rapid that eases after passing the bridge. You can easily see this rapid from the CA 267 bridge.

Leaving town, the gradient steepens. The river turns into a long, steep technical boulder drop with a few logs tossed in for good measure. At 800 cfs, broadsiding a boat has immediate penalties, and swimming is undesirable. The railroad runs along the left bank and provides some scouting and portage routes. The rapid continues where the railroad and river diverge near the Glenshire Drive fishing access.

Toward the regional wastewater treatment plant and Martis Creek, the rapids ease. The river bends to the north as it carves against an exposed canyon slope. The new bridge is Glenshire Drive, traditional site of a take-out on river right.

Glenshire Drive Bridge to Gray Creek

Length: 9.4 miles.
Average run time: 3 to 5 hours.
Class: II.
Skill level: Intermediate.
Average gradient: 27 feet per mile.
Optimal flow: 400 to 800 cfs (Truckee River at Farad gauge).

Like the last part of the previous run, this reach starts with rapids that are easy in a kayak and a little more demanding in a canoe. We brought kayakers with limited experience here to hone their skills.

At first, both I–80 and the railroad parallel the river. Sagebrush and scattered Jeffrey pines vegetate the landscape. Below the Glenshire Drive bridge, a fly-fishing club claims private property rights to 2.5 miles of the right bank. Their land extends past Prosser Creek to the approximate midpoint between the first and second freeway bridges. You paddle past their expansive clubhouse.

After the third freeway crossing, a steeper rapid requires some accurate maneuvering. Soon the discharge from Boca Reservoir enters on the left. This is a good put-in/take-out point.

Some minor rapids stretch between Boca and the last freeway crossing. Except for a prominent boulder, the river runs two fast miles to Hirshdale. Although the railroad stays close to the river, I–80 retreats across the canyon 0.5 mile above the river. An old bridge crossing at Hirshdale has good access for boaters and people fishing.

This stretch is the prettiest part of the river below Truckee. The river winds deep in the canyon between sage- and pine-covered slopes. Sandbars and gravel bars invite a relaxing lunch or fishing. You can see much of this run from the Gray Creek shuttle road. What is not visible is a sharp Class II rapid at a bend in the river. That rapid broke boats before the era of plastic craft.

The railroad crosses the river at the Gray Creek confluence. Since it collects snowmelt from the 9,600-foot Rose Knob, Gray Creek runs well into the summer. Enjoy the sparkling clear water and the scenery. A house of new construction stands above the creek. A gravel bar provides an easy take-out on river right above the creek and bridge. If you continue, expect some serious whitewater or a lengthy portage.

Gray Creek to Floriston

Length: 1.9 miles.

Average run time: 1 to 2 hours.

Class: III to IV.

Skill level: Expert.

Average gradient: 42 feet per mile, with sections more than 60 feet per mile.

Optimal flow: 400 to 800 cfs (Truckee River at Farad gauge).

Put in at Hirshdale or the Gray Creek confluence. To this point the canyon of the Truckee has provided little warmup for the rapids ahead. Fortunately they do not start abruptly. Several rapids place increasing demands on the boater. Then the last 1.3 miles drops 62 feet per mile.

At normal summer flows, the rapids are demanding boulder slaloms. Use the eddies to plot your next move. While swimming after missing an eddy here, I saw a piece of steel rebar protruding from underwater concrete. The good news is that the railroad runs along

The Truckee River Canyon above Gray Creek is the prettiest part of the river below Truckee.

the right bank and affords an excellent means to scout the rapids or portage your boat. Take out by the bridge at Floriston and appreciate your paddling accomplishment.

Access: Bell's Landing is 0.1 mile upstream of River Ranch along CA 89. A highway turnout and limited free public parking are adjacent to the bicycle trail. The rafting outfitters charge a fee to use a larger parking lot on the other side of CA 89.

Silver Creek Campground: 7 miles south of I–80 from Truckee on CA 89. The easiest put-in is beside the private bridge near the upstream end of the campground.

Granite Flat Campground: 1.5 miles south of I–80 from Truckee on CA 89.

Donner Creek Confluence: 0.5 mile south of I–80 from Truckee on CA 89, turn east onto West River Street. Look for the riverside turnout with concrete panels standing in the Donner Creek confluence.

Railroad: In Truckee go 0.4 mile north on CA 89 past the CA 267 junction. Turn east on Old Highway 40/Glenshire Drive. Proceed about 1.2 miles down the hill to a well-used informal parking area next to the transcontinental railroad. The boulder-strewn river is 200 yards through the sagebrush.

Glenshire Drive bridge: Continue east another 2.4 miles to the new high bridge across the Truckee. Tahoe National Forest provides a parking area at the east end of the bridge.

Boca: Exit I–80 at the Boca turnoff and go toward Boca Reservoir. Cross the Truckee River and put in by the railroad tracks where the outflow from Boca Reservoir joins the Truckee.

Hirshdale: This tiny hamlet is downstream from Boca. From the I–80 exit follow the paved road 1.2 miles on river right. Bear left at the junction with Glenshire Drive (a shortcut over the hill to the Glenshire Drive bridge) to the old bridge across the river. Put in beside the old bridge.

Gray Creek: From the center of Hirshdale follow the narrow, unpaved road 3.5 miles along the canyon wall with fine views of the river. At Gray Creek it drops closer to the river with a rough road to a gravel bar.

Floriston: Exit I–80 at Floriston to the secondary road by the bridge. That take-out gives an excellent view of the last steep rapid.

Shuttle: Silver Creek to Donner Creek: 7 miles (10 minutes). Donner Creek to Glenshire Drive bridge: 5.3 miles (15 minutes). Boca to Gray Creek: 5 miles (30 minutes). Boca to Floriston: 5.5 miles (10 minutes).

For more information: (See Appendix B for phone numbers, websites, and street addresses.) Visit the Internet or telephone the federal watermaster for streamflows.

Lake Tahoe near Emerald Bay

Character: Spectacular high Sierra scenery at one of America's most beautiful lakes, quite possibly the clearest lake in North America.

Size: Length 21 miles, width 12 miles.

Elevation: 6,230 feet.

Class: Large lake. SCRS I to III.

Skill level: Beginner to intermediate.

Best season: Late spring through autumn.

Craft: Canoes, kayaks, and large power boats.

Hazards: Because of their 1,600-foot depth, Lake Tahoe waters stay extremely cold. Even in late summer, only the top few feet become warm enough to swim in for more than a few minutes. Afternoon winds typically blow from the west, accelerating down 2,000-foot cliffs before focusing on Emerald Bay. The California Department of Boating and Waterways advises that "wind-driven waves can build to a height capable of capsizing or swamping small craft." The most frequent hazard is man-made—the scenic wonders of Emerald Bay attract a constant line of power boats, even 100-passenger tour boats. Although they observe the 15-m.p.h. speed limit, their wakes unnerve canoeists. Outside the bay, there is no speed limit, so power boat wakes become choppy waves. Open canoes are not recommended when the lake is busy or windy.

Maps: Forest Service Lake Tahoe Basin Management Unit, USGS 7.5 Emerald Bay.

Overview: Lake Tahoe is world famous for its incredibly clear water, fabulous mountain setting, and recreational playground. Emerald Bay is one of the most popular vistas at Tahoe. Visitors look down from the mountain highway or circle the bay aboard large and small boats. Campgrounds abound in the area but are so popular in summer that reservations are advised. The least crowded times are early morning or early autumn weekdays.

The paddling:

D. L. Bliss Campground Beach to Mouth of Emerald Bay

Length: 2.8 miles.

Average paddling time: 1.0 to 1.5 hours.

Put in at beautiful Lester Beach below the campground. Head south past little Calawee Cove Beach, an idyllic anchorage for sailboats. Soon you will round Rubicon Point, where granite cliffs plunge directly into the water. The breathtaking color of the lake changes from emerald green to indigo blue as the depth abruptly increases. Look south past Tahoe Keyes, South Shore, and the ski trails of Heavenly Valley to the 10,000-foot peaks of Jobs Sister, Freel Peak, and Round Top.

The shoreline to and including Emerald Bay is within state parks. The cliffs give way to steep mountainsides of brush and boulders without good landing spots. Although protected from the worst of the westerly winds, this shore is open to the wakes of hundreds of

Lake Tahoe near Emerald Bay

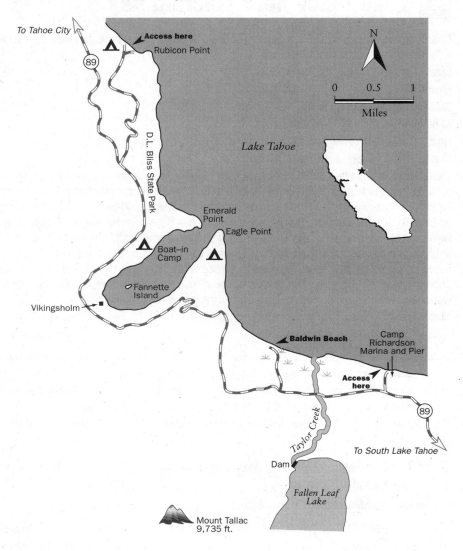

power boats. Sea kayaks resist swamping and capsizing better than canoes, so canoes should stay very close to shore. Experienced sea kayakers can actually surf some waves.

From the north, the mouth of Emerald Bay is obscure. The lowlands leading to Emerald Point are the first clues. Look for the two small beaches close to where the ridge drops to the water. Continue to paddle around Emerald Point. Immediately the awesome views of 9,735-foot Mount Tallac jump into sight. Stay close to the shallow north shore to avoid the larger boats.

For the return trip, looking north from the mouth of Emerald Bay; two distant points protrude into the lake. The farthest is Sugar Pine Point. If you aim for it until you reach the cliffs just south of Rubicon Point, the course will save you distance, but it will take you as much as 0.5 mile from shore.

Camp Richardson to Baldwin Beach

Length: 1.5 miles.

Average paddling time: 30 to 45 minutes.

In sharp contrast to the state parks' controlled tranquility, Camp Richardson can be a hubbub of activity. The Beacon Bar and Grill provides a great view from their deck next to the beach and marina. From the marina you can rent sit-on-top kayaks or even take a guided trip to Emerald Bay. The long pier is a landmark. Going north past Keyes Beach, the sandy coastline to Baldwin Beach is flat and covered with pine. Land at the small point south of Baldwin Beach about 0.8 mile from Camp Richardson, and follow the foot trails to the marvelous stream profile chamber featuring rainbow trout and kokanee landlocked salmon in Taylor Creek. It is well worth the 0.4 mile (one way) walk.

Besides the mountains circling the lake, the low shoreline permits great westward views to the mountains in the Desolation Wilderness Area. Remember to keep an eye open for power boats.

Baldwin Beach to Mouth of Emerald Bay

Length: 1.9 miles.

Average paddling time: 45 minutes to 1.5 hours.

This broad, sandy beach provides an easy put-in and is the closest to Emerald Bay. Paddling north beyond the beach, the shore gets steeper and chateau-like houses line the shore. Many have their own private pier. The buildings cease where the shoreline becomes part of Emerald Bay State Park.

An osprey nest sits atop a tall snag on the lake side of Eagle Point.

Emerald Bay

Length: 1.6 miles long. 0.5 miles wide.

Average paddling time: 30 to 45 minutes.

On warm weekends, many boats parade through the narrow, shallow mouth of Emerald Bay. On the north shore, the beach on Emerald Point is a lovely place to relax and enjoy the view. The only access is by foot trail or shallow draft boat.

Inside the bay, the mountains pull like magnets at your eyes—Mount Tallac with its snow bowl, the bare slope of the gigantic landslide, and the monumental granite cliffs rising nearly 3,000 feet to Jakes Peak in the Desolation Wilderness Area. Flowing out of the mountains, Eagle Falls punctuates the scene with soaring snowmelt.

Lake Tahoe's Emerald Bay is popular for boats of every size.

At lake level, the beauty is still sublime. The only island in all of Lake Tahoe, little Fannette Island rises 150 feet with an old granite "tea house" crowning the summit. The southwest corner is rocky but provides the easiest landing site. A partly obscured trail climbs rocky steps to the top.

Vikingsholm presides over the western end of the bay with a delightful beach. Hand hewn of local granite and timber, the sod-covered house was built to incorporate Scandinavian architecture of ages past. To participate in a tour, you must obtain tickets from the visitor center up the trail toward California Highway 89.

For those boaters wishing to camp away from cars, the north side of Emerald Bay harbors twenty boat-in campsites operated by the state park. The park provides mooring buoys, a dock, and a small beach. A discrete distance up the hill, tent sites have steel containers for bear protection, vault toilets, tables, and fresh water. They allocate campsites on a first come, first served, fee basis.

Access: D. L. Bliss State Park borders CA 89 on the west shore of Lake Tahoe 17 miles south of Tahoe City and a couple of miles north of Emerald Bay. From the entrance, follow the park road down past the campground kiosk, pay the day-use fee, and bear right to Lester Beach.

The access road to Baldwin Beach Picnic Area is about 4 miles north of the "Y" where CA 89 splits from U.S. Highway 50 in South Lake Tahoe. Turn right after 0.5 mile to the beach that is a fee area.

Camp Richardson has a privately operated marina on Jameson Beach Road. From the South Lake Tahoe "Y," go north on CA 89 about 2.5 miles. Turn right to the lake. Rental sit-on-top kayaks are available.

For more information: (See Appendix B for phone numbers, websites, and street addresses.) For information on the surrounding Forest Service facilities, contact the Lake Tahoe Basin Management Unit. Camp Richardson provides accommodations, dining, and rental kayaks. D. L. Bliss State Park has campgrounds, and day-use beaches and hiking trails. Emerald Bay State Park contains the Vikingsholm, boat-in campgrounds, and Eagle Point campgrounds, all of which operate seasonally. For operations information and camping reservations, call Emerald Bay State Park. The California parks Internet site provides a summary of Emerald Bay's history and accessibility. Sugar Pine Point State Park provides camping even during the abundant winter snows. For dining, hotels, and activities, the Lake Tahoe Chamber of Commerce provides excellent information sources via Internet.

65 East Fork Carson River

Character: This Sierra high-country gem offers lots of Class II whitewater, spectacular scenery, great campsites, and hot springs.

Length: 20 miles.

Average run time: 4 to 7 hours, often spread over 2 days.

Elevation at put-in: 5,480 feet.

Class: II.

Skill level: Intermediate.

Optimal flow: 600 to 2,000 cfs (Markleeville or Gardnerville gauges).

Water source: Snowmelt.

Average gradient: 26 feet per mile.

Best season: Spring and early summer.

Craft: Whitewater canoes, kayaks, rafts, and inflatables.

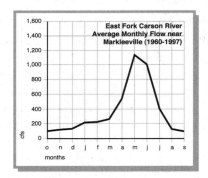

Hazards: Like other Sierra snowmelt rivers, the water is cold and swift. No easy access exists between the put-in and take-out. Unlike other rivers, a deadly broken dam awaits the unwary paddler 400 yards below the take-out.

Maps: Humboldt-Toiyabe National Forest, Carson Ranger District, USGS 7.5 Carters Station, Heenan Lake, Markleeville.

Overview: The East Fork of the Carson River is one of my favorite places. Days are delightfully warm, high elevation makes the air feel light, night skies sparkle with stars, hot springs soothe the body, and constant rapids refresh the spirit.

The East Fork of the Carson well deserves its designation as a California Wild and Scenic River. The Humboldt-Toiyabe National Forest and the Bureau of Land Management administer most of the lands bordering the river. These agencies are studying proposals to include the E. F. Carson in the National Wild and Scenic River System.

In January 1997, a flood changed parts of the river, including the put-ins. At high water, little space remains on the beach at Hangman's Bridge for organizing gear. An alternative is to go 0.6 mile upstream to a pebble beach near the East Fork Carson River Resort.

Flows above 600 cfs are suitable for large rafts plus kayaks and canoes. Higher water generates faster currents and bigger waves. Below 600 cfs, it is generally unsuitable for rafts, and below 300 to 400 cfs even small boats encounter more work than fun.

Both California and Nevada require fishing licenses for their respective portions of the river. Wild trout-fishing restrictions stipulate use of artificial flies, or lures with barbless hooks (no bait), and a two-fish limit with minimum size of 14 inches. The Forest Service or Alpine County Chamber of Commerce will issue free campfire permits. All floaters must secure a river permit available from the Carson Ranger District or at the put-in.

East Fork Carson River

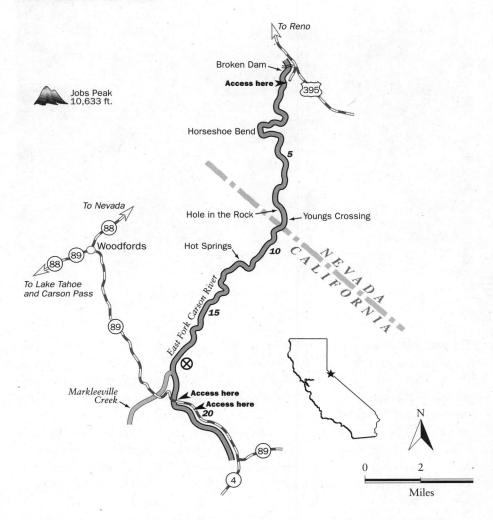

While you are waiting for the shuttle (unless you have invested in a shuttle service), the story of Hangman's Bridge may be told. On December 18, 1872, Ernest Reusch murdered E. H. Errickson at the Fisk's Hotel in Silver Mountain City (5 miles upstream). Reusch was apparently jealous that Errickson had recently won the affection of Reusch's new bride. Reusch turned himself in to the authorities. Many months later, when Reusch was being transported to trial at Bridgeport, masked vigilantes intercepted Reusch at this bridge and threw Reusch over the side with a hangman's noose around his neck. So they call this place Hangman's Bridge. (From *The Lore and Legend of the East Fork*, by Shane Murphy.)

Boaters young and old enjoy the alpine whitewater on the East Fork Carson River.

The paddling: At the put-in, the 50-feet-per-mile gradient makes for some fast boating. Choose carefully which side of Hangman's Bridge to paddle. The channel under the bridge changes with successive floods but always thrusts into a low cliff on river right just downstream. The fast current continues to twist and turn into low cliffs and undercut ledges that can easily snare the unwary boater.

Opposite Markleeville Creek is a wide bar suitable for camping, but why stop here when you have just begun? Take advantage of the reduced gradient (30 feet per mile) to catch an eddy and enjoy the specular upstream views of 9,000-foot Markleeville and Jeff Davis Peaks. At 1,200 cfs, downstream rapids provide fun-filled, splashy, 2- to 3-foot waves mile after mile.

Progressing downstream, you enter the Humboldt-Toiyabe National Forest where the river has carved a canyon 800 feet below the ridgetops. Steep cliffs alternate with riverside terraces ready-made for camping. The Forest Service strongly encourages low-impact camping, such as bringing stoves and packing out all trash and human waste with you.

On river left, a high cliff with a bright sulfur-yellow ravine marks the approach to the hot springs. Wide terraces on the right provide ample campsites. Beyond another brisk rapid are more campsites on both sides of the river. Volunteer off-road vehicle clubs have helped to maintain these campsites. The 1997 flood washed away the Class III rapid, known as Sidewinder, that once guarded the approach to the hot springs.

In recent years, natural hot spring pools of different sizes have been carved from the banks on both sides of the river. Those on river right are large enough for only two or three adults. On river left, the largest is perched on a ledge immediately above the river and gives paddlers below an "in the boat" hot shower.

To preserve this natural area, establish your camp at least 200 feet from the water and do not alter the hot springs.

Here, the canyons open up to reveal vistas of hills swathed in sage, and piñon and Jeffrey pine. In 1990, the Toiyabe National Forest planted thousands of Jeffrey pines to replace trees lost to the 1987 wildfire. The gradient slackens to 25 feet per mile in volcanic bedrock that includes imbedded gravel and cobbles. Its rough texture encourages "clean" boating. The geology also creates some curious rock pillars with undercut bases.

About 2.5 miles below the hot springs, two fences mark the old Von Schmidt and current state lines. A half mile beyond is Youngs Crossing, one of the largest areas of privately owned land along the river. Look up at the rock outcropping on the left to see "hole in the rock." Several pleasant beaches line the nearby shore. Beware of the rapids immediately below, as they require some precise maneuvering.

Downstream 3 miles is a delightful boulder slalom. Between turns, enjoy the magnificent views of Jobs Peak (10,633 feet) and Freel Peak (10,881 feet). These mountains are 10 miles from the river and only 7 miles southwest of Lake Tahoe.

A long, straight reach with abruptly rising cliffs on the right marks the beginning of Horseshoe Bend. Dam proponents have proposed building a dam in this canyon. The resultant reservoir would inundate most of the whitewater run. Designating the river as a National Wild and Scenic River would prohibit such a dam. Write your congressional representative to encourage Wild and Scenic Status.

A large sign and a long, willow-shrouded sandbar mark the take-out on river right. **You must stop here.** Four hundred yards downstream, the fast currents drop over the broken 30-foot high Ruhenstroth Dam. The good news is that the cars can be parked only a few yards above the take-out.

Access: To reach the put-in from California Highway 88 at Woodfords, turn south on CA 89. Go through Markleeville 1.5 miles to Hangman's Bridge over the E. F. Carson, or continue another 0.6 mile to a flat adjacent to the river.

To reach the take-out, return to Woodfords, then follow CA 88 northeast to Minden, Nevada. At Minden, go south about 6.5 miles on U.S. Highway 395, cross the river, and immediately turn right (east) where a local road parallels the river. Follow the road 0.75 mile along the south side of the river (river right). Ignore the bridge over the river and go up the hill overlooking the breeched dam to the reconstructed parking areas, loading zone, and toilets. Go down to the river so you will know what the take-out looks like. Do not miss the take-out!

Dangerous Ruhenstroth Dam is located a brief 400 yards below the take-out.

Shuttle: 30 miles (45 minutes).

For more information: (See Appendix B for phone numbers, websites, and street addresses.) To reserve shuttle service, contact Family Mountain Shuttle Service by phone. Call the Forest Service for the names of professional river outfitters on the Carson. Grover Hot Springs State Park, with its geothermal heated swimming pool, is a great place to camp before a river trip. For details on services available, call them or check their Internet site.

Appendix A:
Flows, Tides, Waves, and Storms

National Weather Service Forecasts

Northern California from Monterey and Fresno to Eureka and Redding: *www.wrh.noaa.gov/mtr*
Sacramento and Central Valley: *nimbo.wrh.noaa.gov/sto/*

National Oceanographic and Atmospheric Administration (NOAA) Weather Radio
frequencies—especially important for marine forecasts for sea kayakers.

Sacramento to Oroville	162.40 MHz
Sacramento to Modesto	162.55 MHz
Northern Sacramento Valley	162.55 MHz
San Francisco Bay Area	162.40 MHz
South San Francisco Bay and Monterey Bay Area	162.55 MHz
Monterey Marine	162.450 MHz
Eureka	162.400 MHz
Point Arena and Ukiah	162.550 MHz

Tides

Center for Operational Oceanographic Products and Services: *co-ops.nos.noaa.gov*

Daily tides: *tidesonline.nos.noaa.gov/geographic.html*

NOAA tidal differences and other constants: *co-ops.nos.noaa.gov/tide_pred.html*
  —scroll down to map, choose state
  —for tide tables, choose a location and then click on the Reference Station

NOAA instructions for using tidal predictions: *co-ops.nos.noaa.gov/t2help.html*

Winds and Waves

National Weather Service coastal and buoy data including wind, wave, and temperatures
conditions: *www.wrh.noaa.gov/mtr/bouy.php*

Buoys	ID number
Saint Georges	46027
Eel River	46022
Blunts reef	46030
Point Arena	46014
Bodega	46013
San Francisco	46026
Half Moon Bay	46012
Monterey	46042

River Flows, Reservoir Inflows, and Releases

Dream Flows—West wide river reports: *www.dreamflows.com*

Jef's CA DWR CDEC Interface
—graphical downloads of stream gauge data: *www.acme.com/jefflow/cdec.html*

California Department of Water Resources—California Data Exchange Center
(uses DWR ID letters): *cdec.water.ca.gov*
  Daily reservoir report: *cdec.water.ca.gov/cgi-progs/current/RES*
  Current river conditions: *cdec.water.ca.gov/river/rivcond.html*
U.S. Geologic Survey Water Resources in California
  (uses USGS gauge numbers): *ca.water.usgs.gov*
  USGS real-time flow conditions: *waterdate.usgs.gov/ea/nwis/rt*

Rivers are listed in alphabetical order and from upstream to downstream.

Gauge Name	USGS Number	DWR ID
American River, Middle Fork near Oxbow Powerhouse		OXB
American River, North Fork at North Fork Dam	11427000	NFD
American River, South Fork at Chili Bar		CBR
American River, Lake Natoma Release (Nimbus Dam)		NAT
American River at Fair Oaks	11446500	AFO
Bear River into Lake Combie—Call Nevada Irrigation District Operations at 530–823–2466.		
Bear River near Wheatland	11424000	BRW
Cache Creek, North Fork releases from Indian Valley Reservoir		INV
Cache Creek at Rumsey		RUM
Cosumnes River at Michigan Bar	11335000	MHB
East Fork Carson River below Markleeville	10308200	
East Fork Carson River at Gardnerville		GDV
Eel River at Fort Seward	11475000	FSW
Eel River, South Fork at Leggett	11475800	LEG
Eel River, South Fork at Miranda	11476500	MRD
Feather River near Gridley		GRL
Mokelumne River near Mokelumne Hill	1319500	
Mokelumne River Pardee Reservoir Inflow		PAR
Mokelumne River, Camanche Reservoir Outflow		CMN
Mokelumne River at Berson's Ferry near Thorton		BEN
Navarro River near Navarro	11468000	NRN
Russian River at Cloverdale	11463000	CLV
Russian River near Healdsburg	11464000	HEA
Russian River near Guerneville	11467000	

Sacramento River, Bend Bridge	11377100	BND
Sacramento River at Ord Ferry		ORD
Sacramento River at Colusa	11389500	COL
Stanislaus River at Orange Blossom		OBB
Stanislaus River at Ripon	11303000	
Trinity River release from Lewiston outflow	11525500	LWS
Trinity River Flow Schedule from Lewiston Reservoir posted on U.S. Bureau of Reclamation Central Valley Operations: www.mp.usbr.gov/cvo		
Trinity River at Douglas City		DGC
Trinity River at Hoopa	11530000	HPA
Truckee River—Call the Federal watermaster at 775–784–5241 x 25		
Truckee River at Tahoe City	10337500	TTC
Truckee River near Truckee	10338000	TRK
Truckee River at Farad	10346000	FAR
Tuolumne River at LaGrange	11289650	LGN
Tuolumne River—Discharges to river from Hickman Spillway, call 209–883–8301 or 209–883–8300		
Tuolumne River at Modesto	11290000	MOD
Yuba River below Englebright Dam	11418000	YRS
Yuba River near Marysville	11421000	MRY

Appendix B: For More Information

Ahjumawi State Park
24898 Highway 89
Burney, CA 96013
530–335–2777

Albion River Campground & Fishing Village
P.O. Box 217
Albion, CA 95410
707–937–0606

American River Natural History Association
www.arnha.org

American River Parkway Foundation
P.O. Box 188437
Sacramento, CA 95818–8437
916–456–7423

Angel Island State Park
415-435-3522
415-435-1915 Recorded info
415–435–5390 Ranger station
www.angelisland.org

Auburn State Recreation Area
P.O. Box 3266
Auburn, CA 95603
530–885–5648

Bidwell Sacramento River State Park
12105 River Road
Chico, CA 95926
530–342–5185

Bigfoot Rafting Co.
P.O. Box 729
Willow Creek, CA 95573
800–722–2223 or 530–629–2263
Fax: 530–629–1157
www.bigfootrafting.com/index.htm
E-mail: fun@bigfootrafting.com

Blue Waters Kayaking
12938 Sir Francis Drake Boulevard
Inverness, CA 94937
415–669–2600 & 415-663-1743
Fax: 415–669–7835
bwKayak.com
E-mail: info@bwkayak.com

Bureau of Land Management in California
www.ca.blm.gov/caso

Bureau of Land Management
Eagle Lake Field Office
2950 Riverside Drive
Susanville, CA 96130
530–257–0456
Fax: 530–257–4831
www.ca.blm.gov/eaglelake

Bureau of Land Management
Folsom Field Office
63 Natoma Street
Folsom, CA 95630
916–985–4474
Fax: 916–985–3259
www.ca.blm.gov/folsom
E-mail: caweb018@ca.blm.gov

Bureau of Land Management
Redding Field Office
355 Hemsted Drive
Redding, CA 96002
530–224–2100
www.ca.blm.gov/redding

Bureau of Land Management
Ukiah Field Office
2550 N. State Street
Ukiah, CA 95482
707–468–4000
www.ca.blm.gov/ukiah

Cache Creek Regional Parks
Yolo County Parks Department
292 West Beamer St.
Woodland, CA 95695
530–666–8115

California Department of Boating & Waterways
2000 Evergreen Street, Suite 100
Sacramento, CA 95815-3888
916–263–4326 or 888–326–2822
Fax: 916–263–0648
www.dbw.ca.gov

California State Parks Camping Reservations
800–444–7275
www.parks.ca.gov/travel/parkindex/
www.reserveamerica.com

Catch-a-Canoe & Bicycles Too
P.O. Box 487
Mendocino, CA 95460
707–937–0273
www.catchacanoe.com

Chesbro Reservoir County Park
298 Garden Hill Drive
Los Gatos, CA 95032
408-779-9232
www.parkhere.org/
E-mail: parkinfo@prk.sccgov.org

China Camp State Park
Route 1, Box 244
San Raphael, CA 94901
www.parks.ca.gov - click on "find a park"

City of Berkeley Recreation Office
510-981-6700
www.ci.berkeley.ca.us/parks

Coastal Traveler
www.coastaltraveler.com/

Coloma Online
www.coloma.com

Colusa Weir Recreation Area & Colusa Levee Scenic Park
425 Webster
P.O. Box 1063
Colusa, CA 95932
530–458–5622

Colusa-Sacramento River State Recreation Area
P.O. Box 207
Colusa, CA 95932
530–458–4927
www.parks.ca.gov

Corps of Engineers
Reservoir Report for Corps Operated Reservoirs
www.spk-wc.usace.army.mil

Cosumnes River Preserve
13501 Franklin Boulevard
Galt, CA 95632
916–684–2816
www.cosumnes.org

County of Santa Clara
Parks & Recreation Department
298 Garden Hill Drive
Los Gatos, CA 95032
408–358–3741
www.parkhere.org
E-mail: parkinfo@prk.sccgov.org

CSUS Aquatic Center
1901 Hazel Avenue
Rancho Cordova, CA 95670
916–278-2842
www.csusaquaticcenter.com

D. L. Bliss State Park
530–525–7277
www.parks.ca.gov

East Bay Municipal Utility District
Recreation
500 San Pablo Dam Road
Orinda, CA 94563
925–284–9669
www.ebmud.com/services/recreation/recmain.html

East Bay Municipal Utility District
Mokelumne River
209–722–8204

East Bay Regional Parks District
2950 Peralta Oaks Court
P.O. Box 5381
Oakland, CA 94605
510–562–7275
www.ebparks.org
E-mail: info@ebparks.org

El Dorado County Parks & Recreation
3000 Fairlane Court, Suite 1
Placerville, CA 95667
530–621–5349
www.co.el-dorado.ca.us/parks
E-mail: southfork@co.el-dorado.ca.us

Elkhorn Slough Foundation
P.O. Box 267
Moss Landing, CA 95039
831–728–5939
www.elkhornslough.org
E-mail: esf@elkhornslough.org.

Emerald Bay State Park
530–541–3030
www.parks.ca.gov

Family Fun Publications
P.O. Box 21-4152
Sacramento, CA 95821
916–481–7422

Family Mountain Shuttle Service
19750 State Route 89, Number 9
Markleeville, CA 96120
530–694–2966
Fax: 530–694–2966

Folsom Lake State Recreation Area
7806 Folsom-Auburn Road
Folsom, CA 95630-1797
916–988–0205
Fax: 916–988–9062
www.parks.ca.gov

Fort Bragg–Mendocino Coast Chamber of Commerce
P.O. Box 1141
Fort Bragg, CA 95437
707–961–6300
Fax: 707–964–2056
www.mendocinocoast.com
E-mail: chamber@mcn.org

Friends of the River
915 20th Street
Sacramento, CA 95814
916–442–3155
Fax: 916–442–3196
www.friendsoftheriver.org
E-mail: chare@friendsoftheriver.org

Golden Hinde Inn
12938 Sir Francis Drake Boulevard
Inverness, CA 94937
415–669–1389
www.goldenhindeinn.com
E-mail: reservations@goldenhindeinn.com

Grover Hot Springs State Park
P.O. Box 188
Markleeville, CA 96120
530–694–2248
Fax: 530–694–2502
www.parks.ca.gov

Hendy Woods State Park
18599 Philo-Greenwood Road
Philo, CA 95466
707–895–3141
www.parks.ca.gov

Historic Camp Richardson Resort
P.O. Box 9028
1900 Jameson Beach Road
South Lake Tahoe, CA 96158
800–544–1801 or 530–541–1801
www.camprichardson.com
E-mail: info@camprichardson.com

Humboldt Lodging Guide
www.visitormags.com/humboldt/

Humboldt Redwoods State Park
P.O. Box 100
Weott, CA 95571
707–946–2409
www.humboldtredwoods.org
www.parks.ca.gov
E-mail: hrsp@humboldtredwoods.org

Humboldt-Toiyabe National Forest
Carson Ranger District
1536 South Carson Street
Carson City, NV 89701
775–882–2766

Indian Grinding Rock State Historic Park
14881 Pinegrove-Volcano Road
Pinegrove, CA 95665
209–296–7488
www.parks.ca.org

Lake Tahoe Basin Management Unit
35 College Drive
South Lake Tahoe, CA 96150
530-543-2600
www.fs.fed.us/r5/ltbmu

Lassen National Forest
2550 Riverside Drive
Susanville, CA 96130
530–257–2151
www.fs.fed.us/r5/lassen

Lassen Volcanic National Park
P.O. Box 100
Mineral, CA 96063-0100
530–595–4444
www.nps.gov/lavo

Lawson's Landing
P.O. Box 57
Dillon Beach, CA 94929-0067
707–878–2443
www.lawsonslanding.com
E-mail: lawsonslanding@aol.com

Lexington Reservoir County Park
408–356–2729
www.parkhere.org
E-mail: parkinfo@park.sccgov.org

Marin County Department of Parks
3501 Civic Center Dr.
San Raphael, CA 94903
415–499–6387
www.co.marin.ca.us/depts/pk/

Marshall Gold Discovery State Historic Park
P.O. Box 265
Coloma, CA 95613
530–622–3470
Fax: 530–622–3472
E-mail: coloma@jps.net

Mendocino Coast State Parks
c/o Russian Gulch SP
P.O. Box 440
Mendocino, CA 95460
707–937–5804
Fax: 707–937–2953

Monterey Bay Aquarium
886 Cannery Row
Monterey, CA 93940
831–648–4888
www.mbayaq.org

Monterey Bay Kayaks
693 Del Monte Avenue
Monterey, CA 93940
800–649–KELP [5357]
www.montereybaykays.com

Monterey Bay National Marine Sanctuary
299 Foam Street
Monterey, CA 93940
831–647–4201
Fax: 831–647–4250
bonita.mbnms.nos.noaa.gov

Monterey Bay State Seashore
2211 Garden Road
Monterey, CA 93940
831–649–2836
Fax: 831–649–2847
www.parks.ca.gov

Monterey Office of the Harbormaster
City Hall
Monterey, CA 93940
831–646–3950; 831–594–7760 after 5:00 P.M.
Fax: 831–646–5674
www.monterey.org/harbor
E-mail: scheibla@ci.monterey.ca.us

Monterey Peninsula Visitors and Convention Bureau
P. O. Box 1770
Monterey, CA 93942-1770
831–649–1770
www.montereyinfo.org

National Recreation Reservation Service
Campsites of the Forest Service and U.S. Army Corps of Engineers
www.ReserveUSA.com

Navarro River Redwoods State Park
707–895–3141
www.parks.ca.gov

Nevada Irrigation District Operations Center
530–823–2466 or 530–273–8571

North Coast Redwoods District Headquarters & Sector Headquarters
P.O. Box 2006
Eureka, CA 95502-2006
707–445–6547
Fax: 707–441–5737
E-mail: ncrhq@parks.ca.gov

Orbend Park Butte City Launch Facility
125 South Murdock
Willows, CA 95988
530-934-6545

Oroville Area Chamber of Commerce
1789 Montgomery Street
Oroville, CA 95965
800–655–GOLD (4653)
www.lakeoroville.net

Pacific Gas & Electric Co.
916–386–5164
www.pge.com/recreation

Placer County Dept. Facility Services
Parks and Grounds
11476 C Avenue
Auburn, CA 95603
530-886-4901
www.placer.ca.gov/facility/parkgrnd.htm

Plumas National Forest
P.O. Box 11500
Quincy, CA 95971
530–283–2050
www.fs.fed.us/r5/plumas

Point Reyes National Seashore
Point Reyes Station, CA 94956-9799
415–464–5100
www.nps.gov/pore

ReserveAmerica (for California State Parks)
800–444–7275
www.reserveamerica.com

Richardson Grove State Park
1600 U.S. Highway 101
Garberville, CA 95440–3318
707–247–3318

River Journey
14842 Orange Blossom Road
Oakdale, CA 95361
800–292–2938
Fax: 209–847–4671
www.riverjourney.com
E-mail: info@riverjourney.com

Round Valley Lake Resort
P.O. Box 959
Greenville, CA 95947
530–258–7751
www.rvlr.com
E-mail: camping@rvlr.com

Sacramento County American River Parkway
4040 Bradshaw Road
Sacramento, CA 95827
916–875–6672
www.sacparks.net

Santa Clara County Parks and Recreation Department
298 Garden Hill Drive
Los Gatos, CA 95032
408-355-2200
Fax: 408-355-2290
www.parkhere.org

Save The American River Association
www.sarariverwatch.org

Scotty's Boat Landing
12609 River Road
Chico, CA 95973–8911
530–893–2020

Shasta Cascade Wonderland Association
1699 Highway 273
Anderson, CA 96007
800–4SHASTA
www.shastacascade.com

Shasta-Trinity National Forests
Weaverville Ranger Station
P.O. Box 1190
Weaverville, CA 96063
530–623–2121
www.r5.pswfs.gov/shastatrinity

Shasta-Trinity National Forests
Star Route 1, Box 10
Big Bar, CA 96010
530–623–6106
Fax: 530-623-6123
www.r5.pswfs.gov/shastatrinity

Six Rivers National Forest
Lower Trinity Ranger District
P.O. Box 68
Willow Creek, CA 95573
530-629-2118

Skunk Train–Sierra Railroad
Fort Bragg, CA 95437
866-45-SKUNK
www.skunktrain.com

Smithe Redwoods State Reserve
707–247–3318

Sonoma Lake, U.S. Army Corps of Engineers
3333 Skaggs Springs Road
Geyserville, CA 95441-9644
707–433–9483
Fax: 707–431–0313
www.sp.usace.army.mil/lakesnoma/index

South Lake Tahoe Chamber of Commerce
3066 Lake Tahoe Boulevard
South Lake Tahoe, CA 96150
530–541–5255
Fax: 530–541–7121
www.tahoeinfo.com
E-mail: sltcc@sierranet.com

Standish-Hickey State Recreation Area
69350 U.S. Highway 101
Box #2
Leggett, CA 95455
707–925–6482
www.parks.ca.gov

Stanislaus River Parks, U.S. Army Corps of Engineers
P.O. Box 1229
18020 Sonora Road
Knights Ferry, CA 95361-9510
209–881–3517
Fax: 209–881–3203
www.spk.usace.army.mil/organizations/cespk-co/lakes/stanislaus.htm
E-mail: stanislaus-info@spk.usace.army.mil

Sugar Pine Point State Park
530–525–7982
www.parks.ca.gov

Sunshine Adventures, Inc.
P.O. Box 1445
Oakdale, CA 95361
209–848–4800 or 800-829-7238
Fax: 209–848–1381
www.raftadventure.com

Tahoe National Forest
Big Bend Visitor Center
P.O. Box 830
Soda Springs, CA 95728-0830
530–426–3609
www.fs.fed.us/r5/tahoe/

Tehama County River Park
P.O. Box 421
Red Bluff, CA 96080
530–527–4630

The Fish Sniffer Magazine
P.O. Box 994
Elk Grove, CA 95759-0094
800–748–6599
www.fishsniffer.com/maps
E-mail: steelhead@fishsniffer.com

The Fly Shop
4140 Churn Creek Road
Redding, CA 96002
800–669–FISH
www.theflyshop.com

Thousand Trails and NACO Snowflower Camping Preserve
P.O. Box 40
41776 Yuba Gap Drive
Emigrant Gap, CA 95715
530–389–9614
www.thousandtrails.com

Tomales Bay State Park
Star Route
Inverness, CA 94937
415–669–1140
www.parks.ca.gov

Trinity County Visitors Guide
800–487–4648 or 530–623–6101
www.trinitycounty.com

Trinity River Flow Schedule
www.usbr.gov/mp/cvo/

Truckee Donner Chamber of Commerce
10065 Donner Pass Road
Truckee, CA 96161
530–587–2757
www.truckee.com
E-mail: info@truckee.com

Truckee River Raft Rentals
185 River Road
P.O. Box 1799
Tahoe City, CA 96145
877–583–0123 or 530–581–0123
www.truckeeriverraft.com

Turlock Lake State Recreation Area
22600 Lake Road
LaGrange, CA 95329
209–874–2056
www.parks.ca.gov

Van Damme State Park
707–937–5804
www.parks.ca.gov

Wild and Scenic Rivers
www.nps.gov/rivers

William B. Ide Adobe State Historic Park
21659 Adobe Road
Red Bluff, CA 96080
530–529–8599
www.parks.ca.gov

Woodson Bridge State Recreation Area
Route 1, Box 325
Corning, CA 96021
530–839–2112
www.parks.ca.gov

Yolo County Flood Control Field Office
530–662–0266

Appendix C: Further Reading

Biking and Hiking the American River Parkway, The American River Natural History Association, 1998

California Coastal Access Guide, Fifth Edition, State of California, California Coastal Commission, San Francisco, 1997

California Wildlife Viewing Guide, Jeanne L. Clark, Falcon Press, Helena, Montana, 1996

The Coastal Kayaker's Manual, Third Edition, Randel Washburne, The Globe Pequot Press, Guilford, Connecticut, 1998

Extreme Sea Kayaking, Eric Soares and Michael Powers, Ragged Mountain Press, 1999

Guide to Expedition Kayaking, Fourth Edition, Derek C. Hutchinson, The Globe Pequot Press, Guilford, Connecticut, 1999

A History of the Lower American River, William C. Dillinger for The American River Natural History Association, 1991

Marin, text by Beth Ashley, photography by Hal Lauritzen, Chronicle Books, San Francisco, 1993

Mendocino County Remembered—An Oral History, by Bruce Levene and William Bradd, Lana Krasner, Gloria Petrykowski, Rosalie Zucker; The Mendocino County Historical Society, Mendocino County, California, 1976

Monterey Bay Area: Natural History and Cultural Imprints, Burton L. Gordon, The Boxwood Press, Pacific Grove, California, 1974

Point Reyes the Solemn Land, Second Edition, Jack Mason, North Shore Books, Inverness, California, 1972

Point Reyes Secret Places & Magic Moments, Phil Arnot, World Wide Publishing/Tetra, San Carlos, California, 1987

Sea Kayaking: A Manual for Long-Distance Touring, John Dowd, Douglas & McIntyre Vancouver, University of Washington Press, Seattle, 1986

Appendix D: California Paddling Organizations

American Whitewater Association
www.americanwhitewater.org

Bay Area Sea Kayakers
c/o Penny Wells
229 Courtright Road
San Rafael, CA 94901
www.baskers.org

California Floaters Society
www.cfsonline.org

Chico Paddle Heads
12428 Centerville Road
Chico, CA 95928-8320

Friends of the River
915 20th Street
Sacramento, CA 95814
916–442–3155
www.friendsoftheriver.org

Gold Country Paddlers
P.O. Box 1058
Lotus, CA 95651
www.gcpaddlers.org

Kern River Alliance
15400 Via Mileno
Bakersfield, CA 93306

Leaping Lounge Lizards
c/o Rick Norman
3437 East Green Street
Pasadena, CA 91107

Loma Prieta Paddlers, Sierra Club RTS
c/o Riptides & Rapids
650-961-1240
www.lomaprieta.sierraclub.org/lpp

Paddlers News Bulletin
Sierra Club/RTS
5960 S Land Park Dr #117
Sacramento, CA 95822-3313

Popular Outdoor Sport Trips (POST)
Kit Hewitt
510-526-3997
www.canoecal.org

Sequoia Paddling Club
P.O. Box 1164
Windsor, CA 95492
www.sequioapc.org

Shasta Paddlers
Mark Twitchell
530-243-7436
www.shastapaddlers.org

Sierra Club RTS Angeles Chapter
1355 N. Laurel Ave #4
Los Angeles, CA 90046
angeles.sierraclub.org/rts/

Sierra Sea Kayakers
Sacramento, CA
groups.yahoo.com/group/sierraseakayakers/

INDEX

A

Agate Beach, 74
Ahjumawi Lava Springs State Park, 183–84
Alameda Estuary, 34
Alameda Island, 35
Alan Sieroty Beach, 50
Albion, 70
Albion Cove, 64, 65, 72
Albion River, 64–66, 72, 75
American River, 148, 214–18, 223–30
American River Parkway, 152–58
Americano Creek, 52
Anderson, 105, 106, 107
Anderson Creek, 109
Anderson Valley, 58, 59, 60
Angel Island, 36–38
Angel Island State Park, 36
Ansil Hoffman Park, 154, 158
Antelope Lake, 196
Arrowhead Marsh, 34
Asilomar beach, 16
Auburn, 212, 213, 219, 220, 221, 223, 225
Avalis Beach, 49, 50
Ayala Cove, 36

B

Back Ranch Meadows Campground, 39
Baldwin Beach, 243
Balls Ferry, 105–13
Barge Hole, 111, 112
Barking Dog, 229
Battle Creek, 109, 111
Bay Bridge, 32
Beals Point, 144, 145, 148
Bear Creek, 134–37, 235, 237
Bear River, 204–6
Bedrock Park, 124, 126, 128
Bell Gulch, 94
Bell's Landing, 231, 233, 240
Benbow Lake, 76, 78–79, 80, 83
Bend Bridge, 111, 113
Berkeley, 32, 33
Berkeley Aquatic Park, 30
Berkeley Hills, 32
Bidwell Sacramento River State Park, 120
Big Bar, 98
Big Chico Creek Beach, 120

Big Flat, 96, 97, 98, 100
Big French Creek, 99
Big Lake, 183, 184
Big River, 67–69, 70, 73
Big Rock Trinity River, 103, 104
Black Mountain, 187
Blackberry Island, 114
Bliss State Park, 244
Blue Cliffs, 142
Blue Gum Beach, 49
Boca Reservoir, 231, 235, 238, 240
Bodega Head, 52
Boggs Bend, 121
Bogus Thunder, 216
Bouncing Rock Rapid, 229
Brockman Flat Lava Beds, 186
Brush Creek, 55
Buck Bay, 187
Buck Island, 135–36, 137
Buck Point, 187
Buckeye Point, 40
Bucktail Hole, 95
Bull Creek, 85
Bullet Hill, 40
Bullhead Flat, 40, 41
Bunch Creek, 216
Burnt Ranch, 100
Bushy Lake Nature Preserve, 156
Butler Slough, 115
Butte City County Park, 122
Butte County, 120

C

Cache Creek, 134–43
Camp Richardson, 243, 245
Cannery Row, 15–17
Canyon Creek, 94, 95, 100
Capay Valley, 134, 140, 142–43
Cape Horn, 60
Cascade Range, 2, 120, 185
Caspar, 74, 75
Castle Peak, 207
Cedar Flat, 96–100
Central Valley, 1–2, 22, 87, 90, 159
Chamberlin Falls, 216
Cherokee Bar, 223, 224
Cherry Creek, 55

Chesbro Reservoir, 22–23
Chicken Coop Hill, 40
Chico, 118, 120, 121
Chili Bar, 226–30
China Camp, 39–42
China Cove, 36
China Creek, 116
China Gulch, 92
Chinese Rapids, 111
Christie Beach, 186
Cisco Butte, 207
Clair Engle Lake, 89
Clear Lake, 134, 138
Clements, 168, 169
Cloverdale, 56
Coastal Range, 1, 2, 87,107, 120
Codfish Creek, 217
Colfax, 204–6, 214–18
Colfax–Iowa Hill Bridge, 214, 218
Coloma, 226, 227, 230
Colusa, 118–23
Colusa-Sacramento River River State Recreation
Area, 121, 121, 123
Coopers Bar, 97
Copeland Bar, 116
Corning, 117
Cortina Ridge, 136
Cosumnes River Preserve, 159–64
Cottonwood Creek, 109
Cow Creek, 107
Craig Creek, 114
Creamery Bay, 45
Current Diver, 229

D

Daguerra Dam, 129
Daguerra Point Dam, 131
Damon Marsh, 34
Deer Creek, 116
Deer Park, 236
Del Loma, 99, 100
Del Valle Regional Park, 26
Denny Creek, 98
Desolation Wilderness Area, 243
Dibble Creek, 111
Dillon Beach, 50, 51
Discovery Park, 156, 158
Dog Bar, 204–6
Don Juan Point, 100
Donner Creek, 235, 240

Donner Lake, 235
Dora Creek, 78
Douglas City, 89, 92, 93
Drakes Cove, 45, 46
Drakes Estero, 43–47, 53
Drakes Head, 46
Dry Creek, 55, 85, 130–31, 132, 133
Duck Island, 50

E

Eagle Cliffs, 189
Eagle Creek, 97
Eagle Falls, 243
Eagle Lake, 185–88
Eagle Mountain, 210, 211
Eagle Point, 85
East Beach, 26
East Fork Baker, 38
East Fork Carson River, 246–50
East Sand Slough, 111
Eel River, 87–88
Eel Rock, 88
El Dorado Hills, 230
El Estero Park, 17
El Manto Access, 154
Elder Creek, 114, 116
Electra Run, 165–69
Elkhorn Slough, 18–21, 53
Emeryville, 32, 33
Emeryville Marina, 32, 33
Englebright Reservoir, 129
English Bar, 199
Estero Americano, 52–54

F

Fannette Island, 244
Feather River, 124–28, 132, 198–200
Federation Grove, 85, 86
Fir Crags, 233
Fisherman's Wharf, 16, 17
Fishtale, 98
Five Fingers Slough, 21
Floodgate Creek, 59
Floriston, 235–40
Folsom Lake, 144–47, 226–30
Fordyce Creek, 209
Fort Bragg, 70
Fort Seward, 87
Foster Island, 120
Fowler's Rock, 229

Fox Grove Park, 180–82
French Bar, 99, 100
French Meadows Reservoir, 221–22, 223

G

Galletin Peak, 187
Gallinas Slough, 39
Garberville, 80, 82
Garden Club Grove, 85
Garretson Point, 34
Genesee, 196
Glenn County, 120
Goethe Park, 152, 154, 155, 158
Golden Gate, 1, 8, 30, 32, 37, 38
Gonelson Canyon, 207
Goose Meadows, 237
Goose Ranch, 92
Gould Bar, 86
Grand Canyon, 176
Granite Bay, 145
Granite Chief Peak, 221
Granite Flat, 236, 237, 240
Grass Valley Bald Mountain, 201
Gray Creek, 235, 238, 240
Great Basin Desert, 185
Greenville, 192
Greenwood, 223, 225
Greenwood Bridge, 223–25
Greenwood Creek, 229
Greenwood Ridge, 59
Grouse Ridge, 207, 208
Grove Park, 181
Grover Hot Springs State Park, 250
Guinda, 143
Gunsight Rock, 228

H

Hamilton Bend, 121
Hamilton City, 121
Hangman's Bridge, 248
Harrington, 155, 158
Hartly Island, 121
Hartsook Creek, 79
Hawkins Bar, 101–4
Hayden Flat, 98, 99, 100
Healdsburg, 56
Heart's Desire Beach, 49, 51
Hell Hole, 98
Hell Hole Reservoir, 223
Hendy Woods State Park, 58, 60, 61, 63

Henningsen–Lotus County Park, 228, 229, 230
Hetch Hetchy Canyon, 176
Highway Rapid, 229
Hirshdale, 238, 240
Hog Island, 49, 50
Home Bay, 45
Horr Pond, 183, 184
Horseshoe Bar, 221
Horseshoe Bay, 36, 38
Horseshoe Bend, 249
Horseshoe Road Recreation Area, 171–72, 174
Hospital Bar, 229
Humboldt Redwoods State Park, 76, 80, 83, 86
Humboldt-Toiyabe National Forest, 246, 248, 249

I

Ida Adobe State Historic Park, 111
Indian Beach, 49
Indian Creek, 79
Indian Grinding Rock State Historic Park, 165, 166
Indian Valley Reservoir, 134, 138
Inks Creek, 111
Inverness, 46, 49, 51
Iron Canyon, 111
Irvine Finch River, 121

J

Ja She Creek, 183, 184
Jackson, 165
Jacob Meyers Park, 174, 175
Jake's Island, 40
Jakes Peak, 243
Jeff Davis Peaks, 248
Jelly's Ferry, 111, 112, 113
Jenny Lind Bend, 120
Jensen Grove, 85
Johnson Point, 94
Junction City, 89–100
Juniper Lake, 189–90

K

Keddie Ridge, 194
Kenebec Bar, 223
Kennedy Flats, 134
Keyes Beach, 243
Kilkenny Beach, 49
Kimtu Bar, 103, 104
Kirby Park, 18, 19, 21
Knights Ferry, 170–75
Kopta Slough, 114

L

La Grange, 176–79
La Porte, 201
Lafayette Reservoir, 28
Lahonton Reservoir, 231
Lairds Landing, 49
Lake Clementine, 214–20
Lake Combie, 204, 206
Lake Del Valle, 26
Lake Natoma, 148–51
Lake Red Bluff, 109, 111, 113, 116
Lake Shasta, 105
Lake Sonoma, 55–57
Lake Spaulding, 207–9
Lake Tahoe (near Emerald Bay), 241–45
Lake Valley Reservoir, 210–11
Lansdale Bar, 85
Lassen National Forest, 185, 188
Lassen Peak, 2, 105, 109, 114, 189, 194
Lassen Volcanic National Park, 189, 190
Lawson's Landing, 51
Leatherwood Bar, 85, 86
Leggett, 76–82
Lewiston, 89–95, 101
Lewiston Lake, 89
Lexington Reservoir, 24
Limantour Bay, 46
Limekiln Gulch, 92
Little Grass Valley Reservoir, 201–3
Little Prairie, 98
Little Swede Creek, 99
Lodi, 168
Lone Rock, 196
Long Point, 196, 217, 220
Lookout Mountain, 111
Lost Slough, 162, 164
Lotus, 226, 227, 228
Lovers Point, 16
Lower Cache Creek Park, 136, 141
Lower Dominici Creek, 177
Lower Sunrise, 154

M

Mackerricher State Park, 70
Mad Mike Rapid, 134, 135
Maine Bar, 223
Mammoth Bar, 223–25
Marin Headlands, 30
Markleeville Creek, 248
Marshall Beach, 49

Marshall Gold Discovery State Historic Park, 228, 230
Martin Luther King Jr. Regional Shoreline, 34, 34–35
Martis Creek, 237
Marysville, 129, 131, 132, 133
McArthur–Burney Falls Memorial State Park, 184
McHenry Recreation area, 170–75
McInnis Park, 39, 40, 41, 42
McNears Beach, 41, 42
Meatgrinder Rapid, 228
Mendocino, 67, 70–75
Merrills Landing, 120
Middle Fork American River, 223–25
Middle Fork Feather River, 198–200
Middle Slough, 160, 161, 162
Mill Creek, 116, 117
Miller County Park, 50
Millerton Point, 49, 50
Milsap Bar, 198
Miranda, 85
Mississippi Bar, 149
Modoc Lava Plateau, 185
Mohawk Valley, 198
Mokelumne Hill, 165
Mokelumne River, 161, 162, 164, 165–69
Monterey Bay, 15–18, 21
Monterey Bay Aquarium, 15, 16
Monterey Beach State Park, 17
Monterey Harbor, 15
Mormon Ravine, 146
Moss Landing Harbor, 19, 20, 21
Moss Landing State Wildlife Area, 18
Moulton Weir, 121
Mount Caroline Livermore, 36
Mount Harkness, 189
Mount Shasta, 105, 109, 114
Mount Tallac, 242
Mountain Meadow Reservoir, 194–95
Municipal Wharf, 15, 16, 17
Murders Bar, 225
Myers Flat, 85, 88

N

National Estuarine Research Reserve, 18, 21
Navarro Beach, 62, 63
Navarro River, 58–61
Navarro River Estuary, 62–63
Negro Bar, 148, 149, 151
Nelson Point, 198–200

New Bullards Bar, 129
New Don Pedro Reservoir, 176
Nick's Cove, 50
Nimbus Dam, 149
North Fork American River, 214–18
North Fork Trinity River, 97
North Fork, 58, 60, 61
Norton's Ravine, 229
Nunes Rapid, 111

O

Oakdale, 172, 174, 175
Old Man Mountain, 207
Old Scary, 228, 230
Olema, 49
Ordbend County Park, 120, 122
Oregon Creek, 94
Oroville, 124–28

P

Pacific Grove, 15
Pacific Grove State Marine Gardens Fish Refuge, 15
Packer Island, 121
Paper Mill Creek, 49
Paradise Beach, 156
Parks Bar, 129, 130, 132, 133
Paynes Creek, 111
Peaslee Creek, 178
Pelican Point, 49, 186
Peninsula Point, 36
Perles Beach, 37
Phillipsville, 85
Picket Fence, 99
Pierce's Wharf, 49
Piercy, 78–79, 80
Pigeon Point, 96, 97, 98, 100
Pilot Hill, 230
Pilot Peak, 203
Pin Ball, 98
Pine Creek, 120, 121, 122
Placer Big Trees Grove, 221
Plumas National Forest, 192, 194, 195, 196, 200, 203
Plumtree Crossing, 206
Point Blunt, 36
Point Cabrillo, 16
Point Pinole Regional Shoreline, 41
Point Reyes, 48, 50
Point Reyes National Seashore, 13, 48

Poker Bar, 92
Ponderosa Park, 228
Ponderosa Way, 216, 217, 218
Posse Park, 105, 107
Poverty Bar, 223, 224
Princeton, 121, 122
Prosser Creek, 238
Prosser Reservoir, 231
Pyramid Lake, 231

Q

Quarry Beach, 36, 37
Quincy, 203

R

Raccoon Strait, 36
Racehorse Rapid, 228
Rainbow Bridge, 148
Ralston Afterbay
Ramparts, 233
Rat Rock, 40
Rattlesnake Bar, 145
Reading Bar, 93
Reading Island, 109, 112
Red Bluff, 109–17
Red Bluff River Park, 113
Red Bridge, 199
Redding, 105–8, 184
Redway, 76–82
Richardson Bay, 36, 37
Richardson Grove State Park, 76, 79, 80, 83
River Ranch, 231–40
Riverbank, 174, 175
Riverfront Park, 132
Robbers Roost, 219
Roberts Ferry, 176–82
Robinson Creek, 85
Rock Bar Creek, 98
Rocky Point, 185, 186, 187, 188
Rollins Reservoir, 204
Round Valley Lake, 192, 193
Round Valley Reservoir, 192–93
Rubicon Point, 243
Rubis Creek, 20–21
Ruck-A-Chucky Rapids, 223, 225
Rumsey Canyon, 135, 136, 137, 138–41, 142, 143
Rush Creek (Hog Hole), 92, 95
Russian Gulch State Park, 70, 73, 74, 75
Russian Rapid, 171

S

Sacramento, 149, 150
Sacramento Bar, 114, 115
Sacramento National Wildlife Refuge,
    114, 115, 120
Sacramento River, 105–23
Sacramento–San Joaquin Delta, 124, 129, 159
Saddle Mountain, 189
Sailor Bar, 152, 154, 156
Sailor Rapid, 98
Salmon Falls, 230
Salmon Plaza, 116
Salt Flat, 92
Salyer, 102–3, 104
San Andreas Rift Zone, 24, 48
San Francisco, 30, 36, 37, 176
San Francisco Bay, 1, 30, 36–38
    East, 32–33
San Joaquin County, 174
San Joaquin River, 176
San Juan Rapid, 154
San Leandro Bay, 34–35
San Pablo Bay, 39
Sand Point, 50
Sandy Bar River, 100
Santa Clara Valley, 22
Santa Cruz mountains, 24
Satan's Cesspool, 229
Sausalito, 36
Schneider's Bar, 99
Schooner Bay, 45, 46
Schoonmaker Point, 36, 37
Scotty's Landing, 120, 122
Seabird Park, 33
Shad Park, 131, 132
Shasta County, 183
Shell Beach, 49
Shirttail Canyon, 216
Sidds Landing, 121
Sierra Nevada, 1, 2, 3
Sierra Valley, 198
Silver Creek, 236, 240
Skid Gulch, 59
Skunk Point, 98
Sky Mountain, 211
Sloat, 198–200
Smithe Redwoods State Reserve, 78, 80
Snaden Island, 120
Sonoma Creek, 88
Sore Finger Point, 216

South Bay, 24
South Fork American River, 226–30
South Fork Eel River, 76–82
South Fork Trinity River, 101, 103
South Yuba River, 208, 209, 210
Spalding Tract, 187, 188
Sproul Creek, 79
Squaw Peak, 221
Squaw Valley, 236
Staircase Rapid, 216
Standish Hickey State Park, 76, 78, 80
Stanislaus River, 170–75
Steel Bridge, 89, 91, 92, 95
Steiner Flat, 89, 93, 94
Stillman L. Magee County Park, 168
Stillwater Creek, 107
Stone Landing, 188
Stuart Point, 37
Sugar Pine Point, 243
Sugar Pine Reservoir, 212
Suicide Bend, 154
Sunrise, 154, 156, 158
Sutter Buttes, 121
Sutter's Landing, 156
Sylvandale, 83–86

T

Table Mountain, 111
Tahoe City, 231–34
Tahoe National Forest, 212, 222
Tall Forest, 161, 162
Taylor Crossing, 204
Taylorsville, 196
Teachers Beach, 49
Tehama Bridge, 117
Tehama County River Park, 114, 116, 117, 121
Thermalito, 124, 126, 128
Thomes Creek, 116
Thornton, 161
Thunder Cliffs, 233
Tiburon, 36
Tihuechemne Slough, 161
Tiscornia Parks, 156, 158
Todd Island, 115
Tom's Point, 50
Tomales Bay, 1, 48–51
Tomales Beach, 49
Tomales Point, 52
Tooby Park, 82
Trinity Alps, 94, 114

Trinity River, 89–105
Triple Threat, 228
Troxel Point, 187
Truckee River, 231–40
Tule Rivers, 183
Tuolumne River, 176–82
Turlock Lake, 177, 179
Turtle Back, 40
Turtle Park, 107
Twin Crags, 233

U
Upper Indian Creek, 196
Upper Sunrise, 154

V
Vallejo, 36
Valley Ford, 54
Valley Oak Recreation Area, 172, 175
Van Damme State Park, 70, 72, 75
Vikingsholm, 244
Vitzthum Gulch, 93

W
Walker Creek, 50
Warm Springs Creek, 55
Waterford, 178, 181, 182

Weott, 83–86
Westwood, 194
White Gulch, 49, 50
White Gulch Beach, 49
Whites Bar, 98, 100
Whitlow (Sequoia), 87–88
William Pond Recreation Area, 155
Williams Grove, 85
Willough Slough, 160, 161, 164
Willow Creek, 101–4, 150
Willow Scrub Meadow, 162
Wilson Valley, 134
Wood Duck Slough, 161
Woodfords, 249
Woodson Bridge, 114–23
Woodson Bridge State Recreation Area, 114, 116,
    117, 118, 123

Y
Yolo County Cache Creek Parks, 137, 138, 143
Yorty Creek, 55, 56
Yosemite National Park, 176
Yuba River, 129–33

About the Author

For 35 years, Charlie Pike has enjoyed paddling smooth streams and roaring whitewater. While in college, the Appalachian Mountain Club introduced him to whitewater canoeing; soon it became a passion. Wherever he has lived—upstate New York, New England, Missouri, Arkansas, or the West Coast—he has enjoyed paddling. In each location he has organized training sessions and river trips. He now lives in Northern California, where he and his sons enjoy paddling lakes, rivers, and coastal waters. When not on the water, he develops water conservation programs for the California Department of Water Resources. He may be reached by e-mail at pike@garlic.com.